The Origins of Louth

The Origins of
LOUTH

Archaeology and History in
East Lincolnshire
400,000 BC–AD 1086

Caitlin Green

THE LINDES PRESS

To Frances

Published by The Lindes Press
Louth, Lincolnshire

Copyright © Caitlin Green, 2011

This edition of *The Origins of Louth* was issued in 2014 with slightly revised front matter. Revised front matter is © 2014 Caitlin Green

The right of Caitlin Green to be identified as the Author of this work has been asserted in accordance with the Copyrights, Designs and Patents Act 1988.

All rights reserved. No part of this book may be reprinted or reproduced or utilised in any form or by any electronic, mechanical or other means, now known or hereafter invented, including photocopying and recording, or in any information storage or retrieval system, without the permission in writing of the Author.

A catalogue record for this book is available from the British Library.

ISBN 978-0-9570336-2-7

Contents

	List of Figures	vi
	Acknowledgements	viii
	Preface	xi
1	The First Humans in the Louth Region, *c.* 400,000–23,000 BC	1
2	After the Ice: Hunters, Farmers and the Changing Landscape, *c.* 20,000 BC–AD 43	13
3	Forgers, Fortresses and Religion in the Romano-British Louth Region, *c.* AD 43–410	41
4	Natives, Immigrants and the Emergence of a Regional Centre, *c.* 410–650	59
5	The Middle Saxon Minster and Market at Louth, *c.* 650–870	79
6	Vikings, Bishops and the Origins of Louth, *c.* 870–1086	95
7	Louth – Past, Present and Future	111
	An Archaeological Gazetteer of the Louth Region	131
	Further Reading and Notes	151

List of Figures

1	Map of the Louth region as defined in this study	xii
2	Lower Palaeolithic finds from the Louth region	2
3	A Lower Palaeolithic handaxe found in Calcethorpe and Kelstern parish	3
4	The Marine Oxygen Isotope Record	6
5	The approximate coastline of Lincolnshire and East Anglia during the Hoxnian Interglacial	8
6	Woolly mammoths, woolly rhinoceros and other fauna typical of western Europe in the Late Pleistocene	11
7	Lincolnshire during the Late Devensian glaciation	15
8	Reindeer migration routes and the extent of Doggerland during the Younger Dryas	18
9	Mesolithic finds from the Louth region	20
10	The latter stages of the flooding of Doggerland	21
11	Cross-section derived from multiple boreholes in North Somercotes parish	23
12	The rise in relative sea-level in the Lincolnshire Marshes area	24
13	A Neolithic polished axe from the Great Langdale 'axe factory' in Cumbria, found at Legbourne	26
14	Neolithic finds and sites in the Louth region	27
15	The round barrows at Bully Hills, Tathwell	30
16	Bronze Age finds and sites in the Louth region	32
17	Iron Age finds and sites in the Louth region	35
18	Five of the Late Iron Age coins assigned a 'Louth' findspot in the Celtic Coin Index	37
19	Romano-British finds and sites in the Louth region	42
20	Romano-British silver ring inscribed ToT, found at Stenigot	44

21	A silver Roman coin found at Fulstow, probably a contemporary copy of one of Constantius II (337–61)	45
22	A lead tablet containing the impression of a Roman coin of Valens (364–78)	47
23	A fourth-century crossbow brooch, found at Welsdale, Donington on Bain	48
24	A fragment of a fourth-century Roman lead font, found in Calcethorpe with Kelstern parish	51
25	Romano-British finds and sites in the Louth region, plotted against all of the potential routeways of this period	53
26	The location of Yarburgh, plotted against the suggested Late Roman/post-Roman coastline	56
27	The distribution of the major Early Anglo-Saxon cremation cemeteries of Lincolnshire	62
28	A British proto-hand-pin, found in Welton le Wold parish	65
29	Early Anglo-Saxon finds and cemeteries in the Louth region	67
30	The territorial context of the South Elkington-Louth cremation cemetery	70
31	Early Anglo-Saxon place-names of the Louth region	73
32	David Robinson's reconstruction of the Early Anglo-Saxon coastline of Lincolnshire	76
33	Coins of two ninth-century kings of Mercia, Burgred (852–74) and Ludica (825–7)	81
34	Possible local devotional foci and ecclesiastical sites associated with the Middle Saxon minster at Louth	86
35	The Louth region in the Middle Saxon period	89
36	Scandinavian place-names in the Louth region	97
37	The front and rear of an incomplete cast lead Viking disc brooch from North Ormsby	99
38	The Louth region in the Anglo-Scandinavian period	101
39	An eleventh-century horse harness link from Yarburgh	104
40	Thomas Espin's map of Louth, 1808	116
41	Robert Bayley's map of Louth, 1834	122
42	Map showing those parts of the Louth region that could be affected by a sea-level rise of two metres	126
43	Map showing those parts of the Louth region that could be affected by the melting of the Greenland and West Antarctic ice sheets	127

Acknowledgements

The present work has benefitted considerably from the help and kindness of a significant number of people and institutions, and I would like to take this opportunity to briefly thank them and acknowledge their contribution. In particular, thanks are due here to John Aram, Nick Barton, Mark Bennet, Chris Clark, Adam Daubney, Martin Foreman, Phil Gibbard, Richard Gurnham, Geoff Hill, Dave Holmes, Mark Jones, Kevin Leahy, Michael Lewis, Daniel Pett, John Pygott, Tom Redmayne, Ian Richardson, David Robinson, Ian Shennan, John Sills, Stuart Sizer, and Chris Stringer for their help, assistance and advice.

With specific regard to the figures used in this book, the following acknowledgements need to be made. Figures 3, 20, 21, 22, 24, 33, 37, and 39 are used by kind permission of the Portable Antiquities Scheme, and were created by the PAS's Finds Liasion Officers working in the following host organisations: Lincolnshire County Council (Figs 20, 21, 22, 24, 39), North Lincolnshire Council (Figs 3, 37), Surrey County Council (Fig. 33), and Birmingham City Council (Fig. 33). Figure 6 is by Mauricio Anton and was published in the *Public Library of Science* journal (*PLoS Biology* 6.4, 2008: e99) under a Creative Commons Attribution 2.5 Generic license; the outline of a mammoth used on the front cover is also derived from this image and used under the same license. Figures 13 and 23 are used by kind permission of Louth Museum. Figure 18 consists of images from the Oxford Celtic Coin Index, used by kind permission. Figure 28 is copyright of the Trustees of the British Museum and is used by kind permission. Figure 32 is used by kind permission of David Robinson. Figures 8, 10, and 12 contain material copyright of The Geological Society, which is used by kind permission of both this society and Professor Ian Shennan. Figure 4 is based on P. L. Gibbard and K. M. Cohen, 'Global chronostratigraphical correlation table for the last 2.7 million years', 2010 (archived at http://www.quaternary.stratigraphy.

org.uk/correlation/chart.html) and is used by kind permission. Figure 5 is based on C. Stringer, *Homo Britannicus* (London, 2006), and is used by kind permission. Figure 7 is based on C. D. Clark et al, 'Map and GIS database of landforms and features related to the last British Ice Sheet', *Boreas*, 33.4 (2004), 359–75, and is used by kind permission. Figure 8 is based on N. Barton, *Ice Age Britain* (London, 2005), and is used by kind permission. Figure 11 is based on Environment Agency, *Donna Nook Managed Realignment Scheme* (November 2009), and is used by kind permission. Figures 26, 29, 31, 42, and 43 are based partly on public domain NASA Shuttle Radar Topography Mission data, via http://flood.firetree.net. Figures 1, 2, 9, 14, 16, 17, 19, 25–27, 29, 31, 34–36, 38, 42, and 43 use material derived from OS OpenData, which is made freely available under the Open Government Licence v1.0 with the following attribution statement: Contains Ordnance Survey data © Crown copyright and database right 2011. The front and rear cover photographs were taken by the author: the front cover photograph shows the view of St James' Church, Louth, from the vicinity of the Early Anglo-Saxon cremation cemetery; the rear cover photograph shows the Bully Hills barrows at Tathwell and also appears as Figure 15.

Preface

By and large, most historical accounts of Louth and its surrounding villages have tended to focus on the events of the past thousand years, largely due to the fact that the documentary record for this area only really begins in earnest with the compilation of Domesday Book in 1086. However, whilst this is understandable, it is also problematical. First and foremost, humans have been active in the area around Louth for considerably longer than a thousand years. The earliest material found in Louth itself dates from the Later Mesolithic and Neolithic periods, and tools found only a little way from the town (at Welton le Wold) were made by humans who lived there hundreds of thousands of years ago. In other words, the documentary record covers only a small fraction of the actual human history of this part of Lincolnshire. Second, it seems clear that the fundamental origins of the medieval and modern Louth region lie beyond this documentary horizon. Louth was already a market town by the time of Domesday Book, and most of the surrounding villages had been founded before this point too. In consequence, if we are interested in origins, then we need to be looking at what happened in the period before written records become common.

This is the starting point for the present study. Whilst written references are certainly rare before the Norman Conquest, other types of evidence – notably archaeological, linguistic, environmental and geological – do exist, and together these can be used to investigate the early history and origins of Louth and its hinterland, even in the absence of documentary evidence. In what follows, a study zone of 10 km radius around Louth (the 'Louth region') is established, in order both to pull together enough of this material for a meaningful analysis and to enable Louth's development to be placed within its local context. Louth, after all, has always had a close relationship with its hinterland, and only by adopting this approach can we really hope to understand how and when it began to emerge as the dominant settlement here.

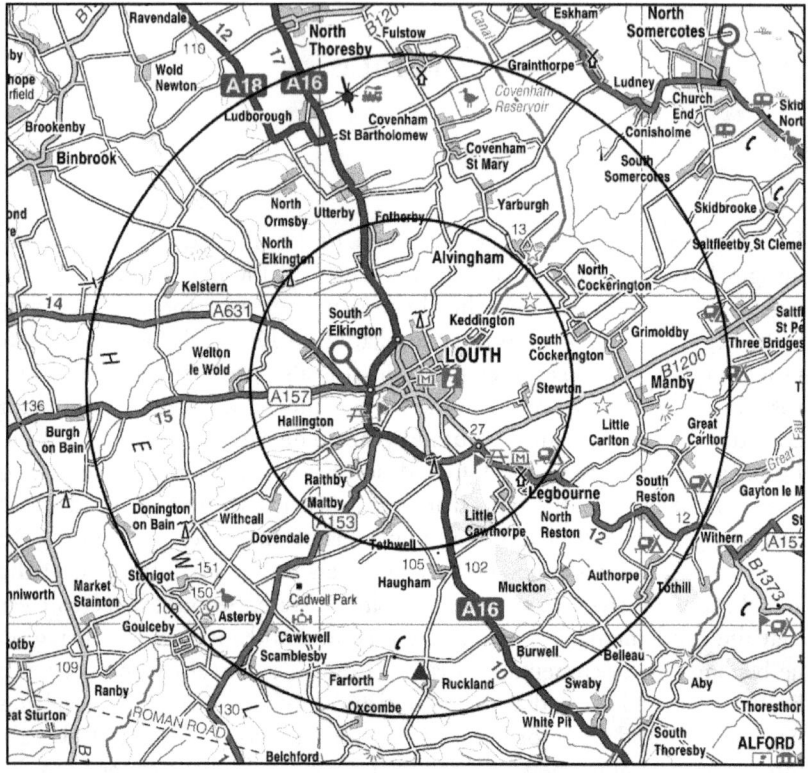

Figure 1: Map of the Louth region as defined in this study, showing areas lying within 5 and 10 km of the centre of Louth.

Needless to say, such an analysis of the pre-Norman history of the Louth region faces problems. In particular, although there is now a substantial corpus of archaeological material available from this part of Lincolnshire, this has not previously been published and it resides in a number of independently compiled databases, only some of which are easily accessible. As such, the first task in researching this volume was to gather all of this material together for the first time. This was undertaken over the summer and autumn of 2010, and the results can be seen in both the archaeological gazetteer included here as an appendix and the maps in the main text. Further details of the datasets used are provided in the gazetteer; it should be noted that the inherent limitations of the various databases are responsible for the adoption of a 10 km radius survey area, rather than one based on the boundaries of the nineteenth-century Louth Rural District or the medieval Louthesk wapentake. There are also issues over the interpretation of the linguistic and archaeological material that comes from the Louth region, if this is treated as a stand-alone, isolated corpus. In consequence, an effort has been made to analyse all of the available evidence in light of recent scholarship and comparative evidence from elsewhere in Britain. By doing this, a more detailed and developed understanding of both the significance of the surviving evidence and the early history of our study zone is achievable. Finally, for the most distant periods, even archaeological evidence is exceedingly scarce. In these circumstances, the likely course of events has largely had to be reconstructed from non-archaeological sources and in light of academic and scientific research into both the area around Louth and the wider region.

This, then, is the background to the following analysis of the origins of Louth. By utilizing all of the available evidence, a reasonably detailed picture of the development of Louth and the evolution of human activity in this region – from around 400,000 years ago until the time of Domesday Book – can be offered. Before turning to this, however, two final points ought to be made. First, further information as to the earlier scholarship upon which this study and its conclusions build and depend can be found in the 'further reading and notes' section at the end of this volume. Second, for the sake of clarity and accessibility, I have avoided using diacritics and historical linguistic conventions in the following text, so that, for example, *Lindēs is rendered below as *Lindes*, *hlūde as *hlude*, and *tūn* as *tun*.

1

The First Humans in the Louth Region, *c.* 400,000–23,000 BC

Quite when the first humans arrived in Britain remains a matter of debate. Until relatively recently, it was thought that members of the genus *Homo* only reached Britain after the Anglian glaciation (*c.* 478,000–424,000 years ago), which buried Britain under ice as far south as North London. However, such a position is no longer tenable. First, excavations at Boxgrove (Sussex) in the 1980s and 1990s saw Lower Palaeolithic tools discovered alongside both animal remains dating to around 500,000 years ago and a partial tibia of a male *Homo heidelbergensis*. The latter was a human species that may be the ancestor of both Neanderthal man (*Homo neanderthalensis*) and our own species (*Homo sapiens*); it stood around six feet tall and had a brain not too dissimilar in size to that of modern humans. Second, in the past few years, finds from East Anglia have extended the human history of Britain even further back in time, initially to around 700,000 years ago with finds from Pakefield (Suffolk) made in 2005, and now to between 970,000 to 814,000 years ago based on new finds from Happisburgh (Norfolk). Unfortunately, the latter artefacts were not found associated with any human remains, but the only type of human known to be in Europe around this time was *Homo antecessor* ('Pioneer Man') and so they have been tentatively ascribed to members of this species. *Homo antecessor* had a slightly smaller average brain volume than modern humans do, stood between five and a half and six feet tall, and may have occasionally practiced nutritional cannibalism, in light of the evidence from the Gran Dolina site in the Sierra de Atapuerca, northern Spain.

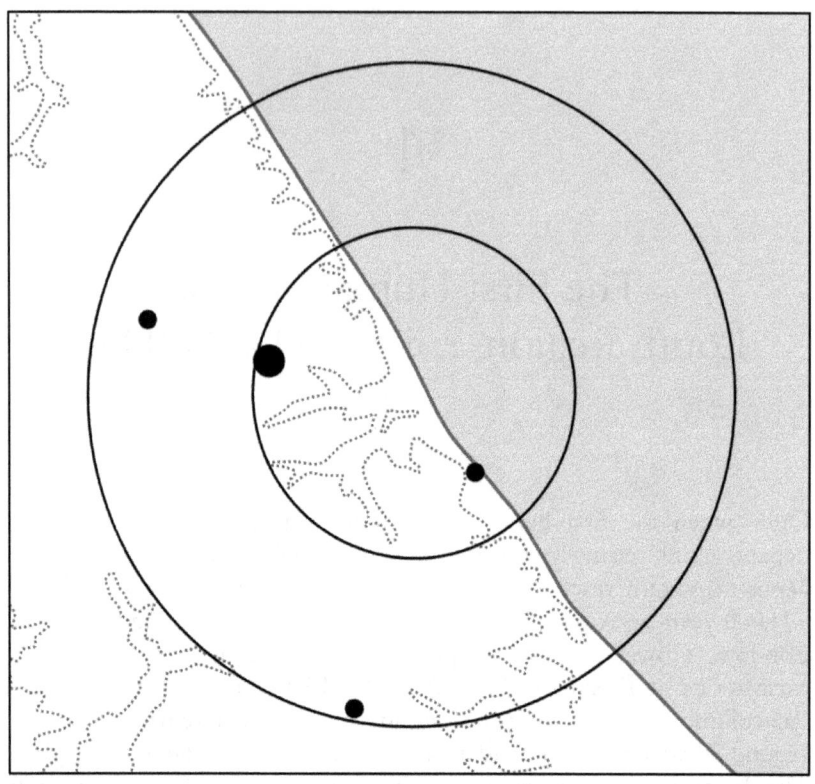

Figure 2: Lower Palaeolithic finds from the Louth region; symbol size reflects the number of finds. Finds are shown against an outline of modern topography; any evidence for Lower Palaeolithic human activity east of the line running northwest-southeast is irretrievably lost, as this was eroded away by the sea around 115,000 years ago, during the Ipswichian Interglacial. The line marks the Ipswichian cliff-edge, which would have had a flint beach at its foot. As sea-levels fell again after this time, the exposed wave-cut platform become a flat plain.

As to whether such pre-Anglian humans were ever present in the Louth region, this remains uncertain. On the one hand, the recent Happisburgh finds demonstrate that areas such as this one are not too far north for such early humans to have ventured, contrary to the previous assumption that they were active only in warmer climes. Indeed, not only is Happisburgh located only around 50 km to the south of Louth, but the faunal evidence found with the tools here also indicates that when the site was inhabited the climate was colder than today, being more akin to that presently experienced in southern Sweden or Norway. Furthermore, the main physical obstacles for any early humans moving north from Suffolk and Norfolk into eastern Lincolnshire, namely the Wash and the Fens, didn't actually exist before the Anglian glaciation (they are thought to have been gouged out as the Anglian ice sheet moved south-westwards). On the other hand, there is currently no solid evidence for the presence of pre-Anglian humans in the Louth region. This doesn't, of course, mean that they were necessarily absent from this region. Around half of the Palaeolithic landscape here was eroded away by the sea during the Ipswichian Interglacial (Marine Isotope Substage 5e, which ran from around 130,000 to 115,000 years ago), and that which was not – the modern Wolds – has few contexts that might preserve pre-Anglian human artefacts, unlike the coast of East Anglia (the only possible exception here is the Calcethorpe Till, on which see below). In such circumstances, an absence of positive evidence for human activity before 478,000 years ago is to be expected, especially given the rarity of this material even where relevant contexts survive and are accessible.

Figure 3: A Lower Palaeolithic handaxe found in Calcethorpe and Kelstern parish. Image used by kind permission of the Portable Antiquities Scheme; PAS find reference number NLM-54EC10.

Whatever the case may be with regard to pre-Anglian humans, both Lincolnshire and the Louth region certainly saw at least some human activity in the period after the end of the Anglian glaciation 424,000 years ago. In particular, a number of Lower Palaeolithic handaxes are now known from Lincolnshire, with the total being added to considerably in recent years by detailed field-walking specifically designed to look for such artefacts. Indeed, the success of this field-walking project – focussed on the Tetford-Salmonby area, just to the south of our study zone – suggests that the relative rarity of such post-Anglian Palaeolithic material in Lincolnshire may be more apparent than real, deriving primarily from issues surrounding preservation and collection rather than anything else. Looking specifically at the Louth region in this era, three Palaeolithic handaxes have been discovered from the surface of the Wolds here, all of which probably date from between around 424,000 and 191,000 years ago (after the latter point Britain appears to have been totally abandoned by humans until approximately 60,000 years ago). The first of these was found at Kenwick Farm in 1930, just to the south of Louth in Legbourne parish; the second was reported in 2005 from Maidenwell parish, just to the north of the main Tetford-Salmonby cluster; and the third handaxe was found in 2010 during metal-detecting in Calcethorpe and Kelstern parish. Whilst these are sufficient to demonstrate that some early humans were active in our region at one or more points during the almost inconceivably long Lower Palaeolithic era, they can tell us little more than this. Potentially more informative, however, are a small number of artefacts from Welton le Wold.

The artefacts in question consist of three Lower Palaeolithic handaxes and a worked flake, which were discovered in the Upper Gravels of Welton le Wold quarry alongside fossil animal bones and teeth. Both the artefacts and the fossils appear to have been incorporated into the Upper Gravels after being eroded away from their original location(s), something confirmed by their random dispersal within these gravels, the evidence for abrasion on the artefacts and fossils, and the fact that the Upper Gravels were probably formed by erosion and mass-movement during an arctic climate whilst the fossils belong to temperate species, such as elephant, red deer and horse. Nonetheless, given both the limited amount and nature of the abrasion and the fact that these items were all found within a relatively small area of the quarry, it is unlikely that they had moved very far. As such, whilst they were found in a disturbed and secondary context, the artefacts and fossils from this site would seem to strongly indicate the presence of Lower Palaeolithic humans actually within the Welton le Wold valley, probably during a temperate period. So, when was this?

There are two possible approaches to establishing the date of these artefacts and faunal remains. The first is to look at the probable age of the materials that overlie and postdate the Upper Gravels at Welton le Wold. In particular, we need to ask when the Welton Till was laid down, as this glacial till (a sediment deposited by a glacier as it melts or retreats, also known as boulder clay) forms the layer immediately above the Upper Gravels and its date of deposition should consequently provide a *terminus ante quem* for both the gravels and the artefacts they contain. With regard to this, the Welton Till is itself overlain by two further glacial tills that can help to narrow its date. One of these is the Marsh Till, which is present above the Welton Till in the eastern part of the quarry. This is believed to have its origins in the most recent glaciation of our region (the Late Devensian, which began around 22,000 years ago) and looks to have been laid down some considerable time after the Welton Till, given the degree to which the latter had apparently been eroded before this occurred. The other till is the Calcethorpe Till, which lies above the Welton Till in the western part of the quarry. This till is present elsewhere on the top of the Wolds and must derive from a significant glaciation of the region that saw ice sheets flowing right across the Wolds, unlike in the Late Devensian glaciation. Indeed, the Calcethorpe Till has been correlated with the chalky tills of East Anglia and elsewhere and treated as Anglian in date. If this is correct, then it implies that the Welton Till must either be of Anglian or pre-Anglian date, and thus that the handaxes and temperate fossils that are preserved in the Upper Gravel are pre-Anglian in origin, dating either from the preceding temperate epoch, Marine Isotope Stage (MIS) 13, which lasted from 533,000 to 478,000 years ago, or even from an earlier warm period such as MIS 15, 621,000–563,000 years ago. With regard to the names and dates of these eras, Marine Isotope Stages are now commonly used to understand the climatic fluctuations of the past few million years. They are derived from deep-sea core samples, with datable fluctuations in the proportions of different oxygen isotopes in these cores reflecting changes in global ice volume and thus temperature. This material reveals a regularly alternating pattern of cold and warm epochs, which are numbered backwards from the present era (MIS 1), with warm stages assigned an odd number and cold stages an even one.

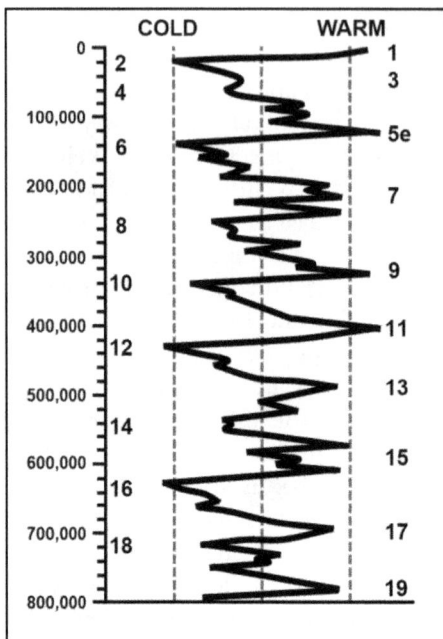

Figure 4: The Marine Oxygen Isotope Record, showing the fluctuating climate over the past 800,000 years along with the associated Marine Isotope Stage numbering; cold stages are assigned even numbers and warm stages odd. Image based on Gibbard and Cohen, 2010, and used by kind permission.

The second approach to dating these artefacts is to try to date the gravel itself using modern scientific dating methods. This has recently been attempted using a method for determining how much time has passed since minerals such as quartz were last exposed to light, known as Optically Stimulated Luminescence (OSL) dating. Although not all of the samples taken from Welton le Wold were able to provide absolute date ranges using this method, offering merely 'minimum age' estimates, and some of the results are only preliminary, together they imply a rather different reconstruction to that based on the suggested correlations between the tills at Welton and elsewhere in England. In particular, a sample from the Lower Gravels – which underlie and so antedate the artefact- and fossil-containing Upper Gravels – indicates that these were deposited around 365,000 ± 28,000 years ago. Given that the Lower Gravels were probably formed in cool temperate conditions rather than a glacial climate, this implies an origin sometime in the latter part of the Hoxnian Interglacial (MIS 11, 424,000–374,000 years ago). Similarly, two very preliminary OSL age estimates from sediments found between the Upper Gravels and the Welton Till suggest that the sequence of glacial tills here probably began at some point late in the MIS 6 glacial epoch, which came to end around 130,000 years ago, rather than in the Anglian era. Finally, OSL samples taken from within the Upper Gravels themselves indicate that these gravels are likely to be at least 337,000 years old.

In light of the above, it seems clear that an Anglian or pre-Anglian date for the Upper Gravels and the overlying tills – and thus a pre-Anglian date for the early humans who made and used the three handaxes and worked flake – is difficult to sustain. The data we currently possess instead supports a sequence of events that saw the Lower Gravels formed in the later Hoxnian Interglacial (MIS 11), the artefact-containing Upper Gravels deposited on top of them during the following MIS 10 glacial epoch (374,000–337,000 years ago), and the Upper Gravels being finally buried under the Welton Till towards the end of MIS 6 (which ran from around 191,000–130,000 years ago). This in turn implies that our early humans are likely to have lived during the Hoxnian Interglacial, between 424,000 and 374,000 years ago, given that both the artefacts and the animal fossils are thought to have their origins in a pre-Upper Gravels temperate context (their survival from an earlier, pre-Anglian, warm stage until they were eroded into the Upper Gravels in MIS 10 is unlikely, due to the intervening highly extensive and destructive Anglian ice sheet).

If the earliest datable inhabitants of the Louth region were thus probably active here around 400,000 years ago, what else can be said about them? If they were like their contemporaries who lived elsewhere in Britain, such as 'Swanscombe man' (actually a woman), then they would have had brains of a similar volume and physical structure to our own and are likely to have been pre- or ancestral Neanderthals, lying on the evolutionary line leading from *Homo heidelbergensis* to *Homo neanderthalensis*. In terms of their everyday lives, they almost certainly survived via hunting, scavenging and gathering. They may also have used fires for cooking and warmth, given that the first good evidence for the existence of hearths in Britain comes from this period. As to the landscape they inhabited, in this era the Wolds still extended well to the east of the modern coastline, and the people who were active here had probably arrived by following a minor river inland (the Welton valley in this period contained a river that ran north-west to the south-east, with its head somewhere in the vicinity of the present-day heads of the Bain valley). In doing this they may have been relatively adventurous by the standards of the time, with Lower Palaeolithic sites being more often located in significant river valleys and on lower-lying land, although it is worth noting in this context that the Lower Palaeolithic finds from the Tetford-Salmonby area are similarly located well inland and on high ground.

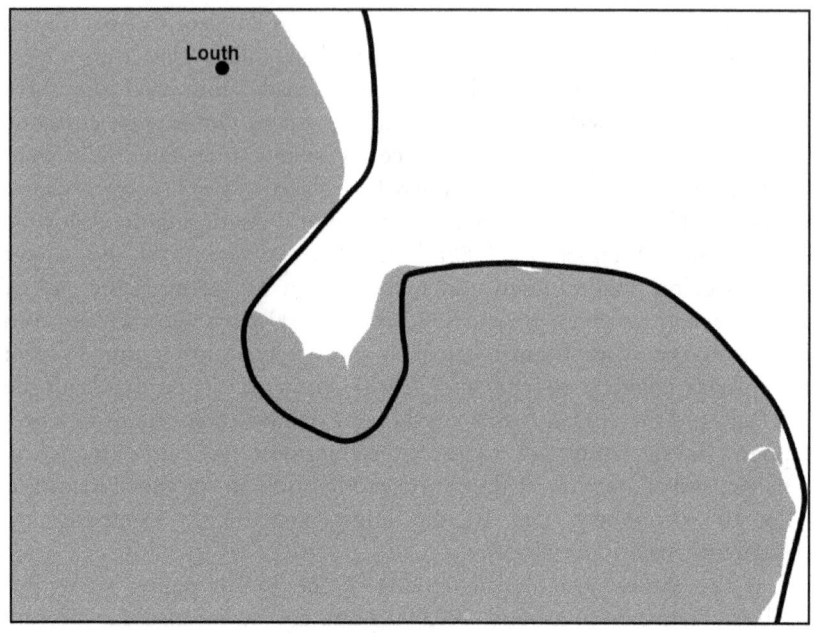

Figure 5: The approximate coastline of Lincolnshire and East Anglia during the Hoxnian Interglacial, mapped against the current coastline in grey. Image based on Stringer, 2006, and used by kind permission.

It is likely that both the Louth region and Britain as a whole were largely abandoned after the end of the Hoxnian Interglacial, with the subsequent MIS 10 cold period having no definite archaeology associated with it. Whether our region was later reoccupied like other parts of Britain during the Purfleet Interglacial (MIS 9, 337,000–300,000 years ago) is uncertain, as we lack any further stratified Lower Palaeolithic artefacts. Nonetheless, it seems credible that it was, and it has been suggested that the handaxe from Calcethorpe and Kelstern belongs, typologically, to the early part of the MIS 8 cold stage (300,000–243,000 years ago), which would tend to support this. The following warm stage, MIS 7 or the Aveley Interglacial (243,000–191,000 years ago), is equally obscure for our region – there may have been activity here but as yet there is no clear evidence for this. However, even if there was, after around 191,000 years ago the evidence for humans in Britain appears to dry up entirely, and we can say with a fair degree of certainty that the Louth region was uninhabited from at least this time right the way through until around 60,000 years ago.

Even though it was devoid of humans, the 130,000 years after the end of MIS 7 were undoubtedly important from the perspective of the developing landscape of the Louth region. For example, the MIS 6 glacial epoch – recently defined as the 'Tottenhill Glaciation' – appears to have been especially severe and saw ice sheets moving over our region, depositing as they melted not only the Welton Till, but also probably the Calcethorpe Till across the top of the Wolds. The subsequent Ipswichian Interglacial (MIS 5e, beginning around 130,000 years ago) was even more significant for this region. This period was one of the warmest in recent geological history, and Britain from Yorkshire southwards was inhabited by exotic fauna including lions, hyenas, hippopotamuses, elephants and rhinoceroses. It was also the era in which around half of the Palaeolithic landscape of our region disappeared. As was noted above, the Wolds originally extended well to the east of the current coastline, but in the Ipswichian Interglacial the sea gradually eroded this landscape away until it reached the modern eastern edge of the Wolds. The last glaciation, which began around 22,000 years ago, has covered the resultant Ipswichian landscape with glacial till, but around 115,000 years ago the edge of the Wolds would have been marked by a line of white cliffs with a flinty beach at its foot and a wave-cut chalk platform extending eastwards from this: the present-day Louth hospital and cemetery stand roughly on this cliff-edge, and the Lincolnshire Marshes now lie above the ancient wave-cut platform.

After about 15,000 years, this period of warm temperatures and relatively high sea-levels came to an end, to be followed by an erratic decline into the next cold epoch, MIS 4 (71,000–57,000 years ago). During MIS 4, Britain and the Louth region probably experienced a climate akin to that of present-day northern Scandinavia and temperatures dropped to around −20°C in winter months. Only with the end of this global cold stage did humans return to Britain. These new human inhabitants of Britain were true Neanderthals, *Homo neanderthalensis*, and they brought with them new and diagnostic stone tools, notably *Bout coupé* handaxes. The latter have been considered indicative of the MIS 3 recolonization of Britain, and whilst none are known from our study zone, two have been found in Lincolnshire, at Risby Warren and Harlaxton. In consequence, it is by no means implausible that the Neanderthals of MIS 3 at least hunted in or passed through the Louth region. With regard to the landscape of this district, it is worth noting that MIS 3 is sometimes referred to as a 'failed interglacial', with an unstable climate that swung from relatively mild to cold. As a result, sea-levels remained as much as 80 metres lower than today, and the Ipswichian wave-cut platform here would have been exposed as a flat plain sloping gently eastwards in this period. Of course, any archaeological evidence for Neanderthal activity on this plain would have been destroyed by the Late Devensian glaciation of 22,000 years ago, which saw it first scoured by an ice sheet and then buried under many metres of glacial till as the ice retreated.

If the initial human recolonization of Britain and Lincolnshire was undertaken by Neanderthals, around 35,000 years ago they appear to have been joined by our own species of humans, *Homo sapiens*. Unlike Neanderthals, who are thought to have evolved within Europe, modern humans evolved in Africa, with a small population of a few thousand then migrating into the Middle East during the last 100,000 years, where they interbred with the local Neanderthals before moving on into Europe and Asia (up to 4% of the genome of present-day non-Africans results from this interbreeding). This migration of *Homo sapiens* into Britain led to the introduction of their Upper Palaeolithic material culture too, and some examples of these artefacts are known from Lincolnshire, including a classic Upper Palaeolithic blade core found just to the south of the Louth region at Fulletby. Of course, a key question is how these two species of humans interacted during the time when they both lived in Britain. Unfortunately, there is no relevant evidence for this, either from our region or from Britain and Europe as a whole. A degree of violence or warfare is certainly possible, but there may also have been local interbreeding and more generally increased competition for resources and hunting grounds during a period of escalating climatic instability. Whatever the case may be, by about 30,000 years ago it seems clear that *Homo neanderthalensis* had disappeared from the scene and *Homo sapiens* stood alone as the sole human species to occupy Britain, as the world began to enter the final Ice Age before the current Holocene epoch.

This, then, is the general picture that emerges of the Louth region before the last Ice Age. Although the surviving archaeology is meagre in light of the vast period of time under study, when put together with the geological and scientific evidence and comparative material from

Figure 6: *Woolly mammoths, woolly rhinoceros and other fauna typical of western Europe in the Late Pleistocene, MIS 5–MIS 2 (Image credit: Mauricio Antón).*

elsewhere in the country, it is possible to reconstruct a broad outline of events. From the perspective of early human activity, it appears likely that the Louth region was occupied from at least as early as the Hoxnian Interglacial, 400,000 years ago, based on the archaeology and geology from Welton le Wold quarry. Furthermore, both the evidence from our region and Britain as a whole strongly indicates that this occupation was non-continuous, with periods of tens of thousands of years in which there seems not to have been a single human active in Britain. This long phase of minimal and discontinuous occupation by a very small number of humans only begins to change significantly after the last glaciation, and the subsequent emergence of a more permanent and numerous human community in our region is the focus of the following chapter.

2

After the Ice: Hunters, Farmers and the Changing Landscape, *c.* 20,000 BC–AD 43

The last global cold stage – known as the Late Devensian – saw Britain once again emptied of people after approximately 23,000 BC, with mean annual temperatures dropping to as low as −6 or −7°C and midwinter temperatures of around −40°C, colder than parts of Siberia today. As *Homo sapiens* either retreated to 'refuges' in areas such as south-western France and northern Spain – where weather conditions were less severe – or died out trying to cling on to their homelands, the ice sheets moved down the east coast from Scotland and northern England. Radiocarbon dating indicates that the ice arrived in Holderness sometime around 20,000 BC and something similar is likely to apply to its advance up to and onto the edge of the Lincolnshire Wolds too, where it rose to a maximum of about 114 metres above the current sea-level (Ordnance Datum). At the same time, the development of these massive ice sheets both here and elsewhere led to global sea-levels dropping to approximately −120 metres (−395 feet) OD. As a direct result, the bottom of the North Sea became dry land as far north as Shetland, although both this plain and those parts of modern Britain that remained ice-free formed an uninhabitable arctic desert at the height of the Ice Age.

Even though there were no people still living in the region to witness it, the presence of the glacier clearly had an enormous impact on the landscape of Lincolnshire. Further south and west, massive lakes such as 'Lake Humber' built up covering large tracts of the county, as the ice sheet prevented the rivers draining properly. In our study area, one of the most significant developments before the final retreat of the glacier was the cutting of a number of meltwater channels on the eastern edge of the Wolds, which can still be traced today. Of these, the channel that formed due to the blocking of the Hallington valley by the decaying ice and its thick deposits of till (glacial sediments) is of particular interest from the perspective of Louth. This blockage meant that the water that would have drained along this valley from the springtime snowmelt on the Wolds backed up to form a large lake covering Hallington and Raithby, which then overflowed northwards across the chalk ridge. The resulting waterfall off the ridge into the Welton valley rapidly cut a steep-sided channel backwards through the chalk over the course of perhaps as little as two or three hundred years. This event is, needless to say, the origins of the modern Hubbard's Hills gorge, which thereafter acted as the new permanent channel for the Hallington and Raithby/Tathwell Becks.

Further major changes for the region came when the climate began to take a significant and rapid turn for the better *c.* 12,700 BC, as the warm period known as the Late Glacial, or Windermere, Interstadial began. Temperatures rapidly increased over the course of just a few years, to the extent that the early part of this period was as hot as today, and the ice sheet retreated northwards to leave the old, flat, wave-cut chalk platform that extended eastwards from the Lincolnshire Wolds covered in a thick layer of glacial till. This undulating till forms the present Middle Marsh and underlies the Outmarsh; it also extended out beyond the current coastline onto the North Sea plain, which began to slowly flood in the north around Scotland as sea-levels rose by perhaps 50 metres due to the glacial melt. The pollen records suggest that Late Glacial eastern Britain was initially a dry and open, treeless landscape of grasses and sedges, albeit with a growing presence of downy birch, willow and juniper. However, between about 12,000 and 11,000 BC climatic conditions became both wetter and a little cooler, and this is associated with a rapid rise in birch pollen and a corresponding decline in non-arboreal pollen, which can be observed both in the records from Holderness and Aby Grange, just to the south-east of our study zone. In other words, the open grassland of the earlier Windermere Interstadial in our region gave way to birch woodland in the latter part of this period, with previously-present species such as sea-buckthorn being shaded out by the developing tree canopy.

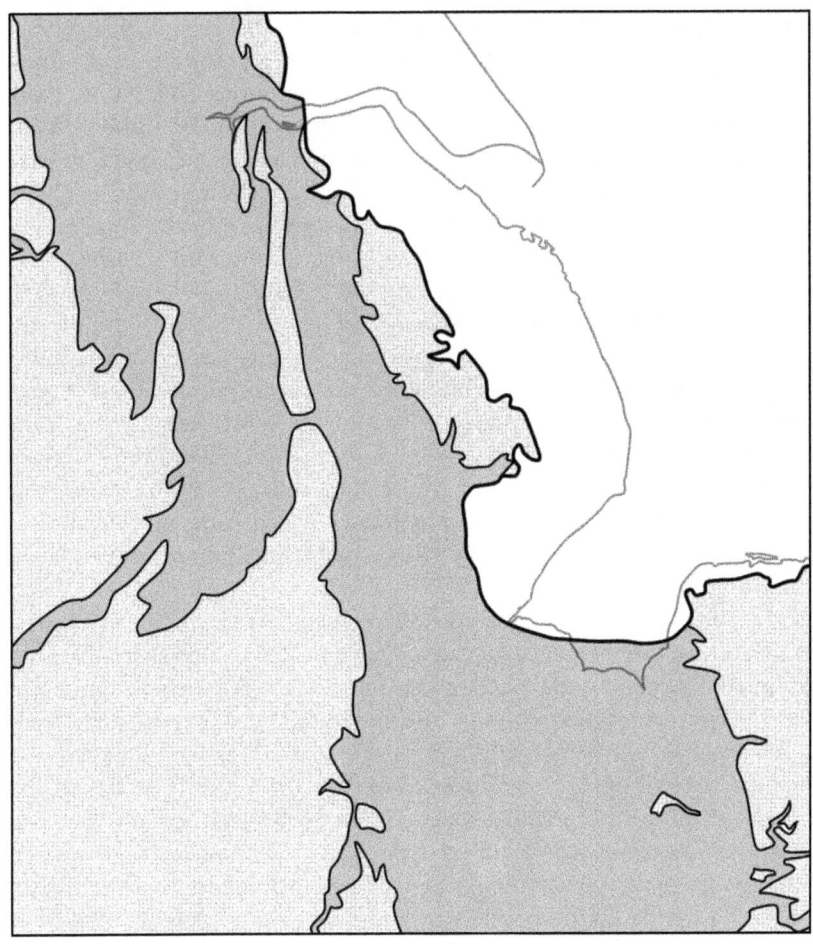

Figure 7: Lincolnshire during the Late Devensian glaciation. The present-day coastline is shown as a grey line; areas covered by the ice sheet are in white, areas covered by glacial lakes are rendered in dark grey, and ice- and water-free land is in light grey. It should be noted that the large glacial lake to the south of the Wash is speculative and its existence has been disputed. Image based on Clark et al, 2004, and used by kind permission.

As the ice retreated and the landscape warmed and changed, a variety of animals migrated to Britain across the exposed grass- and scrub-covered plain that linked Britain to the Continent. These included arctic foxes and hares, brown bears, wolves and – most importantly – mammoths, red deer, and herds of wild horses. These game animals seem to have been followed into Britain by the groups of Ice Age hunters who lived off them. Certainly there was a group of people living at Gough's Cave in Chedder Gorge, Somerset, around 12,700 BC, who were primarily hunting the herds of wild horses that flourished on the grasslands of this period, although this group can also be shown to have practiced nutritional (as opposed to ritual) cannibalism. In fact, evidence for the presence of people in Britain in the early part of the Windermere Interstadial is reasonably widely spread, being found both at cave sites such as Gough's Cave, Cresswell Crags (Derbyshire and Nottinghamshire), and King Arthur's Cave (Herefordshire), and also increasingly at open-air locations in central and eastern Britain too. Similarly, there is now a sizeable body of material indicative of human activity in the succeeding period of woodland growth too, although the lifestyle of these people is likely to have been somewhat different, given the change in vegetation (which must have restricted mobility) and the fact that both the mammoths and many of the herds of wild horses probably largely vanished from Britain with the disappearance of the earlier open landscape.

With specific regard to the Louth region, there is as yet no positive evidence for the presence of such Late Glacial hunters here, be they cannibals or otherwise. However, it is more than credible that the region saw at least occasional visits by the Late and Final Upper Palaeolithic hunter-gatherers of this period. In this context it is worth noting that mammoth remains that probably date from the Late Glacial era are known from both Ingoldmells and Saltfleetby St Clement. Equally, it is important to recognize that there have been a number of finds of Late and Final Upper Palaeolithic flints in Lincolnshire. The most significant of these come from the Scunthorpe and Risby Warren areas, but perhaps more relevant here are a knife and a shouldered point from the neighbouring parishes of Fulletby and Salmonby, located only around three kilometres to the south of our study zone. These finds imply that the Louth region may well have seen at least a degree of hunting activity at this time, especially given that the Late Upper Palaeolithic hunters of the earlier part of the Interstadial appear to have been extremely mobile over significant distances.

Around 10,900 BC the environment of the Louth area changed dramatically once again. The start of the Younger Dryas, or Loch Lomond Stadial, saw temperatures fall significantly as Britain returned to glacial conditions, with mean annual temperatures reaching a minimum of between −5 and −2°C at the height of this cold period (*c.* 10,500 BC). The root cause of this plunge in temperature appears to have been a failure of the ocean thermohaline circulation – the 'conveyer belt' of ocean currents that warms Britain via the 'Gulf Stream'. Exactly why this shut-down of the Gulf Stream happened is still uncertain. The usual explanation is that the retreat of the Laurentide ice sheet in North America led to a sudden flood of 9300 km^3 of glacial meltwater into the North Atlantic or Arctic Ocean, as a channel opened up from the enormous glacial lake, Lake Agassiz, to the ocean. Alternatively, it has been argued that the flood events and the start of the Younger Dryas ought to be linked to the fragmentation and explosion of a 4.6 km-wide comet above the Laurentide ice sheet, although the evidence for such an impact has been seriously challenged.

Whatever the case may be as to its cause or causes, the Younger Dryas climatic decline would have undoubtedly had a dramatic effect on the people who lived and/or hunted in Lincolnshire at this time, not least because it seems to have been extremely rapid. The initial cooling of 5°C or more is often thought to have occurred over only a decade or so, well within a single human lifespan, and recent work from Ireland suggests that it may even have taken just a few years or even months to complete. Furthermore, the pollen data from Aby Grange and sites elsewhere in Britain confirms the importance and impact of this sudden return to glacial conditions, with the birch forest rapidly dying off except in a few sheltered refuges and the landscape becoming once more one of open tundra dominated by grasses and sedges. In light of this, it is hardly surprising that the continuous human occupation of Britain through the Younger Dryas is open to question, with the presence of hunter-gatherers in this period only becoming certain after about 10,300 BC. With regard to these people, most of the evidence for their existence comes from south-eastern Britain and East Anglia, but none of this material suggests long-term occupation and we are perhaps looking at nomadic hunters who were following migrating reindeer herds. Certainly the available faunal evidence suggests that the cold conditions and tundra landscape of Britain at this time led to reindeer returning to the country, perhaps using the Midlands as breeding grounds in the spring before migrating across the North Sea plain back to Germany for the autumn. In this context, it is interesting to note that the suggested migration route for the reindeer has them passing close to or through our study region, and finds of Ahrensburgian tanged points (arrow tips) have been made from north Lincolnshire. These items not only probably date from the Younger Dryas, but are also identical to finds associated with reindeer hunting in northern Germany in this period.

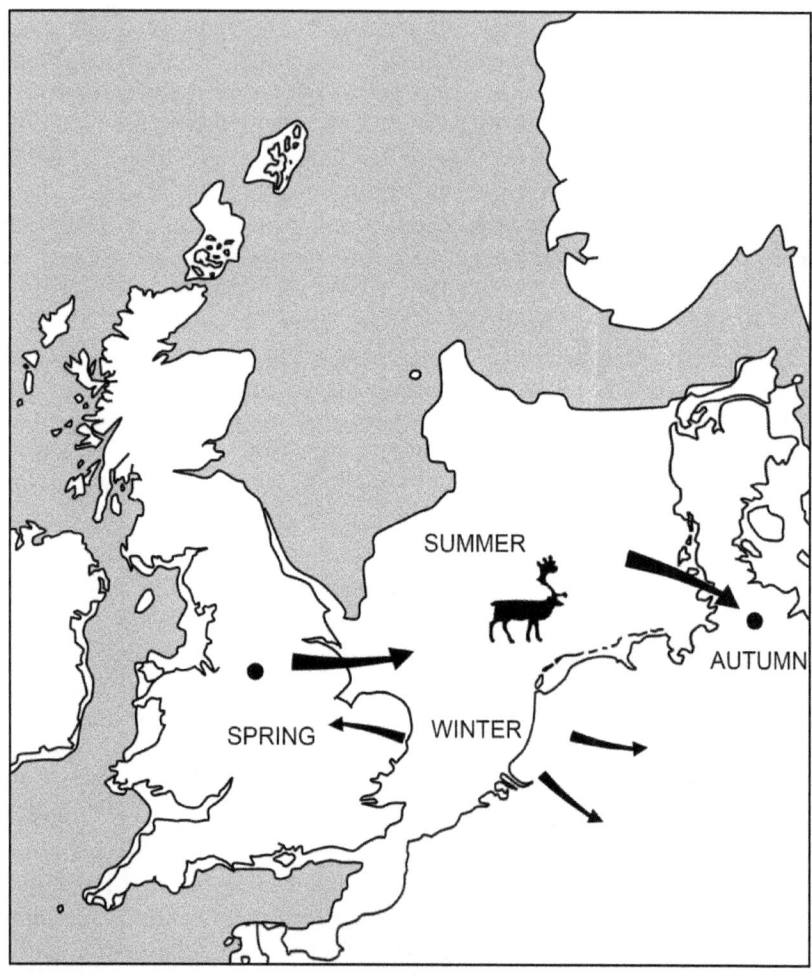

Figure 8: Reindeer migration routes and the extent of Doggerland during the Younger Dryas. Image based on Barton, 2005 and Shennan et al, 2000a, and contains material copyright to The Geological Society; used by kind permission.

If the Younger Dryas began rapidly, it ended in the same way too. Sometime around 9600 BC the temperature began to quickly rise back to levels at least as high as today, probably due to the re-establishment of the Gulf Stream, with this change again appearing to occur over the course of a single human lifespan (between ten and fifty years on most estimates). As a result, birch trees re-expanded from their glacial refuges to form an extensive birch forest whose increasingly dense canopy shaded out other plants. Moreover, in contrast to the Windermere Interstadial, this improvement in the climate and reforestation of the landscape was not a temporary development – the end of the Younger Dryas is generally considered to mark both the beginning of the ongoing Holocene Interglacial and the start of the Mesolithic period, or 'Middle Stone Age'. So, the question becomes, what was happening to the people and landscape of the Louth region as it finally emerged from the Palaeolithic period and into a new, warmer and more climatically-stable era?

With its wooded landscape and hunter-gatherers, the Mesolithic period – which, as a whole, spans the period between $c.$ 9600–4000 BC – doesn't actually appear that dissimilar in character to the latter stages of the Windermere Interstadial. Indeed, some of the stone microlith projectile types found in the Early Mesolithic are largely indistinguishable from those of the Final Upper Palaeolithic. On the other hand, there are some key differences that deserve notice. First and foremost, although Mesolithic artefacts – including a few securely identified as belonging to the earliest part of the period – have been found in some quantity from the intensively investigated area just to the south of our study region (notably in Belchford, Tetford, and Salmonby parishes), unlike in the preceding era a small number of finds of Mesolithic and possibly-Mesolithic date are now also known from the Louth region itself. This does, of course, help to confirm that Mesolithic hunter-gatherers were indeed present in the forests here, including potentially in the Keddington Road area of Louth. Second, the forests of the Mesolithic would appear to have been both denser and more varied than those of the Windermere Interstadial, with species such as elm, hazel and pine increasingly invading the birch forests as soils matured. As a result, the Louth region became covered by a genuine mixed deciduous forest in the period after 8000 BC, with lime becoming a significant component from $c.$ 6400 BC, oak present on the drier ground, and alder flourishing

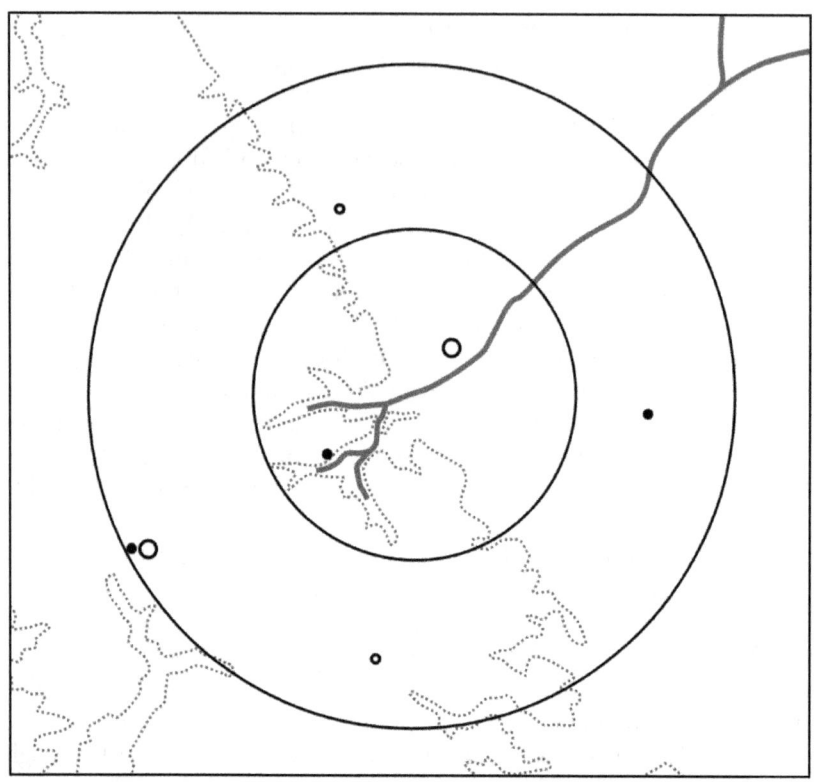

Figure 9: Mesolithic finds from the Louth region. Symbol size reflects the number of finds; filled symbols indicate certainly Mesolithic finds, open symbols indicate Mesolithic-Neolithic finds.

where soil moisture was high, although there were almost certainly numerous large clearings within this forest too. These would have probably been opened up and maintained both by large grazing animals, such as aurochs (wild cattle), bison and wild horses, and possibly by people who used fire for this purpose – it hardly needs saying that these clearings are likely to have formed a significant focus for Mesolithic hunting activity. Third, instead of being peripheral to activity focussed in the southern and western parts of Britain, the Louth region and Lincolnshire as a whole now appears to have been peripheral to the Mesolithic North Sea plain, an area now usually known as 'Doggerland' after the North Sea's Dogger Bank.

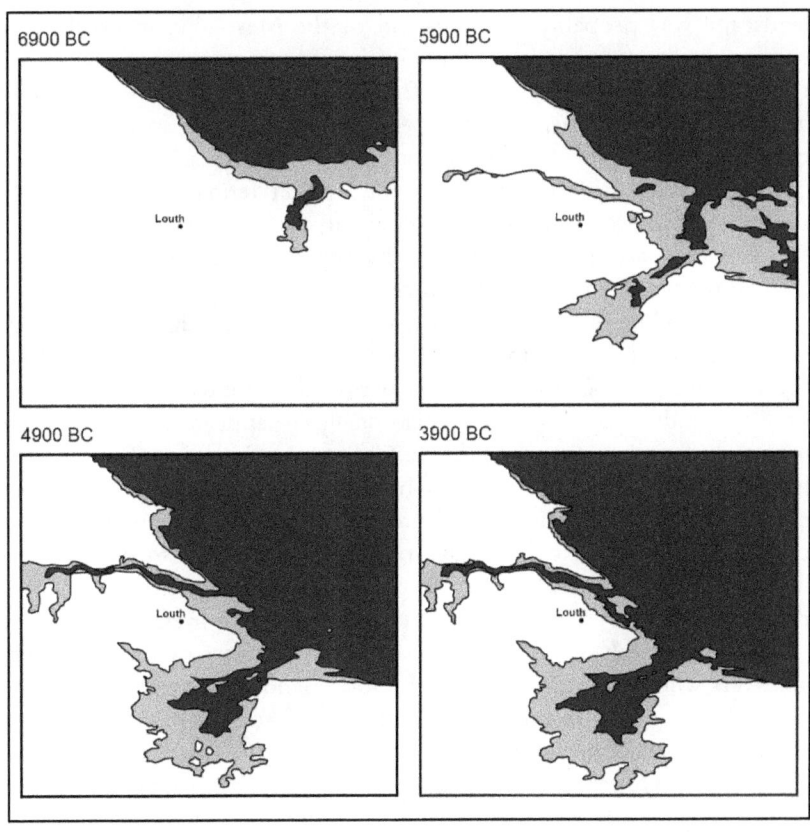

Figure 10: The latter stages of the flooding of Doggerland. Dark grey indicates areas permanently under water; light grey indicates areas probably flooded by the tides; and white indicates land above the high-water mark. Image based on Shennan et al, 2000a, and contains material copyright to The Geological Society; used by kind permission.

Although sometimes treated as little more than a temporary 'land bridge' between Britain and the Continent, Doggerland's importance in the Mesolithic period is now increasingly recognized, particularly in light of the 3D seismic data collected by the North Sea oil and gas industry. This material has recently been used to reconstruct the drowned landscape of Doggerland in far more detail than has previously been possible, and it is now clear that North Sea floor constituted, in the Mesolithic period, a rich landscape of lakes, hills, river valleys, plains, tidal inlets and saltmarshes. Moreover, it has been argued that this landscape was probably the heartland of the Mesolithic in north-west Europe, with areas such as the Louth region consequently likely to represent upland hunting grounds for much of the period, perhaps only visited seasonally by people who spent most of the year on Doggerland, living close to the shifting coastal zone and its resources. This is, in itself, of considerable interest, both generally and in terms of the probable character of the earlier Mesolithic activity in the Louth region. However, Doggerland is also important for the history of this region in other ways too, primarily due to the way in which it was lost.

The flooding of Doggerland began in the Upper Palaeolithic period, when the coastline lay in the area of Scotland, and continued throughout the Mesolithic. Over much of this period the inundation would have been a gradual process, but occasionally it appears to have been extremely fast. For example, the '8.2 kiloyear event' of *c.* 6200 BC saw temperatures drop, temporarily, by between 1 and 5°C and sea-level rise rapidly and permanently by as much as three or four metres, as a consequence of the final drainage of the North American glacial lakes into the Atlantic. From the perspective of the Louth region, this drowning of Doggerland is likely to have had two major effects. The first is that it probably increased the population density, as those hunter-gatherers who had primarily lived on Doggerland were forced to migrate onto higher ground to escape the water. The second is that it led to the death and eventual submersion of the forest that covered the Lincolnshire Outmarsh (a western portion of which is included in our study zone), as the sea first rose close to the level of the land here – raising the water-table and waterlogging the forest – and then beyond.

This waterlogging and flooding is likely to have taken place at different times along the coast, reflecting the fact that the surface on which the forest grew was not the flat alluvial landscape of today, but rather the underlying and undulating stiff clay left behind by the last glaciation, which in some areas lies at or close to the modern surface and in others is buried by many metres of alluvium. Thus, on the one hand, at Chapel Point the peat produced by waterlogging was still forming as late as 2866–2142 BC, with the sea only drowning the land here after this time. On the other hand, at Theddlethorpe the peat had begun to form around 6174–5961 BC, at Immingham the forest looks to have been waterlogged and killed sometime between 5772–5346 BC, and at Marshchapel recent boreholes in the south-west of the parish (just beyond the northern boundary of our study area) indicate that this area had been completely flooded by the sea before the end of the Mesolithic period, *c.* 4000 BC. Similarly, a 1.8 km west–east cross-section in North Somercotes parish, constructed from multiple boreholes, reveals marine silts and clays overlying an undulating till surface that varies in elevation between about twelve metres below the current sea-level to over seventeen metres below. This Mesolithic land-surface would probably have started to flood before 6000 BC based on the relative sea-level graph for the Lincolnshire Marshes, assuming that it was not enclosed by higher ground beyond the eastern limit of the cross-section. Indeed, its low level raises the interesting possibility that any people active on the edges of the Lincolnshire Outmarsh in the Later Mesolithic would have been directly affected by the devastating Storegga Slide tsunami of *c.* 6100 BC. This was generated by a huge underwater land-slide off the coast of Norway and has been seen as potentially responsible for the final physical separation of Britain from the Continent. Current reconstructions of its effects suggest that it flooded a large area of the coastline of Doggerland, which is argued to have then lain not far off the present coast of eastern Lincolnshire. In light of the above, however, it doesn't seem impossible that its effects would have actually been felt by those on the edge of the present Outmarsh too, given that it occurred when sea-levels were at around seventeen metres below present levels

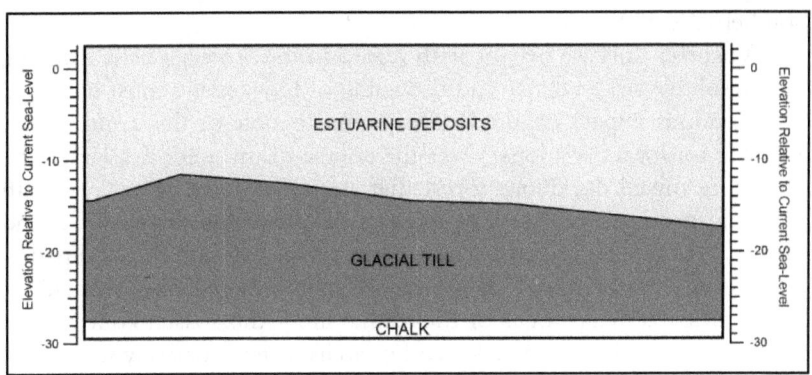

Figure 11: Cross-section derived from multiple boreholes in North Somercotes parish, showing the location of the underlying Mesolithic land-surface (dark grey) relative to the Ipswichian-era chalk wave-cut platform, and the current land-surface and sea-level. Image based on Environment Agency, 2009, and used by kind permission.

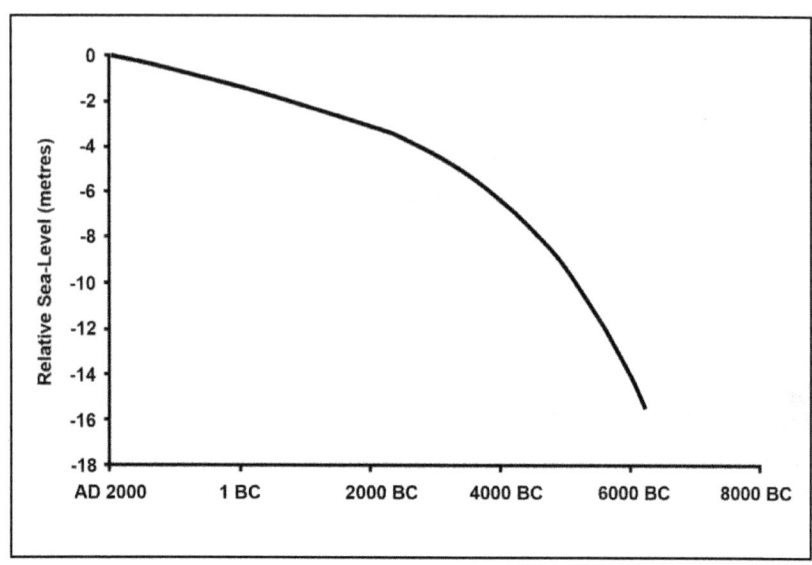

Figure 12: The rise in relative sea-level in the Lincolnshire Marshes area. Image based on Shennan et al, 2000b, and contains material copyright to The Geological Society; used by kind permission.

and may have flooded land up to five metres above this level in the Southern North Sea area.

Whatever the case may be with regard to the Storegga Slide tsunami, the Mesolithic sea-level rise and drowning of Doggerland must have had a tremendous impact on the landscape and people of this region, even allowing for local variations. Over the course of this period, a landscape of mature mixed deciduous forest that stretched down onto the North Sea plain had been replaced, to the east of our region, by wetlands and the sea. At the very least this change must have affected the occupation patterns and seasonal 'rounds' of the Mesolithic population, particularly as the probable main focus of Mesolithic life – the coastal zone and its resources – now lay on the edge and most likely even partially within our region, rather than far away on Doggerland. Although there is currently no local evidence as to how the Late Mesolithic hunter-gatherers interacted with the coastal landscape newly created here, an analogous situation in the Severn estuary can offer some suggestions. Here a mature oak forest was similarly drowned by the rising sea-level in around 5800 BC, with marine silts and saltmarsh forming on top of the old land-surface and in-between the trunks of the trees, but in this case human and animal footprints have been preserved in the silts from this period. These show men, women and children walking singly, together, and potentially in family groups across the landscape, sometimes tracking animals across the silts and other times leading children down to the water's edge to collect shellfish. Needless to say, these footprints preserve a valuable record of Mesolithic life, and there seems little reason to think that the new coastal zone in eastern Lincolnshire wasn't explored and exploited in a similar manner.

Although the flooding of the Lincolnshire Outmarsh continued for some time after the end of the Mesolithic, the subsequent Neolithic period ('New Stone Age', *c.* 4000–2200 BC) saw the start of the next round of major changes to the landscape of the Louth region – the deforestation of the Wolds and the Middle Marsh. However, the cause this time was not climatic decline (as with the Younger Dryas deforestation) or the rising sea, but instead a fundamental change in the way that humans exploited the region, as they adopted a less mobile lifestyle and began to farm the landscape, which in turn required the forest to be cleared in order to provide room for both cereal cultivation and animal herds.

The clearance of the Mesolithic forest by early farmers is likely to have been a process that took several millennia to complete. In the Lincolnshire Marshes, the available pollen cores from Butterbump (Willoughby) indicate that the forest there was largely cleared in the Late Neolithic period and Early Bronze Age (*c.* 2800–1500 BC), with subsequent eras having low levels of tree and shrub pollens and high levels of herbs and cereals. On the other hand, on the Wolds at Skendleby the evidence suggests that the deciduous oak and hazel woodland there was being cleared by *c.* 3500 BC, and at Swinhope (just to the north-west of our study zone) the local area had been cleared to an open grassy landscape with some scrub woodland and at least local arable agriculture by *c.* 3930–3650 BC. Unfortunately the Louth region itself lacks such detailed environmental evidence to date the start of the deforestation and beginning of farming activity on the Wolds and Marshes, but there seems little reason to think that the situation here would have been significantly different. Certainly there are a number of Neolithic axes known from the region, including five from Legbourne parish and one or two from Louth. These objects have often been

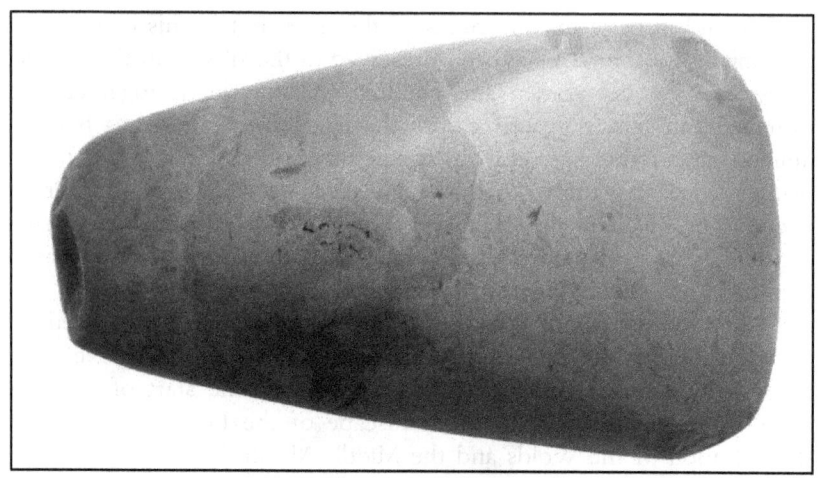

Figure 13: A Neolithic polished axe from the Great Langdale 'axe factory' in Cumbria, found at Legbourne. Image used by kind permission of Louth Museum.

associated with the clearance of forests in this period, although they probably had a symbolic and possibly a ritual significance too. Additionally, a field-system with rectangular plots and access trackways has been identified as underlying Bronze Age features at Donington on Bain and so may be of Neolithic date.

Besides the start of agriculture, the Neolithic period is also likely to have seen more settled communities developing in the region, as a result of the shift to a lifestyle that relied less on hunter-gathering. In the absence of excavated settlements from the region, perhaps the most significant evidence with regard to this comes from the thirteen certain or possible Neolithic 'long barrows' known from this part of eastern Lincolnshire. Long barrows – such as the example measuring approximately 32x12 metres in Tathwell parish, still visible on the north side of the Louth–Horncastle road – represent the earliest evidence we possess for burial and more complex social activity in the Louth region, with the comparable dated examples from Swinhope having their origins between *c.* 4000–3500 BC. These large earthen and chalk monuments functioned as communal burial sites for bodies that had been previously defleshed, almost certainly by being left outside (perhaps on a platform) until the soft tissues had rotted or been scavenged away. It seems

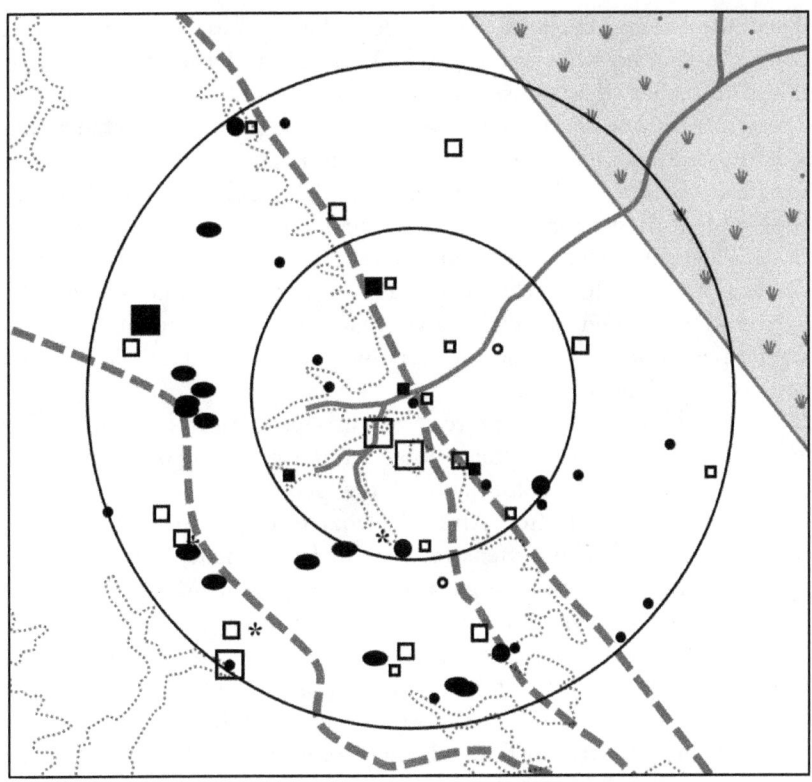

Figure 14: Neolithic finds and sites in the Louth region. Symbol size reflects the number of finds; filled symbols are certainly Neolithic, open symbols are Neolithic-Bronze Age. Ovals are long barrows; circles are axes; squares are stone tools other than axes; stars are other types of finds, including pottery and field-systems. The approximate position of the Neolithic coastline is shown, along with the inter-tidal zone in light grey; possible areas of saltmarsh and sand/silt within this are also depicted here, as they are on later maps that show the coastal zone too. Also illustrated are the key north-south prehistoric routes that may have been in existence by this point.

probable that these burials were in some way special, sacrificial or symbolic, in order to justify the time and effort that this burial-rite and mound-building must have entailed. As such, long barrows are unlikely to reflect the normal method of dealing with the remains of the dead in this era, and they have instead been credibly interpreted as ritual sites that represented a permanent link between the community that used them, its ancestral dead, and the surrounding landscape. In other words, these tombs are likely to have been the shrines of more settled communities who were farming in the local area and were laying claim to this land, rather than those of hunter-gatherers. In this context, it is interesting to note that the barrows at Swinhope were constructed within a deforested and at least partially farmed landscape and there is evidence for tillage of the pre-barrow soil at Skendleby. It is also important to observe that these monuments usually stand at the head or on the edge of a valley, sited where they could have been seen on the skyline from the nearby valley floor. This would tend to support the notion that the barrows functioned in the above manner, and it certainly seems suggestive with regard to the location of the primary settlements associated with these sites.

If there is evidence for more settled groups engaged in farming after 4000 BC, this is not to say that mobile hunter-gathering didn't continue to play a major role in the lives of the people of this region in the Neolithic period and after. After all, what evidence we have suggests there were probably still extensive tracts of forest throughout the region well into the Neolithic, particularly on the Middle Marsh (given the environmental evidence discussed above) and also potentially on the Wolds too. In this respect, the numerous sites that have produced flint tools and debitage – waste material from tool production – of Neolithic and Neolithic/Bronze Age date are perhaps significant. Some of the larger of these scatters of flints may well represent settlement sites. The dense scatter of Neolithic material at Kelstern has, for example, been seen in this light, and there are other large Neolithic/Bronze Age flint scatters known from Raithby (north of Brock a Dale plantation, close to the Louth bypass), Louth (to the east of the southern entrance to Hubbard's Hills), and Asterby (in the valley of the Scamblesby Beck), to which this interpretation might also apply, although the Asterby site is currently categorized as simply a 'lithic (stone) working site' and the others could be too. In many other cases, however, the scatters are smaller in scale, and at least a proportion of these are likely to reflect temporary transit or hunting camps resulting from continuing hunter-gathering activity, perhaps located in clearings within the remaining forest that were, in some cases, repeatedly returned to. Certainly such an interpretation might help to explain the small scatters of material found across our region, including the Mesolithic–Neolithic/Bronze Age scatter found in the Keddington Road area of Louth, to the north of Lyndon Way.

There is, of course, considerable room for debate as to what such a coexistence of farming and hunting activity in the region might signify. First and foremost, it is worth emphasising that this probably doesn't mean that there were two entirely discrete groups living in the region, farmers on the cleared parts of the Wolds and hunter-gatherers elsewhere and especially on the Marshes. Although such a situation has been hypothesized for other parts of north-western Europe – most notably in the Netherlands – there doesn't really seem to be sufficient evidence to justify it here. Indeed, it can be pointed out that items usually associated with the new Neolithic farming culture (specifically polished axes and leaf-shaped arrowheads) are found both on the low-lying Middle Marsh and on the Wolds, a pattern replicated both elsewhere in eastern and northern Lincolnshire and across the wider region. This strongly suggests an interconnection between the people living on the Wolds and the Marshes, with them having at the very least similar access to the new Neolithic regional exchange networks that saw these probably prestige-items travelling considerable distances (many Lincolnshire polished axes come from the 'axe factory' at Great Langdale in Cumbria). Needless to say, this doesn't really fit with a scenario whereby two separate and culturally distinct groups inhabited the region in the Neolithic.

Second, if the Neolithic hunter-gatherers and farmers of this region are thus likely to have been one and the same, we do need to consequently ask both whether agriculture or hunter-gathering was the dominant economic activity here during the Neolithic and how rapidly farming was actually adopted. Up until relatively recently, there has been fairly widespread agreement that the hunter-gatherers of Britain only adopted farming gradually as a supplement to their primary and traditional hunting and foraging activities. However, this model has been strongly questioned. In particular, Peter Rowley-Conwy and others have argued that the evidence for the British Neolithic transition to a sedentary, agricultural lifestyle indicates rapid, rather than slow and gradual, change, with hunting and foraging quickly becoming supplemental activities to pastoral and arable farming, instead of remaining the dominant mode of living for much of the period. This interpretation appears to be supported by a recent analysis of the available radiocarbon evidence from Late Mesolithic and Neolithic Britain, and if it can be sustained then it would carry a number of significant implications for this region. Most obviously, it would suggest that farming was likely dominant in the region from the Early Neolithic period onwards, with any hunter-gathering activity becoming a less significant element in the life of the region from a much earlier date than is often assumed. At the same time, it would also imply that the Wolds were indeed the main regional focus of activity in the earlier Neolithic, just as has sometimes been assumed on the basis of the long barrows, given that this is where the environmental evidence suggests that farming was initially focussed.

Finally, if there was potentially a rapid adoption of farming as the primary means of economic support amongst the population of this region and elsewhere, it needs to be asked why this occurred. It has been argued that that farming practices were adopted by the hunter-gatherers of Britain mainly via word-of-mouth and trade. Yet this explanation is perhaps more suited to a model of gradual adoption than one of rapid change, and research into both the DNA and, especially, the radiocarbon data from Britain as a whole suggests that there was in fact a notable episode of immigration into Britain by agriculturalists from the Continent around 4000 BC. In such circumstances, it certainly doesn't seem impossible that farming was first introduced to this region by Continental immigrants, perhaps with the local hunter-gatherers then swiftly adopting the immigrants' new 'Neolithic' material culture and way of life.

Figure 15: The round barrows at Bully Hills, Tathwell.

The Late Neolithic and Early Bronze Age (c. 2800–1500 BC) in the Louth area is likely to have seen further significant woodland clearance across the region, along with the emergence of a new class of funerary monuments, round barrows. These monuments have a considerably wider distribution across our region than the earlier long barrows, and they are found not only more extensively on the Wolds, but also on the Middle Marsh, something which could well reflect the expansion of cleared land in both areas around this time. Thus, for example, several probable barrows are visible on aerial photography from Keddington (just to the south of Louth Park Abbey, and west of River Farm), Alvingham (to the north of the Louth-Alvingham road), and Covenham St Mary (to the west of the Covenham-Yarburgh road), with these sited on land as low as around twelve metres above the current sea-level. In addition, round barrows are more densely distributed than the preceding long barrows, with a substantial number of them appearing to form part of larger 'barrow cemeteries'. This can be most clearly seen at Bully Hills, Tathwell, where a chain of seven round barrows still survives up to a maximum of three metres high and between fifteen and twenty-five metres in diameter, but examples are known throughout the region. Indeed, aerial photography has revealed up to five barrow cemeteries in South Elkington parish alone, each containing between three and six barrows, and one of these cemeteries appears to be associated with Boswell Barrow, a large earthwork barrow that is forty-five metres in diameter and still stands nearly two metres high.

Of course, it once again appears unlikely that everyone living in the region was accorded such a monumental burial. Some in the second millennium BC may have been buried in flat cremation cemeteries, of the type excavated near Long Bennington in south Lincolnshire. Although there is no certain instance from the Louth region, there is a possible example from Donington on Bain where fragments of cinerary urns, along with pieces of human and other bones, were frequently found in the nineteenth century in a field close to other Bronze Age sites. Of the rest of the dead, though, we have no evidence. The only possible hint of their fate comes from Langford in Nottinghamshire, where twelve bodies were recovered from a former river-channel along with fragments of basketwork, all of which had got caught up in a logjam sometime around 2100 BC, presumably after they had been disposed of in the river. If most of the dead of the Bronze Age Louth region were treated in a similar manner, perhaps disposed of by being set afloat on the rivers or at the coast, then their absence from the archaeological record is readily explicable.

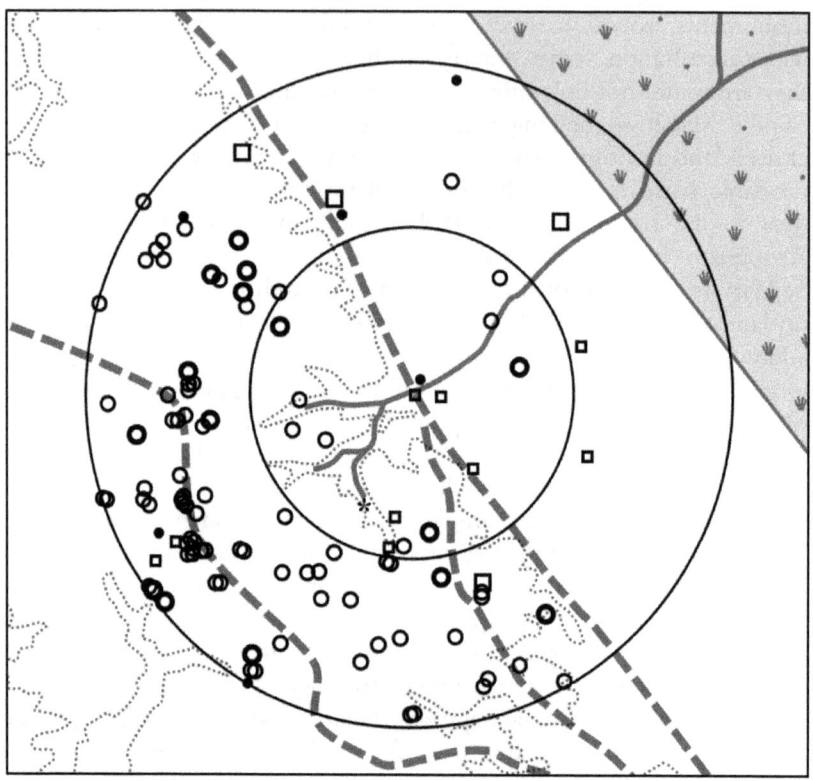

Figure 16: Bronze Age finds and sites in the Louth region. Square symbols indicate stone tools; symbol size reflects the number of finds. Small filled circles indicate metal artefacts. Large open circles are round barrows; those with think borders reflect multiple barrow sites. Stars are other types of finds, including pottery.

Aside from the round barrows and the Neolithic/Bronze Age flint scatters discussed previously, the main evidence for Bronze Age activity in this region consists of some sherds of pottery, stone tools dated specifically to the Bronze Age, and – of course – metalwork. The latter is of particular significance, given that the introduction of metal tools and metal-working is to some degree the defining feature of the Bronze Age. Lincolnshire as a whole actually has a high concentration of such items, but they are rare in this part of the county. Known finds are limited to a palstave – a type of bronze axe – found close to a round barrow in Calcethorpe with Kelstern; a reworked bronze barbed spearhead from Donington on Bain and another spearhead from Scamblesby; a bronze socketed axe, found 'near Louth' in 1914; and a possible wing from a Bronze Age spear or sword from Utterby. Perhaps the most interesting find, however, is a piece of copper-alloy casting waste, found at Fulstow and dated broadly to *c.* 1200–700 BC. This suggests at the very least local bronze casting was happening at this low-lying site, which is intriguing given the relative rarity of Bronze Age metalwork in this region. Moreover, it is interesting to note that the casting waste was actually found on a site that has produced evidence of later (Romano-British) craft activity.

With regard to the other classes of finds, there is equally little Bronze Age pottery from the region when compared with Lincolnshire as a whole, the exceptions being some decorated Beaker-style pottery from the fill of a Bronze Age ring-ditch at Donington on Bain – a type usually associated with individual, as opposed to communal, alcohol consumption – and some Bronze Age pottery from Donington, Raithby cum Maltby, and Tathwell. There are, in contrast, rather more find-spots of stone arrowheads, scrapers, axes and similar items belonging to the Bronze Age, including two from Louth itself. The first of these is an Early Bronze Age (*c.* 2200–1500 BC) scraper – used in the preparation of skins, wood and bone – found at Spout Yard. The lack of wear on this item suggests that it was not deposited by the nearby river, and it consequently seems likely to reflect at least occasional Bronze Age activity in this part of the town. The second item is a barbed and tanged arrowhead found on the school field at Monks' Dyke, which is indicative of local hunting activity. The location of the settlement where the people associated with these artefacts lived is, needless to say, uncertain. There could have been a Bronze Age settlement on the site of the present town, long-since lost below the medieval and later buildings. Alternatively, it is worth recalling that there is a possible Neolithic/Bronze Age settlement site near to the southern entrance to Hubbard's Hills, which may be of relevance here.

Looking eastwards to the edge of our study zone, something ought finally to be said about the role of the coastal zone in the life of this region in both the Neolithic period and the Bronze Age. This area is likely to have remained within the eastern borders of our region from the

Late Mesolithic until the Early Bronze Age as sea-levels continued to rise, and it would almost certainly have been a significant resource for the people of this area. Indeed, not only did this landscape continue to provide opportunities for foraging and food-gathering, as in the Mesolithic, but it also seems likely that the intertidal saltmarshes were used for stock grazing by pastoral farmers in light of comparative evidence from other parts of the country. However, after around 1700 BC this activity potentially moved out of our region, as relative sea-levels temporarily dropped slightly and the coastline moved back eastwards. At Chapel Point, for example, marine clays laid down by the sea were themselves covered by a layer of freshwater peat, dated to 1909–1416 BC, as the sea retreated here. It has to be said, though, that this site was very late to flood in comparison with other sites closer to our region (sometime after 2866–2142 BC, compared to before 4000 BC at Marshchapel and probably even earlier at North Somercotes) and so it would probably have been re-exposed by even a small relative sea-level fall. As such, the deposition of freshwater peat here cannot be taken to indicate that the Bronze Age coastline had moved out to roughly where the present day one is. Nonetheless, it does at least show that a significant marine regression was occurring in the mid-second millennium BC.

Any absence of the coastal zone and saltmarshes from the Louth region was by no means permanent. The retreat of the sea was followed by a new period of marine flooding usually associated with the Iron Age (*c.* 750 BC–AD 43), with relative sea-levels reaching new highs and marine clays containing shells of *Scrobicularia* – the peppery furrow shell or sand gaper, a type of bivalve mollusc – being found overlying the Bronze Age peat at sites like Chapel Point. The Iron Age is notable in other ways too, not least the fact that in its later stages we find evidence for the emergence of both major regional centres and large political units in Lincolnshire. In the period before the Roman conquest of AD 43 the Louth region formed part of the territory of the Corieltavi, an Iron Age tribe whose influence extended from the Humber to the Nene. The heartland of Corieltavian power and wealth appears to have lain in Lindsey and North Kesteven, and within this area major settlements can be identified at sites such as Dragonby, Kirmington and Ludford. Unfortunately, none of these important settlements are found within the present area of study and instead Louth and its immediate vicinity appears to have been largely peripheral in the Iron Age, the region looking to encompass, respectively, the easternmost and northernmost portions of the districts dependent upon Ludford and Ulceby Cross according to recent reconstructions of the Iron Age political landscape. This is not, however, to say that there were no sites of interest in this region, nor that there is nothing that can be said about life here in this period.

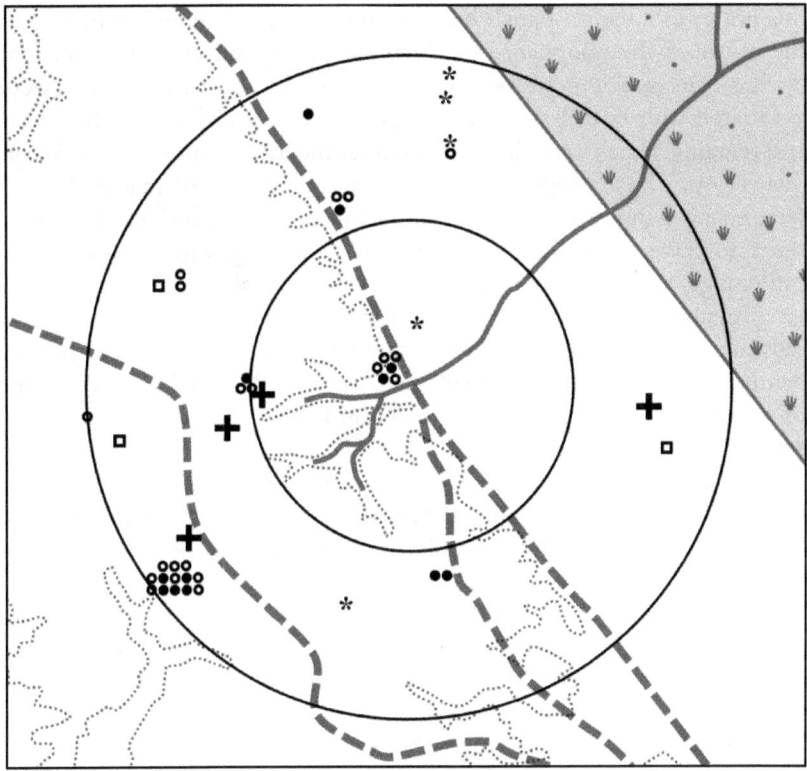

Figure 17: Iron Age finds and sites in the Louth region. Crosses indicate settlement sites; squares refer to metalwork, including brooches; circles are finds of coins – filled circles are gold, open are silver or copper-alloy; stars are other types of finds, including pottery.

The most significant concentration of Iron Age material in the region comes from the Donington-Stenigot area, where there is both an excavated settlement and a collection of thirteen Late Iron Age coins. The latter consists of twelve Corieltavian coins (five gold, six silver, and one copper-alloy) found between 2000 and 2003, along with a single copper-alloy coin of the Cantii tribe of Iron Age Kent, which may suggests a degree of inter-regional trade. All of these coins are assigned to 'Stenigot' in the Oxford Celtic Coin Index, and whilst this database doesn't retain any further details as to the findspot, the number of coins suggests that we are probably dealing with a locally-significant settlement located somewhere in the vicinity of Stenigot. As to the excavated site, this lies in Donington parish but is found only a few hundred metres to the north of the boundary with Stenigot parish and consists chiefly of ditches, pits and the eaves-drip gullies of round houses. These were associated with both Late Iron Age pottery and a variety of other finds and remains, which can begin to give us some idea about Iron Age life in this region. Thus it appears clear that the inhabitants of this settlement were engaged in the arable cultivation of wheat, barley and oat. They also seem to have undertaken some pastoral farming, with the bones of cattle, pigs, sheep and horses found on the site, alongside features that are probably to be associated with stock control. The burnt bones of a redwing or thrush similarly suggest that wild animals formed part of the diet here in the Iron Age, and small amounts of slag, a possible fragment of a loomweight, and an iron needle indicate a degree of local craft activity.

Away from Donington-Stenigot, the available evidence for the Iron Age is sparse. The only other excavated settlement is found at Manby, where pits, ditches and a possible drip gully from a house have been found associated with Middle–Late Iron Age pottery and sheep and cattle bones. There are also two probable Iron Age settlements known from cropmarks in Welton le Wold parish, something supported by finds of three coins of the Corieltavi here. Otherwise our information is restricted to chance finds of metalwork or pottery. Thus two Iron Age silver coin fragments, dated $c.$ 55–45 BC, and a cast copper-alloy Colchester brooch dated $c.$ AD 25–60 suggest that there was some sort of Late Iron Age activity in Calcethorpe with Kelstern parish. Similarly, there are two gold Corieltavian coins from Haugham and one gold (dated $c.$ 60–50 BC) and two silver coins from Utterby, which probably indicate the presence of Iron Age settlements in these parishes. Also of interest are recent finds of Iron Age pottery from the same site in Fulstow parish that has produced evidence of Bronze Age and Romano-British craft activity. However, from the perspective of the present study

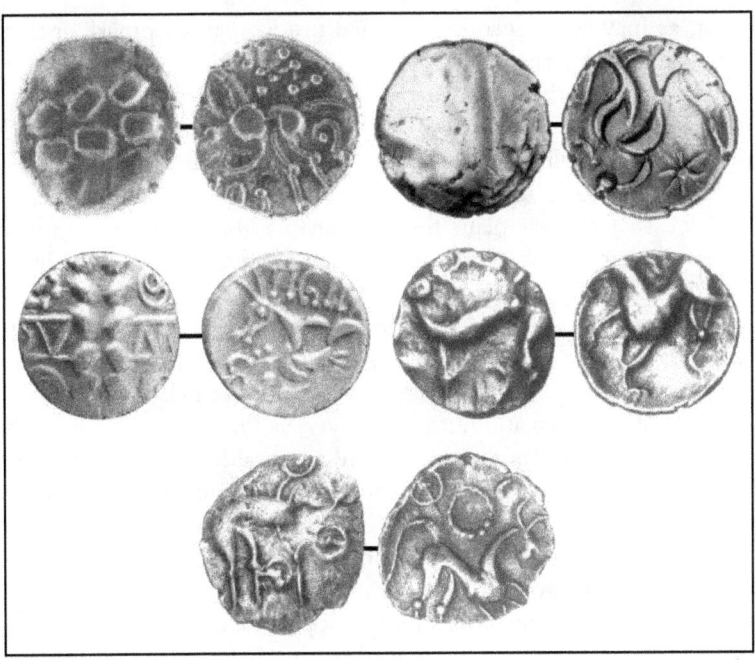

Figure 18: Five of the Late Iron Age coins assigned a 'Louth' findspot in the Celtic Coin Index, showing both sides of the coins. Images of these coins are used by kind permission of the Oxford Celtic Coin Index; CCI reference numbers 95.1181, 03.0516, 02.0055, 01.1010 and 00.0571.

the most intriguing evidence comes from Louth itself, as the Celtic Coin Index actually assigns a 'Louth' findspot to six Corieltavian coins of the Late Iron Age, four of silver and two of gold. In interpreting these finds we do need to be cautious. The Index has no more detailed record of the findspots of these coins than 'Louth', and Louth's status as a modern population centre means that it is not impossible that coins from several different sites, potentially some miles away from the town, could have been reported as having a simple 'Louth' provenance by their finders. On the other hand, these six coins – however poorly recorded – do at least hold out the possibility that there was a Late Iron Age settlement in the immediate vicinity of Louth. In this context, the discovery of a large, unabraded sherd of Iron Age pottery on the Fairfield Industrial Estate (to the north-west of Brackenborough Road) in 2006 may be of especial interest, as may be a recently identified pre-Roman cropmark enclosure near to Fanthorpe Lane.

In conclusion, the period from the end of the last Ice Age to the eve of the Roman conquest is one that saw tremendous changes to both the landscape and people of the Louth region. At the start of the post-glacial era, the region was a tundra- and later grass-covered upland zone, lying to the west of a great plain that stretched right across to continental Europe. As such, it was probably only sporadically visited by hunters who were following animals such as wild horses and mammoths as they passed through. These hunter-gatherers are likely to have become more regular visitors as a dense forest grew up here over the succeeding millennia, probably using clearings within it for the hunting of game and the collection of fruits and nuts. Moreover, as the North Sea plain where they primarily lived was flooded by the inexorably rising sea, the Louth region is likely to have become a zone of regular activity and settlement rather than simply a seasonal hunting ground. With the dawn of the Neolithic around 4000 BC, the amount of archaeological evidence increases dramatically and this may well reflect a genuine population increase, as the people here rapidly adopted a more settled, farming-focussed lifestyle, perhaps influenced in this by the arrival of migrants from the Continent. This new lifestyle led to the gradual clearance of the forest to make room for crops and domesticated animal herds, and a decline in hunter-gatherer activity, first on the Wolds and later on the Marshes. As a result, it is likely that much of the land in the region had been cleared and was being used for either pastoral or arable farming by the end of the Iron Age, including the saltmarshes in the east of the region, which would have provided valuable winter grazing grounds.

With regard to the place of Louth itself in all of this, there is potential evidence for the presence of Mesolithic and later hunter-gatherers in the area to the north of Keddington Road, and a number of finds indicate Neolithic and Bronze Age activity in the town and its environs. Whether there are Neolithic, Bronze Age and/or Iron Age settlements actually buried under (or destroyed by) the medieval and modern town must remain a matter of speculation until opportunities for more extensive excavations present themselves. However, such a situation certainly doesn't seem implausible given the character of the area, and the existence of at least one such settlement on the river terrace itself might well be suspected. In any case, there certainly seem to have been prehistoric settlements in the immediate vicinity of the town. Thus, for example, finds of 'many worked flints' near to the southern entrance to Hubbard's Hills suggest the presence of a settlement site of Neolithic/Bronze Age date. Similarly, the presence of Iron Age pottery, a pre-Roman cropmark enclosure, and six Late Iron Age coins raises the possibility of one or more Iron Age settlements in the area around the town. Indeed, given the general rarity of Iron Age coins in this part of Lincolnshire, if all six 'Louth' finds do come from a single site near to the town, then we may have the first hints that Louth and its environs were developing a degree of local centrality as early as the Iron Age.

3

Forgers, Fortresses and Religion in the Romano-British Louth Region, *c*. AD 43–410

Although the eastern Wolds and Marshes are often left largely blank on maps of 'Roman Lincolnshire', this is a little misleading. In reality, significantly more settlement sites and findspots are known from this region in the first to fourth centuries AD than from the preceding Iron Age or the subsequent Anglo-Saxon period. Partly this is a result of the relative high quality of the artefacts produced in this period, which allows for both easier identification and a better survival rate in the ground, something particularly true with regard to pottery. It is also likely to be a consequence of a wider circulation in local society of such archaeologically 'visible' material, especially during the Late Roman period. So, given this relative abundance of archaeological evidence, what can be said about the Louth region in the Roman period?

The attitude of the Corieltavi of Lincolnshire to the Roman conquest is not documented, but there seems little reason to think that the tribe initially offered significant resistance to the Romans. They may even have been one of the eleven unnamed British tribes who reportedly submitted peacefully and personally to Emperor Claudius in AD 43. On the other hand, it seems clear that the Roman Ninth Legion was based in the territory of the Corieltavi in the years after their arrival, and it has been suggested that the archaeological evidence from Lincolnshire and Leicestershire is consistent with a subsequent partial rebellion of the Corieltavi in AD 47, which led to a more onerous military presence here.

Despite this, there is little evidence for the Roman army in the Louth region. The nearest Early Roman legionary fortifications to Louth are found at Kirmington and, possibly, at Nettleton and Wispington, well outside of our study zone. Moreover, the only explicit evidence for the presence of members of the Roman army in the region is a chance find of part of a Roman first- to third-century sword scabbard from Gayton le Wold.

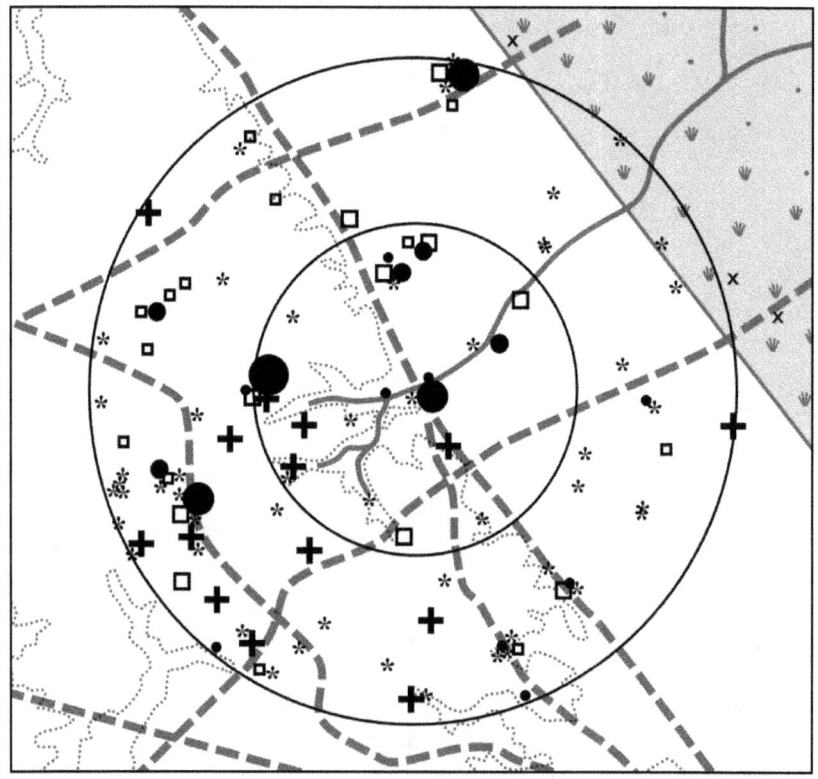

Figure 19: Romano-British finds and sites in the Louth region. Crosses indicate settlement sites; squares refer to metalwork, including brooches and rings, and circles are coin-finds – the size of the symbol reflects the number of finds; stars are other types of finds and sites, including pottery and ditch features; Outmarsh settlements mentioned in text but located outside of the survey area are marked with an 'x'. The approximate position of the Romano-British coastline is shown along with the inter-tidal zone in light grey, as are the major prehistoric and Roman routes that were probably in use in this period.

Part of the reason for this apparent lack of Roman military activity here may simply be the character of the Louth region. The nearest major Late Iron Age centres and subsequent Roman 'small towns' are those of Ludford and Ulceby Cross, both of which are located outside of our study area. Similarly, 'villas' – a term that is generally taken to imply high-status Romano-British estate centres, not necessarily classical in form so much as aspiring towards a Roman style – are rare, although there is probably one at Welton le Wold and another has been postulated at Maidenwell. This is not, of course, to say that there was no significant activity in the Louth area at this time, but rather that the region appears to have been to a large degree peripheral. Just as in the Late Iron Age, the distribution of finds reveals a landscape mainly composed of dispersed small farmsteads and settlements, spread over both the Wolds and the lowlands.

With regard to these farmsteads and settlements, some of them certainly demonstrate a considerable degree of continuity with the Iron Age past. Indeed, it seems likely that a casual observer at the end of the first century would have struggled to see much difference between situation in the Late Iron Age and the Early Roman periods here, aside from the presence of the new major roads that crossed through this region, probably on their way to the salt-making sites on the coast. So, for example, the Late Iron Age settlement site at Donington on Bain appears to have continued in use into the Early Roman period, on the basis of a first-century brooch and sherds of Romano-British pottery found in the upper fills of the excavated features, and the same is probably true at the Iron Age site at Manby too. Similarly, the extensive Romano-British cropmark site at Maidenwell includes probable hut circles, reflecting the pre-Roman building-styles of the region, as do a number of the minor Romano-British settlements or farmsteads visible in the region, such as that at Tathwell. The Romano-British settlements at Welton le Wold also seem likely to have had Iron Age antecedents on the basis of the features seen on aerial photographs. In this context, it is perhaps worth noting the presence of three silver rings from Stenigot and Kelstern, dated broadly to *c.* AD 185–300, which have ToT inscribed on them. To date, 68 such inscribed rings are known and they appear to have been worn almost exclusively by people living within the former territory of the Corieltavi, with the inscription referring to a Romanized Celtic god named or entitled Totatis who was probably the tribe's divine protector. As such, these rings suggest that, even as late as the third century, the people of this region remained at least partially connected to their pre-Roman past and were able to maintain a degree of tribal identity, despite their absorption into the Roman Empire.

Figure 20: Romano-British silver ring inscribed ToT, found at Stenigot. Image used by kind permission of the Portable Antiquities Scheme; PAS find reference number LIN-944EE5.

On the other hand, there is undoubtedly evidence for Romanization as the period progresses too. Imported fine Roman tableware – samian ware or *terra sigillata* – of the first to early third centuries is recorded from a number of sites in the region, including the probable settlement sites at Donington on Bain, Welton le Wold, Fulstow, Fotherby, Muckton, and a buried site at South Somercotes (Scupholme). Early Roman coins also occur at several locations. In particular, eleven silver *denarii* (dating from *c.* AD 69–148) have recently been found at Little Grimsby, and a significant number of first- and second-century coins were recovered from Louth before 1834. The latter finds reportedly included coins of Julius Caesar and Augustus, together with 'a considerable number' of coins of the first-century emperors Tiberius, Caligula, Nero, Galba, Otho, Vitellius, Vespasian, Domitian, Nerva, and Trajan; more recently, a coin of Domitian (dated AD 86) has been found on the corner of Charles Street and Newbridge Hill. Even more interesting is the evidence for the Roman-style usage of brick and tiles in the construction of buildings in the region. Compared to other parts of Lincolnshire, the available evidence is extremely limited, but finds of such building materials are known from a settlement site to the south-west of Donington village, where they are associated with second- to fourth-century pottery and a fragment of a first- to third-century glass vessel; from behind the Greyhound Inn (on the corner of Gospelgate and Upgate) in Louth; and possibly from the site of the probable Roman villa at Welton le Wold.

By the time we reach the fourth century, 'Roman' material is relatively widely distributed throughout the region. A large number of sites have Romano-British greyware pottery on them and most of the Roman coins known from Louth area belong to the third and, especially, the fourth centuries. Of the sites that produce such finds, a handful are particularly worthy of note. One of these is the previously mentioned extensive crop- and soil-mark settlement at Welton le Wold, which probably represents a Roman villa site. These cropmarks are associated with over 300 copper-alloy and silver coins, chiefly dating from the third to the late fourth centuries, although there are some earlier examples. This is a very significant quantity of coins for this part of Lincolnshire: otherwise coin concentrations here are thin, rarely reaching into double figures, although we admittedly don't know how many coins made up the 'plenty of Constantines' found in Louth before 1834. Furthermore, a rare and important silver British proto-hand-pin of the later fourth or fifth century has been found at this site, which suggests that there were

Figure 21: A silver Roman coin found at Fulstow, probably a contemporary copy of one of Constantius II (337–61). Image used by kind permission of the Portable Antiquities Scheme; PAS find reference number LIN-0C4BB1.

high-status and affluent Romano-Britons living at Welton le Wold through to the end of the Roman period or a little beyond.

Another very interesting site is found at Fulstow. This site is only known from metal-detected finds, but these suggest that it was important in the later Roman period. Artefacts recovered include a locally-significant concentration of twenty-six Roman coins, again chiefly of the third to late fourth centuries; metal artefacts, such as a late third- or fourth-century penannular brooch and a possible snake-headed bracelet; and Romano-British pottery, notably sherds of third- to fourth-century mortaria vessels (a specialized item of kitchenware, used to prepare food for a Roman-style diet). Most interesting of all, however, is the evidence for craft activity here. An unworked piece of jet found amongst the Roman finds is suggestive, but the major find has been three drilled lead tablets recovered in 2007. One of these was blank but the other two have a negative impression of a coin of the emperor Valens (364–78) at their centre. Needless to say, the most credible interpretation of these items is that they were dies used in the forging of late fourth-century silver coins, a conclusion which suggests that we have here a highly intriguing site located on the edge of the Late Roman coastal zone.

If we thus have evidence that the Romano-Britons of the Louth region engaged in the counterfeiting of Late Roman silver coins and perhaps other craft activities, is there anything else that might be said of their lives and activities? The evidence we have with regard to the economy of this area is relatively limited, with few detailed excavations or deposits subjected to environmental analysis. However, a number of first- to third-century grain dryers excavated from Cawkwell and a quern stone (used for hand-grinding grain) discovered at Welton le Wold at least confirm that arable farming was taking place and that some of the produce was being consumed locally. On the other hand, the lack of cropmark arable field-systems accompanying the known Romano-British settlements is intriguing, as is the presence of large enclosures at many of the villas on the Wolds, with one of the principal features at Welton le Wold villa being a large double-ditched non-defensive enclosure. This has led to the suggestion that the Lincolnshire Wolds in the Roman period was largely an open range, with the villas here functioning principally as stock farms or ranches, hence the enclosures. In addition to this farming activity, there is also some evidence for local craft and

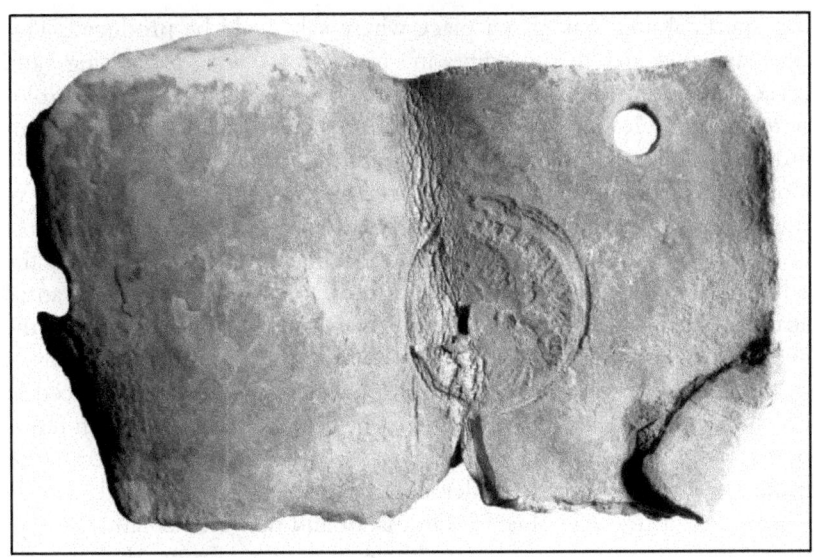

Figure 22: A lead tablet containing the impression of a Roman coin of Valens (364–78). This tablet was probably used in the forging of silver coins and was found at Fulstow. Image used by kind permission of the Portable Antiquities Scheme; PAS find reference number LIN-57B091.

production sites. So, finds of hammerscale – tiny pieces of iron oxide or slag produced as a by-product of iron production and working – from Great Carlton and slag from the base of a probably mid- to late fourth-century iron-smithing hearth at Withcall suggest that there was some local iron-working. Similarly, there is a possible Romano-British pottery kiln at Burwell that may have produced light greyware pottery in the third and fourth centuries, although the evidence for this is open to debate.

For those in the most easterly parts of our study zone, the exploitation of the coastal zone is also likely to have played a major part in their lives. Although sea-levels in the Early Roman period are generally thought to have been a little lower than they were in the Iron Age, the coastal zone is still likely to have extended into the Louth region. Comparative evidence from elsewhere in Britain suggests that the saltmarshes here would almost certainly have provided the local Romano-Britons with stock-breeding grounds for cattle and sheep and a source of winter grazing. Even more important, however, is the fact that the intertidal area was also a place where salt could be produced. This was an essential commodity in terms of food processing and preservation, and the major Roman routeways that run from the Wolds onto the Early Roman saltmarshes are most credibly associated with this industry. Although no salt production-sites, or salterns, are yet known from our region, recent work has revealed an interesting second- to fourth-century settlement in Marshchapel parish, just to the north of both our study zone and the Roman road that ran from Ludford to the saltmarshes. The finds from here indicate a relatively substantial structure that would appear to have been actually situated within the coastal zone, possibly on the saltmarsh itself, and was probably involved in the end-stage processing and transportation of the salt produced at nearby salterns. Moreover, this settlement does not stand alone. In terms of its location, it can be paralleled by a number of other certain or probable Romano-British settlements that are similarly found at low-lying spots on the Lincolnshire Outmarsh and may well be amenable to the same interpretation as to their function. From the present

Figure 23: A fourth-century crossbow brooch, found at Welsdale, Donington on Bain. Image used by kind permission of Louth Museum.

perspective, the most important examples are found in Saltfleetby St Peter, South Cockerington and South Somercotes parishes. Of these, the first two lie just to the east of our study zone, and so are probably to be in some way associated with it, whilst the former (at Scupholme in South Somercotes) does actually lie within our region.

If some people in the east of the region were thus potentially engaged in salt production and processing in the Roman period, then the events of the Late and post-Roman period would have been especially disruptive to their lives, as this time saw sea-levels rise once more to new heights. The earlier Roman land surface of the Lincolnshire Outmarsh was significantly lower than it is today and the rise in sea-level led to this landscape being flooded, with new layers of marine alluvium being laid down on top of the old land surface. So, for example, the mounds of waste from the known Romano-British salt-making sites (salterns) on the Outmarsh – which must necessarily have been elevated when compared to the contemporary ground level – are all buried by up to a metre of alluvium deposited by the sea. Similarly, the previously mentioned probable Romano-British settlement site at Scupholme in South Somercotes, which consists of a large quantity of pottery (including some Early Roman imported pieces) associated with bone and oyster shell, was found buried more than three metres down. Needless to say, such flooding must have seriously disrupted both the salt industry of the coastal zone and the people who lived here. Indeed, even for those settlements not drowned in the Late or post-Roman periods or involved somehow in the salt industry, the flooding of the wetland landscape of Outmarsh must have had serious effects, given the likely use of the flooded saltmarshes for stock-breeding and seasonal grazing.

Turning from economic matters to questions of belief, it was noted above the finds of rings inscribed ToT from Stenigot and Kelstern suggest that some members of the local community continued a pagan tribal-cult of a divine protector named Totatis into the late second or third century. In this context, it is perhaps interesting to note that the first-century Roman poet Lucan (in *Pharsalia*, 1, 444–6) suggests that the pre-Roman Celtic worship of a god bearing the same name – Teutates – involved human sacrifice, with later writers adding that the method used involved the victim being plunged headfirst into a barrel and held there until they drowned. Of course, it is highly unlikely that such rites, if they were ever attached to the Corieltavi's divine protector, continued into the Roman period, and certainly by the end of this era any surviving pagan Celtic religion in the region would have been in severe decline. There is, after all, good evidence for a Christian bishop having been based at Lincoln from as early as AD 314, and the probable sequence of two churches found in the centre of the Roman *forum* at Lincoln may well represent a continuation of this episcopal establishment into the fifth century and beyond. This picture is amplified by a recent find in our area of two deliberately hidden fragments of a fourth-century Roman font from Calcethorpe with Kelstern parish. A study of this font and related items from elsewhere in Lincolnshire and Nottinghamshire has concluded that they all share distinctive decorative elements that are suggestive of a common origin. Furthermore, they seem to be distributed with a focus on Lincoln. Given that the presence of a bishop was required at liturgical events such as baptism, the reasonable inference has consequently been drawn that these lead fonts were actually used by fourth-century Christians who fell under the supervision of the episcopal diocese based at Lincoln. This is, naturally, a point of considerable importance from the perspective of the religious life of the Romano-Britons who lived in the region around Louth.

This, then, is the general picture that emerges of this region in the first to fourth centuries AD. It cannot be denied that this part of Roman Lincolnshire was peripheral to the whole. The major rural settlements – the 'small Roman towns', such as Ludford, Ulceby and Kirmington – all lie outside of our zone of study. Furthermore, whilst fourth-century Roman coins are found reasonably widely throughout this area, they are far less common than they are in other districts, and finds of Roman-style building materials (such as brick and tile) are very rare indeed. Put simply, this part of the eastern Wolds and Lincolnshire Marsh looks to have been home to a reasonably dense but largely economically underdeveloped spread of dispersed farmsteads and settlements, inhabited by people who were probably primarily engaged in farming, although there is evidence for a degree of local iron-working, pottery production, counterfeiting, and potentially salt-making too. This is not, of course, to say that there were no sites of local importance. As in the Late Iron Age, the Stenigot-Donington on Bain and Welton le Wold areas look to have seen relatively significant activity compared to the region as a whole, and there is certainly evidence for high-status activity in the Late Roman period at the latter location. Even more intriguing from the perspective of the present study, however, is the fact that there is also some evidence to suggest that Louth itself may have been the site of one or more locally important settlements in this period.

Figure 24: A fragment of a fourth-century Roman lead font, found in Calcethorpe with Kelstern parish. Image used by kind permission of the Portable Antiquities Scheme; PAS find reference number LIN-E8F806.

The primary support for this comes quite simply from the local context established above. Across the 314 km² covered in the present survey, significant concentrations of Roman coins are extremely rare. In fact, there are actually only three sites from which more than a dozen coins have been recovered: Donington on Bain, Welton le Wold villa, and Fulstow. In this context, the collection of Roman coins from the town that was recorded by Robert Bayley and dispersed before 1834 appears potentially rather more significant than most commentators have given it credit for being. As was noted above, this collection included not only coins of Julius Caesar and Augustus, but also 'a considerable number' of coins minted by eleven named first- and second-century emperors and 'plenty' of fourth-century coins of Constantine the Great, to which may be added three Roman coins found in the town more recently. Needless to say, such a concentration and quantity of Roman coins from Louth is, in the above local context, suggestive not only of there being at least one Romano-British settlement at Louth, but also of this having had some local significance in the Roman period. The recent finds of fragments of Roman brick and tile from behind the Greyhound Inn on the corner of Gospelgate and Upgate offer further support for this position. Once again, such materials are exceedingly rare in this region – indeed, the only other sites across the entire 314 km² from which such items of Roman-style building materials are currently recorded are the settlement to the south-east of Donington on Bain and possibly Welton le Wold villa. As such, it seems more than credible that these finds from Louth do, in fact, derive from a Romanized building constructed in the vicinity using apparently locally-unusual techniques, which again may suggest the presence of a locally-significant Romano-British settlement site in Louth itself.

Also likely to be of relevance with regard to Romano-British activity in the town is the spring dedicated to St Helen, located in the Gatherums off Aswell Street and recorded since the medieval period. Holy wells and springs dedicated to St Helen are now thought to have their origins in an early Christianization of sites dedicated to a Romano-British pagan water-goddess known as Alauna, whose name could easily deformed to 'Helen' – witness, for example, the river Ellen, originally *Alauna*, in Cumbria (the Romano-British veneration of springs, wells and water-courses is, needless to say, well-attested). The presence of such a site in Louth is thus of considerable importance in the present context, and carries with it two major implications. The first and most obvious of these is that there was probably a Romano-British pagan rural cult-site dedicated to the water-goddess Alauna in Louth, located at the present spring site, an important point when considering the possibility of a significant settlement here. The second is that British Christians probably subsequently lived in the immediate vicinity of this spring, in order that the pagan cult-site was Christianized and remembered into the medieval period and beyond. British paganism seems to have died out in lowland

Britain by the middle of the sixth-century, given that their own churchmen accuse the Britons of virtually every possible sin against God at this time except for continued paganism. As such, the at least nominal Christianization of this sacred spring is likely to have occurred before this point, and the only Christians likely to have been in the region then are Britons, as the local Anglo-Saxon immigrant groups (who arrived in the fifth and sixth centuries) don't seem to have converted until the early seventh century. Furthermore, such a scenario certainly has a good context in the evidence for Late and post-Roman British Christians in the Louth region discussed above.

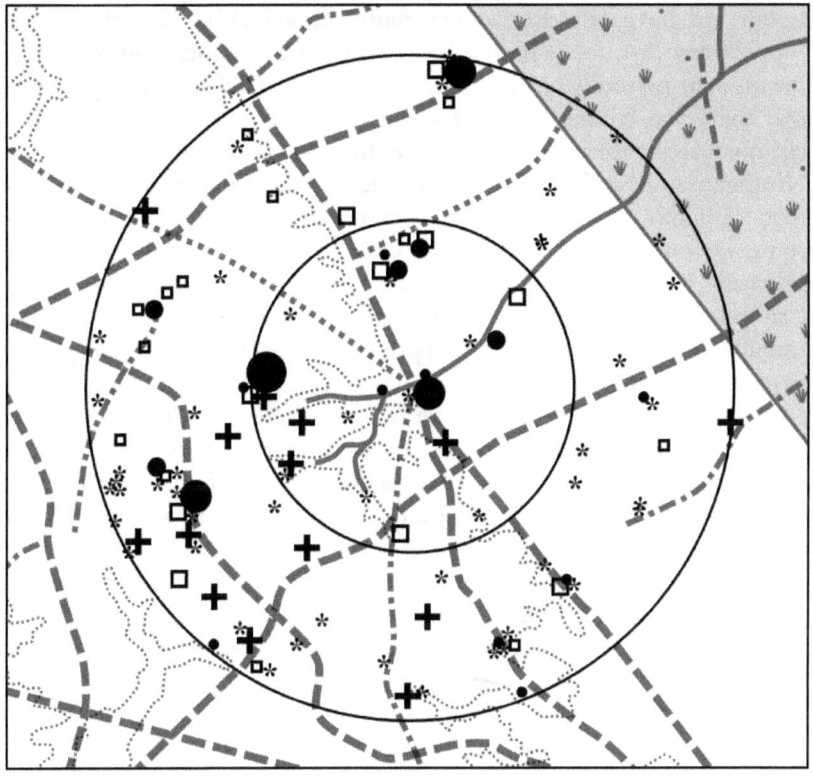

Figure 25: Romano-British finds and sites in the Louth region, plotted against all of the potential routeways of this period, including those proposed by Arthur Owen (1997a). The latter are indicated by a line consisting of dots and dashes; extrapolations of some of these routes to their suggested final destinations are marked by a dotted line.

Whether we ought, or indeed need, to go any further than this is debateable. However, it is perhaps worth noting here that Arthur Owen has made a good case for an Early Anglo-Saxon trackway leading south from Louth through Tathwell and Farforth (in Maidenwell parish) towards Tetford and ultimately Horncastle, and he argues that this was in existence in the Roman period. This suggestion seems to have been accepted by at least some recent academic commentators, as has Owen's argument that a section of another Roman-era routeway running from Caistor to Louth via Binbrook is still traceable. Certainly if one plots the Roman finds and sites from this region against Owen's suggested additional Roman routeways there is a degree of correspondence, and if Louth did have two Roman-era routes aimed at it then this would support any case for it having been a site of some local significance in the Roman period. On the other hand, Owen's subsequent hypothesis that there was a Late Roman fort at Louth is difficult to accept. This claim is based primarily on the notion that the shape formed by modern Northgate and Nichol Hill looks like the outline of part of a Late Roman fort, with this being built here to control the prehistoric north-south route known as Barton Street – Owen suggests that Barton Street originally ran down Broadbank and then through this 'fort' and along Cannon Street, before passing through the modern town, rather than running at least partway down the present Grimsby Road (to the west of Broadbank), as is usually believed. At present, there is no real evidence to support this hypothesis, and the fact that there is no trace of Cannon Street on either Armstrong's 1778 plan of Louth or Espin's more accurate map of 1808 is perhaps telling. Indeed, if there was a Late Roman fort in the vicinity of Louth, then there are two more credible candidates for its location.

The first candidate is on the coast in the vicinity of Grainthorpe, a little beyond our 10 km line. A fort here has often been hypothesized as a northern extension of the Late Roman coastal defensive system, which is likely to have run at least as far north as Skegness on the basis of medieval place-name evidence and Leland's sixteenth-century account of a walled town there being eroded away by the sea (it should, incidentally, be noted that the modern 'Roman Bank' bears no relation to any Roman fortification at Skegness, instead being medieval in origin). However, with regard to Grainthorpe we once again lack solid evidence, as the theory largely derives from a need to explain what the function was of the Roman road that ran from here through to Ludford. Whilst it is certainly not impossible that there was a fort in this vicinity that has since disappeared into the sea, the road itself simply cannot constitute proof of this, not least because some other origin for it – such as the provision of a connection between the major inland settlements and salt-making sites on the coast – is quite conceivable and arguably more plausible. In this context, it is perhaps worth pointing out that the proposed location for the fort does actually appear to have lain significantly beyond the likely spring-tide high-water mark in the Roman period, although a fort might possibly have been constructed in this area on a long-since eroded and buried 'island' of glacial till that stood above the surrounding coastal zone.

The second candidate is Yarburgh, to the north-east of Louth. Owen suggests that there was a Roman road running eastwards towards the coast from here, and his alignment can also be tentatively extended westwards along a track and footpath in the direction of the Roman finds at Fotherby and Little Grimsby, perhaps ultimately to join Barton Street. However, the key evidence here is not the potential presence of a Roman road running from the Wolds to the coast, but rather the derivation of the place-name Yarburgh from Old English *eorð-burh*, 'earthen fortification'. The name *eorð-burh* was applied by the post-Roman Anglo-Saxon immigrants to pre-existing earthen fortifications that they encountered in Britain, and Yarburgh is one of two places to bear this name in Lincolnshire. This is, of course, a point of considerable significance, as it implies that there was indeed a Romano-British or pre-Roman fortification here. Similarly important is the fact that the other site to bear this name is the hillfort of Yarborough Camp, near to Kirmington, and this appears to have been refortified in the late fourth or early fifth century with Roman-style bastions in order that it could function as a significant site in the defence of very Late and post-Roman northern Lincolnshire. Unfortunately, the pre-Anglo-Saxon earthen fortification referred to in the name 'Yarburgh' no longer exists (perhaps because its site developed into a village, unlike that of Yarborough Camp), but the implications of this name when taken together with the nature and usage of its north Lincolnshire etymological twin are, at the very least, extremely suggestive in the present context. Moreover, it has been argued that the construction of the pre-Anglo-Saxon *eorð-burh* at Yarburgh would, in any case, have only made sense during the Late Roman and post-Roman periods, when the sea-level rise of that era

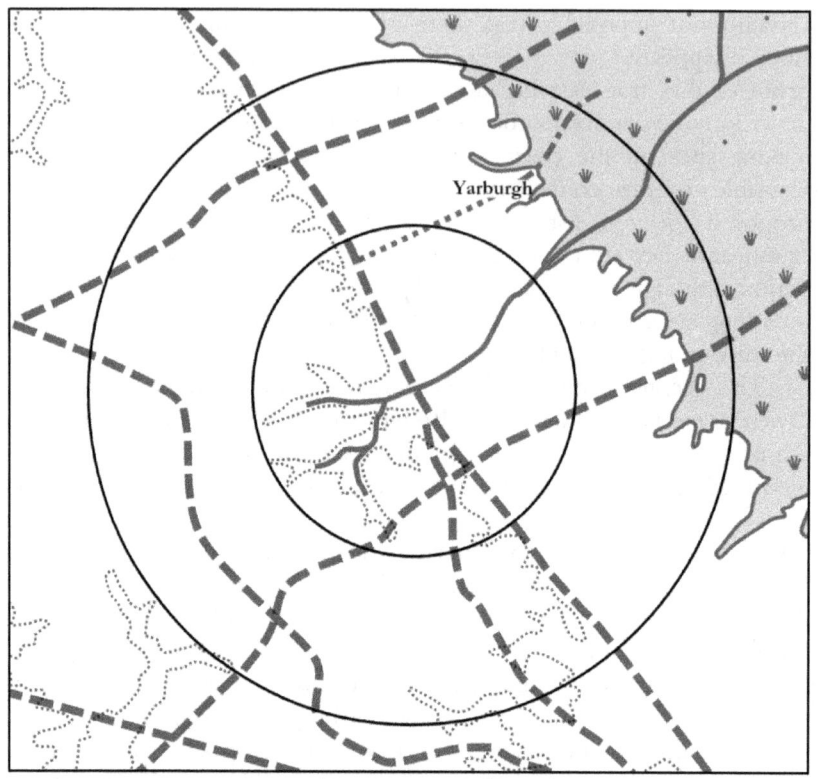

Figure 26: The location of Yarburgh, plotted against the suggested Late Roman/post-Roman coastline and the possible road running from Barton Street to the coast through Yarburgh (see main text).

meant that Yarburgh stood close to the coastline, on a low promontory overlooking a creek flowing east into the sea. In sum, although details are lacking, it seems credible that some sort of earthen fortification was indeed built or refortified here at the end of the Roman period, perhaps as part of the same defensive strategy that led to the refortification of Yarborough Camp.

This, then, really is as far as we can sensibly go with regard to Louth in the Roman period. The evidence is undoubtedly fragmentary, but what we do have is sufficient to suggest that there was at least one locally-significant Romano-British settlement and a rural cult-site at Louth itself, and that there may well have been a Late Roman earthen fortification at Yarburgh to its north-east too. The question thus becomes: how does all of this relate, if at all, to the later development of Louth and its region? Needless to say, in order to address this we need to first ask what evidence there is for events in the period after the fourth century AD.

4

Natives, Immigrants and the Emergence of a Regional Centre, *c*. 410–650

The fifth century AD brought with it enormous changes for the Romano-Britons who lived in this region, not least the fact that Britain ceased to be part of the Roman Empire in around AD 410. Whilst this might be interpreted as the Britons finally regaining control of their own destiny after over three and a half centuries of Roman rule, the reality was in many ways rather less happy. It now seems clear that the rich and vital Romano-British economy and material culture of the third and fourth centuries – which saw low-denomination coinage and relatively good quality pottery (and other artefacts) widely dispersed in Lincolnshire – depended ultimately upon the presence of the Roman Empire, and its withdrawal from Britain led directly to a major economic collapse. Across Britain as a whole this is likely to have caused considerable difficulties and hardship, with towns being abandoned as significant centres of population and mass-production industries disappearing. A 'post-Roman' economic regression of the sort that took place over several hundred years in other parts of Europe was completed in perhaps thirty years or so in Britain, and this cannot but have had a major impact on the former Romano-Britons. At the same time, the disappearance of both Roman coinage and easily identifiable and datable pottery from the archaeological record has the unfortunate side-effect of making the Britons of this period almost completely archaeologically 'invisible'. Often only with considerable luck and extremely careful excavation can post-Roman Britons be identified in the archaeological record, and in some parts of the country they seem not to have generally returned to archaeological visibility until at least the tenth century.

On the other hand, whilst the economic collapse must have been traumatic for some, it needs to be remembered that the Louth region was, economically, relatively underdeveloped even in the Late Roman period. The owners of locally-significant settlements such as that at Welton le Wold would have almost certainly felt the effects of the economic collapse acutely, but it may be that the majority of the inhabitants of the region would have actually escaped relatively lightly. They may no longer have been able to use coinage in their transactions or Romano-British-style material culture in their everyday lives, but then most of them appear to have made relatively little use of these things anyway, especially when compared with the Romano-Britons who lived elsewhere in the country. Indeed, if the local Romano-Britons were primarily engaged in farming, as seems likely, then it is not inconceivable that they were even slightly better off once the Roman state and its army no longer made demands on them. Certainly it has been argued that the post-Roman period in East Anglia saw a de-intensification of land exploitation that can be best associated with the ending of Roman taxation and imperial demand, both of which required a significant agricultural surplus to be produced.

The other major change to affect the region was the arrival of Germanic immigrants from north-western continental Europe in the fifth and sixth centuries. Culturally these immigrants were in many ways distinct from the Britons: they arrived from areas that had always been outside of the borders of the Roman Empire, and so were only subject to minimal Romanization; they were pagans, whereas the Britons by this point were probably almost all at least nominally Christian; they spoke a Germanic language, Old English, whilst the former Romano-Britons spoke a Celtic language (Late British) that is the ancestor of modern Welsh, Cornish and Breton; and they made use of an archaeologically 'visible' material culture and burial rites, unlike the post-Roman Britons. Moreover, it now seems clear that this was not simply an elite migration, made up of a handful of Anglo-Saxon warriors from the Continent, but rather involved a significant number of individuals. Certainly a number of massive cremation cemeteries of the fifth and sixth centuries are known from eastern Britain, the largest of which contain the remains of thousands of people buried in Anglo-Saxon handmade urns.

If the former Romano-Britons of the region around Louth may have been less affected by the post-Roman economic collapse than many others were, the same cannot be said with regard to the arrival of these Germanic migrants. Whilst the region was undoubtedly peripheral in the Late Roman period, it lay at the heart of the area of Early Anglo-Saxon immigration. In fact, one of Lincolnshire's six major cremation cemeteries – which probably originally contained around 1200 cremations, beginning in the fifth century – is actually located on the high ground on the border of Louth and South Elkington parishes, to the east of Acthorpe Top. The question thus becomes, how did such significant immigration to the Louth region in the post-Roman period affect the pre-existing British population?

One suggestion, which was very popular in the nineteenth and earlier twentieth centuries and still finds occasional supporters today, is that this migration was complete catastrophe for the Britons. According to this view, the original inhabitants were largely slaughtered or driven from their homes by the new Anglo-Saxon rulers of eastern Britain. In the words of the great Victorian Anglo-Saxon historian E. A. Freeman, in his *Old English History for Children* (1871),

> there may doubtless be some little British and Roman blood in us, just as some few Welsh and Latin words crept into the English tongue from the very beginning. But we may be sure that we have not much of their blood in us... Now you will perhaps say that our forefathers were cruel and wicked men... And so doubtless it was... But anyhow it has turned out much better in the end that our forefathers did thus kill or drive out nearly all the people whom they found in the land... [since otherwise] I cannot think that we should ever have been so great and free a people as we have been for many ages.

The plausibility of this 'happy genocide' – which ensured that Englishmen were not somehow tainted by native British blood, and so were able to achieve their later greatness – is, naturally, open to very serious question. At the most basic level, there is simply no evidence in the post-Roman environmental record for the kind of massive woodland regrowth that would have occurred if the fifth- and sixth-century British inhabitants of what became England (numbering in the millions) were

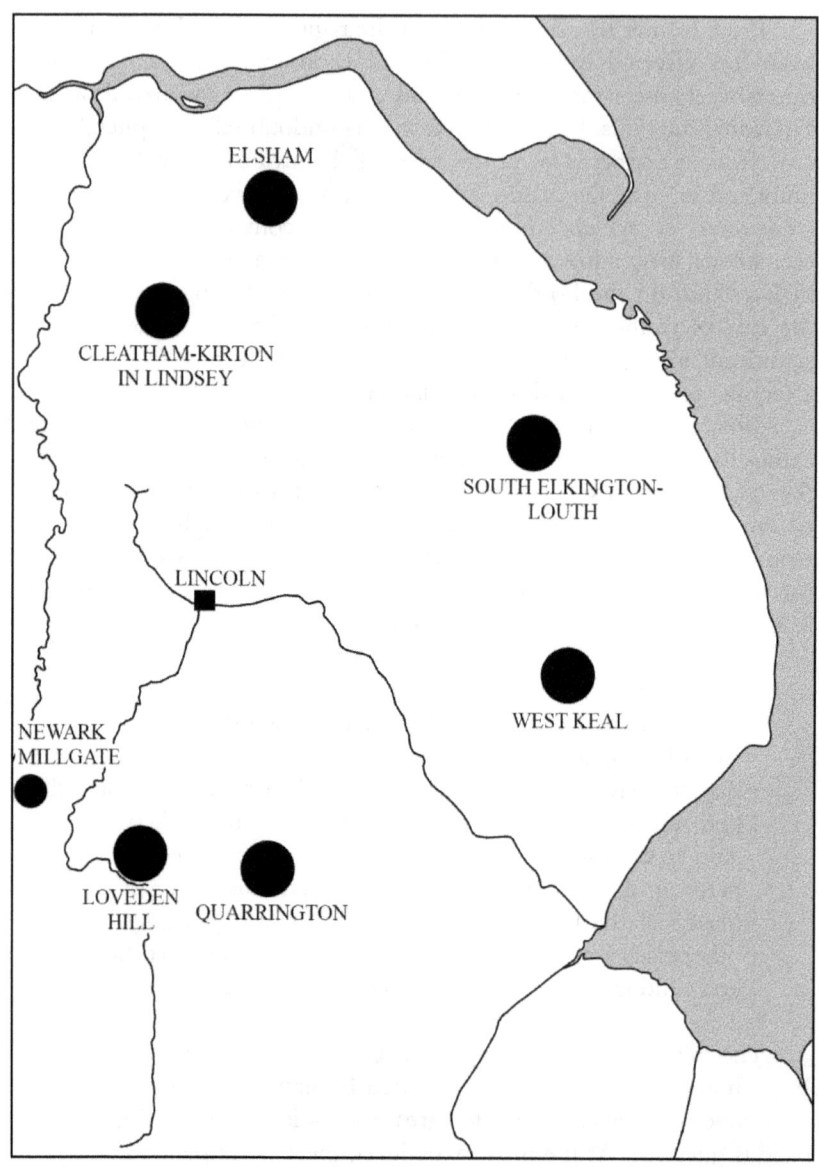

Figure 27: The distribution of the major Early Anglo-Saxon cremation cemeteries of Lincolnshire.

driven out or exterminated by the immigrant Anglo-Saxons (numbering at most around 50,000 to 100,000 people). Moreover, a recent analysis of the very plentiful Early Anglo-Saxon cemetery evidence from Lindsey has concluded that, even if we were to interpret the available data extremely generously, the total number of 'archaeologically visible' Anglo-Saxons it represents are unlikely to have constituted more than five percent or so of the probable total population at that time, something which again implies that the vast majority of the 'archaeologically invisible' Britons probably remained in place even after the arrival of the Anglo-Saxons.

That the arrival of the Anglo-Saxons from the Continent was not quite so devastating for the former Romano-Britons as has sometimes been claimed can be further confirmed by a more detailed examination of the evidence for post-Roman Lincolnshire. This material indicates that Lincoln was actually the centre of a British polity named *Lindes* in the fifth and sixth centuries, which encompassed a large territory to both the north and south of the city. This 'country of *Lindes*' is referred to in early medieval Welsh sources dealing with events in the post-Roman period and it is reflected in other evidence too. So, for example, not only is there a remarkable quantity of British high-status metalwork of the fifth and sixth centuries now known from Lincolnshire, especially given the general archaeological invisibility of the Britons of this period, but the old Roman *forum* at Lincoln also appears to have been used as the site for a significant British Christian church until at least the sixth century. Even more important from the present perspective, however, is the fact that this British polity appears to have been able to control the Anglo-Saxon immigrants in its territory. Whereas the Roman towns elsewhere in eastern and northern Britain often have Anglo-Saxon cremation cemeteries – and hence, by implication, significant immigrant communities – located very close to them, this is not the case here. All six of the major Early Anglo-Saxon cremation cemeteries mentioned above are sited at least 25 km away from Lincoln, and as a group they appear to be arranged in a ring around the city, which is suggestive. This sense that the fifth-century settlement of the Anglo-Saxon immigrants was limited and controlled by the Britons of *Lindes* is further heightened by the fact that these cemeteries are also usually located near to sites that were potentially of some strategic importance in the defence of the British 'country of *Lindes*'. Thus, for example, the Elsham cremation cemetery is located a little way to the west of the Late/post-Roman fortification at Yarborough, discussed in the previous chapter, and the West Keal cemetery is on a high and imposing point overlooking the Witham valley.

This apparent British control over, and use of, the immigrant groups appears to have broken down at some point after the early sixth century, and by the seventh century British *Lindes* had been replaced by the Anglo-Saxon kingdom of *Lindissi* (later known as *Lindesig*, Lindsey, with both names deriving from *Lindes*). There is, however, nothing to indicate that this Anglo-Saxon takeover resulted in the Britons being driven out or killed. Instead, the evidence we have supports the scenario outlined above, namely that the vast majority of the Britons of Lincolnshire stayed in place, gradually adopting the immigrants' culture, ethnicity and language over time. Certainly the British Christian community at Lincoln seems to have continued in existence into at least the early seventh century, and some of the local Anglo-Saxon sub-groups, such as the *Wassingas* of Washingborough, could well have been founded by Anglicized Britons. Indeed, the place-name and documentary evidence suggests that there were still small numbers of people in Lincolnshire speaking the language of the Britons as late as the eighth century. Of course, this is not to say that the takeover by the immigrant groups was benign for the Britons. Some of them may well have died resisting it, whilst others may have fled to areas still under British control in the north or west. Furthermore, those Britons who stayed are likely to have been placed at a significant legal, political, social and economic disadvantage when compared to those who claimed descent from the Anglo-Saxon immigrants. On the other hand, what evidence there is for Anglian-British interaction at this time does suggest a degree of at least toleration towards the British past and culture from the new rulers, and there is even evidence suggestive of intermarriage between the two groups within the ruling house of *Lindissi*.

In general, the Early Anglo-Saxon archaeology of the region around Louth appears to be in harmony with this broad picture of the likely course of events in post-Roman Lincolnshire. The South Elkington-Louth cremation cemetery is, after all, one of those major Anglo-Saxon cemeteries of the fifth and sixth centuries whose distribution speaks of a post-Roman British authority, based at Lincoln, that was able to control the Germanic immigration into the county and confine it – initially at least – to the peripheral parts of *Lindes*. Furthermore, not only does the

Figure 28: A British silver proto-hand-pin, found in Welton le Wold parish. Image copyright of the Trustees of the British Museum and used by kind permission.

immediate vicinity of the cremation cemetery have very good views over the Lincolnshire Marshes towards the post-Roman coastline, but the cemetery is also located only a few miles away from the possible Late/post-Roman coastal fortification at Yarburgh (discussed in the previous chapter). As such, it certainly seems credible that the Anglo-Saxons settled here were indeed being somehow used in the defence of British *Lindes*, as above. This shouldn't really surprise us greatly: similar arrangements were being made between Romanized civilian populations and barbarian groups all across Western Europe during the fifth century. In fact, our main near-contemporary British source – Gildas, writing sometime around AD 540 – makes it clear that the Anglo-Saxon immigrants arrived in the fifth century as federate troops, employed by British civilian leaders to defend their territories.

With regard to the Britons in this part of Lincolnshire, their almost complete archaeological invisibility after the fourth century means that the available corpus of evidence is extremely slight. However, some of the metalwork from the county that is potentially indicative of the presence of high-status, post-Roman Britons does come from the Louth region, with a fifth- or sixth-century British Class 1 penannular brooch apparently found somewhere in this region, and the British proto-hand-pin from Welton le Wold being potentially fifth century in date. There is also the intriguing case of St Helen's spring in Louth. It was suggested earlier that this site, like the other holy wells and springs with this dedication, represented a Romano-British pagan rural cult-site dedicated to the water-goddess Alauna, which was Christianized – probably before the mid-sixth century – by British Christians. Needless to say, the fact that this Christianized cult was maintained through to the later medieval period is important. Such a situation implies that the British Christians who venerated the spring continued to live in Louth (or in its immediate vicinity) into at least the early seventh century, just as is predicted by the wider regional context, as otherwise the cult would have died out before there were local Anglo-Saxon Christians to carry it on. Moreover, it also suggests that relations between the Britons and the immigrants were sufficiently cordial that the latter were able to continue in their religious veneration even after the end of British *Lindes* and the establishment of the pagan Anglo-Saxon kingdom of *Lindissi*.

The name of the river that flows through Louth may also be relevant here. The present name for this watercourse is the Lud, which derives from Old English *hlude*, 'the loud one'. However, downstream of Louth is the parish of North Cockerington, and this place-name – *Cocrinton*, *Cocringtuna* – appears to preserve the original British Celtic name of the Lud, the Cocker or 'crooked river', with Cockerington being 'the village (*tun*) associated with (*-ing-*) the River Cocker'. This is interesting for two reasons. The first is that this British river-name must have been known to the local Anglo-Saxons in order for it to have been used in this Old English place-name, something which obviously implies a degree of Anglian-British contact here. The second is that the place-name 'Cockerington' is unlikely to have been coined before the mid-eighth century, given the general chronology of names involving Old English *tun*. As such, it would appear that the British name for the Lud continued to be used by some inhabitants of the Louth region until at least this late, with it only being completely replaced by the Old English name for this watercourse at some point subsequent to this. Moreover, in this context it is intriguing to note that the tributary of the Lud that flows between Welton le Wold and Hallington parishes is, in fact, still known by a British Celtic stream-name, the Crake.

This is really as far as we can legitimately go in pursuit of the post-Roman Britons of the Louth region, given their lack of archaeological visibility. Nonetheless, the above evidence certainly appears, once again, to accord well with the broad picture of events in post-Roman Lincolnshire detailed previously, implying that this is indeed applicable to this area. All told, the material we have suggests that the Germanic immigrants who founded the major cremation cemetery on Acthorpe Top were probably initially controlled and utilised by the Britons of the Lincoln-based 'country of *Lindes*' as part of a deliberate strategy of coastal defence. It is also likely that most of the Britons of the Louth region remained in place, even after the arrival of the immigrants and the eventual Anglo-Saxon takeover of British *Lindes*. Many of them probably continued to practice their own religion and speak their own language for some considerable time after this, although their lower social, economic, political and legal status is likely to have driven them to increasingly adopt the immigrant culture, language, and finally ethnicity over time. By end of the eighth century most people living in this region would have considered themselves culturally 'Anglo-Saxon', whether or not they were directly descended from the original fifth- and sixth-century immigrant groups.

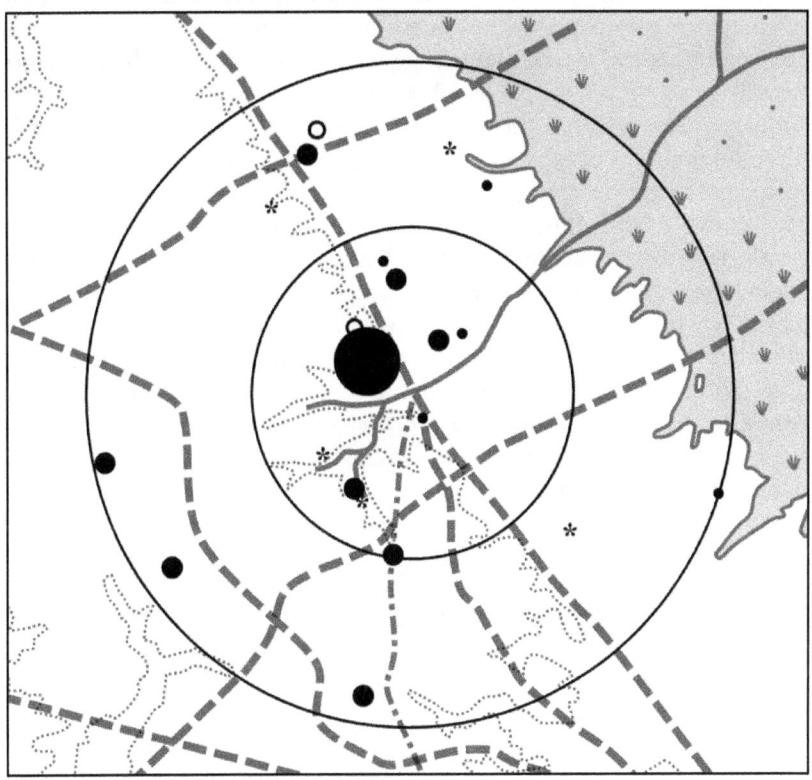

Figure 29: Early Anglo-Saxon finds and cemeteries in the Louth region. The main cremation cemetery is represented by a large filled circle, the seven or eight inhumation cemeteries are medium filled circles, and single finds of metalwork are small filled circles. Stars indicate finds of pottery, open circles coin finds. The approximate Early Anglo-Saxon coastline is also shown, as are significant routeways probably in use in this period.

In light of the above, we need now to turn our attention to what we can know of the Anglo-Saxons of this region. Although the South Elkington-Louth cremation cemetery has already been mentioned, it is still the major site in the area and thus requires further consideration. Looking at the burials themselves, 290 urns were recovered from here in the late 1940s out of a probable original total of around 1200 burials, which makes South Elkington-Louth one of the largest Early Anglo-Saxon cemeteries in England. Interestingly, the site has a number of features that can be paralleled at the fully-excavated Cleatham cremation cemetery located in the west of Lincolnshire, including the possible use of stone cairns to cover the interment sites and the burial of some of the cremation urns on top of and cutting into earlier urns. The latter feature is unlikely to be accidental at either site, especially if there were cairns, and is perhaps best interpreted as an indication that the people buried in these intercutting urns represented members of the same family-group who were being physically reunited in death. On the other hand, whilst around two thirds of the cremation burials at Cleatham contained grave-goods, less than a quarter did so at South Elkington-Louth. It is often assumed on this basis that the community that used this cemetery must have been poor in comparison to those found elsewhere, but this is a potentially dangerous assumption to make. In particular, the use of grave-goods in the early medieval period varies widely from region to region, and seems to have had more to do with such factors as how status and position in the local society were symbolised and reinforced, rather than actual wealth. As such, whilst the paucity of grave-goods in the urns at South Elkington-Louth might be due to the local community being unusually poor, it could simply reflect the fact that they used a slightly different burial rite here, wherein the attitude towards the deposition or use of grave-goods diverged from sites such as Cleatham, perhaps due to a differing local situation. In this context, it is interesting to note that the other major cremation cemetery in eastern Lincolnshire, West Keal, is similarly lacking in grave-goods from the excavated urns, which is perhaps suggestive.

With regard to the cremation cemetery as a whole, there has been a significant body of research dedicated to such sites in recent years. It is now generally agreed that these cemeteries were not designed to serve a single settlement, but rather acted as a central burial place for many farmsteads and settlements in the surrounding region, hence their exceptional size. The dead were probably cremated on pyres located close to the settlement they came from, with their ashes then being placed in urns and carried – possibly in some sort of procession – to the burial site, where the urns were ritually interred. Even more interesting, however, is the fact that recent work suggests that these cemeteries also functioned as social and sacred centres for the people who used them for burial – they were, in other words, the 'central places' of Early Anglo-Saxon society. This was where the Early Anglo-Saxon inhabitants of the region probably assembled to deal with community business, engage in religious festivals, exchange gifts, and potentially even trade items (hence, perhaps, the apparent presence here of burial urns made in the Charnwood Forest area of Leicestershire). In consequence, it is difficult not to see the foundation of one of Lincolnshire's six major cremation cemeteries on Acthorpe Top as a key element in Louth's rise from a merely locally-significant site in the Roman period through to a major centre within Lincolnshire by the time of the Domesday Book. The question is, just how large was the territory that had the South Elkington-Louth cemetery as its central place in the Early Anglo-Saxon period?

In the past, the wide and relatively regular spacing of the large fifth- to seventh-century cremation cemeteries within Lincolnshire has been seen as implying that each served a very extensive region, and there seems little reason to reject this supposition in the case of Louth. Certainly, the existence of a pre-Viking territory focussed on Louth would seem to be confirmed by the Old English place-names Ludborough and Ludford – probably 'the fort belonging to Louth' and 'the ford belonging to Louth' – located to the north and west of Louth, and possibly Meers Bank (a name derived from Old English *(ge)mære*, 'boundary') to its south-east. The Anglo-Saxon territory suggested by these names is perfectly credible as that dependent upon the South Elkington-Louth cemetery/'central place', and it moreover bears an intriguingly close resemblance to the borders of the wapentake of Louthesk, which had its meeting-place at some uncertain spot at or close to Louth (Louthesk means 'the ash tree at Louth').

If we have evidence for a major Early Anglo-Saxon central place and its associated district in the Louth region, can anything else be said about the inhabitants of this? One interesting point is that not every 'Early Anglo-Saxon' in the region made use of the central fifth-century and later burial ground on Acthorpe Top. Although the vast majority

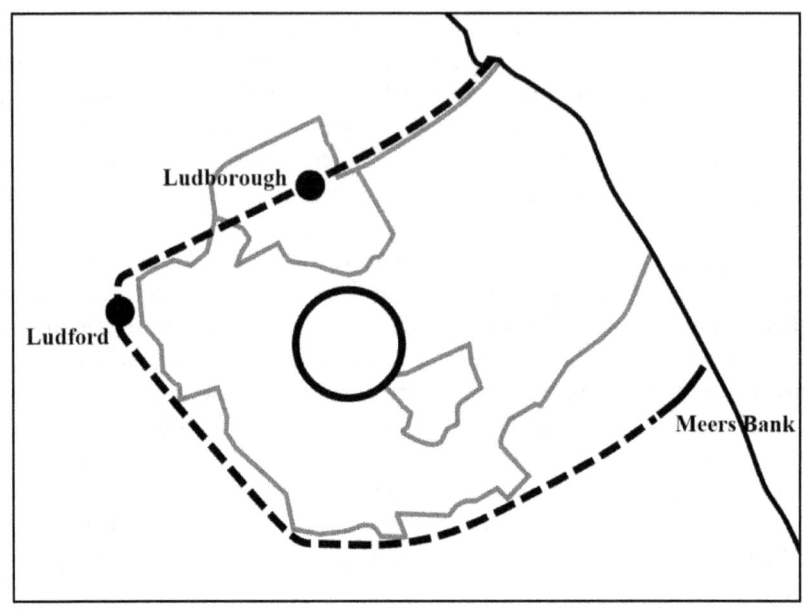

Figure 30: The territorial context of the South Elkington-Louth cremation cemetery. Shown are the cemetery (open circle), the relevant place-names, and the boundaries of Louthesk wapentake (grey).

certainly seem to have done so, within our 10 km radius study zone there also appear to have been seven or eight far smaller Anglo-Saxon inhumation cemeteries, which probably date from the sixth and seventh centuries. In terms of size, the only site from which human remains have been recovered and so can be counted is Stenigot, where three people were buried. However, whilst all of the other inhumation sites are known only from metal-detected finds, the number of pieces from each is consistent with them too being small or very small inhumation cemeteries, perhaps ranging from a handful of burials across their entire period of use to around a dozen at most. Although not large, these inhumation cemeteries are undoubtedly intriguing. So, who were the apparently small number of people being buried in this way in the Louth region, and why did they not make use of the communal cemetery and central place of South Elkington-Louth?

Anglo-Saxon inhumation cemeteries are actually found close to all of the major cremation cemeteries in Lincolnshire, and one plausible suggestion is that at least a proportion of these contained the burials of acculturating Britons who had adopted the immigrants' material culture and so become once more archaeologically 'visible'. Such acculturation may well have begun at an early date amongst the higher-status Britons in the vicinity of the cremation cemeteries, as they attempted to align themselves with the new ascendant power in order to protect their position within local society, and an origin in this for some of the local (family?) inhumation cemeteries of the Louth region would certainly help to explain these sites. After all, inhumation was the normal Late and post-Roman British burial rite, and it seems likely that even acculturating Britons who had adopted elements of the Anglo-Saxon cultural identity would not have chosen to make use of the immigrants' own communal cremation site on Acthorpe Top. Indeed, most such Britons would probably have been prevented from burying there whatever their wishes: the available evidence suggests that, by and large, the Anglo-Saxons continued to draw a distinction between those of immigrant descent and those of British ancestry into at least the seventh century. Finally, it is worth noting that one of the sixth-century Anglo-Saxon cruciform brooches from the small inhumation cemetery at Tathwell was actually enamelled, a British decorative technique that is suggestive in the present context.

If some of the people buried in the local inhumation cemeteries are likely to have been acculturating Britons, could others have been the descendants of the Anglo-Saxon immigrants? Cremation cemetery sites, such as that on Acthorpe Top, probably retained many of their 'central place' functions throughout the whole of the Early Anglo-Saxon period and beyond – so, for example, both the Loveden Hill and West Keal cremation cemeteries appear to have continued to function as assembly-sites for significant districts into at least the Late Saxon period. However, there does seem to have been a general shift away from the use of these sites as communal burial centres by the end of the Early Anglo-Saxon period, with few cremations from the county able to be confidently dated to the seventh century. In consequence, the idea that at least some of the known inhumation cemeteries were used by Anglo-Saxons who had ceased to use the communal site on Acthorpe Top for burial during the sixth or earlier seventh centuries certainly seems credible.

As to why such a change in Anglo-Saxon burial practice occurred, one possible explanation is that there was simply a reduced need to express group-loyalty via communal cremation burial after the first few generations in Britain, with the result that immigrant-descended groups began to increasingly bury their dead locally using the less complex and resource-intensive inhumation rite. This is undoubtedly a plausible scenario with regard to Lincolnshire as a whole, and some of the Early Anglo-Saxon inhumation cemeteries in the Louth region could well result from this. However, other factors may be in play too. In particular, it seems clear that elite lineages were emerging across Anglo-Saxon England during the later sixth and seventh centuries, and these distinguished themselves from the rest of the population through the use of separate grave-sites and unusual rites, such as barrow burial. Certainly, such a situation appears to provide a reasonable explanation for the seventh-century burial site at Stenigot. Not only do the grave-goods from this site include high-status items, such as an imported bronze cauldron and a seax (a single-edged blade) with scabbard fittings, but it also seems that the three bodies found here were interred under a barrow overlooking a tributary of the River Bain. The other potentially interesting site from this perspective is the small burial site at North Ormsby, known only from metal-detecting. In addition to two brooches that may represent a single female burial, we also have a sixth- or seventh-century tinned triangular buckle with gold and garnet decoration from here, which is indicative of a high-status male burial. Interestingly, both the Stenigot and the North Ormsby cemeteries are located on the periphery of the suggested minimum territory dependent upon the South Elkington-Louth cremation cemetery.

The small inhumation cemeteries of this region may thus reflect several different aspects of Early Anglo-Saxon society, including the acculturation of the Britons, the changing burial rites and needs of the Anglo-Saxon immigrants, and the emergence of elite lineages, and it would be a mistake to fix on any one explanation of these sites as being applicable to them all. Unfortunately, learning any more about this period is difficult. It remains a truism that whilst the archaeology of the Roman period is dominated by settlement sites (the only possible Romano-British grave comes from Maidenwell), that of the Early Anglo-Saxon period is dominated by burial grounds. There is, in fact, very little archaeological evidence whatsoever for Early Anglo-Saxon settlement sites in the Louth region. Unless some of the single finds of Anglo-Saxon brooches and pins reflect such sites, we are restricted to five possible find-spots of Early Anglo-Saxon pottery and two coins. The latter are perhaps the most interesting finds, as both are forgeries of high-status Merovingian gold coins (*tremisses*) from the Continent. Such coins are generally very rare in this part of Britain, with only twelve *tremisses* known from the whole of Lindsey. Given that the two from the Louth region are both single finds, they may thus represent high-status settlement sites of the period *c.* 600–75, and in this context the find-spots – which are only general, not specific – are interesting. One is from 'Louth', perhaps the Acthorpe area (in the neighbourhood of the cremation cemetery) to judge from the available information. The other is from 'Ludborough', and so could be somehow associated with the previously mentioned high-status male burial from neighbouring North Ormsby parish.

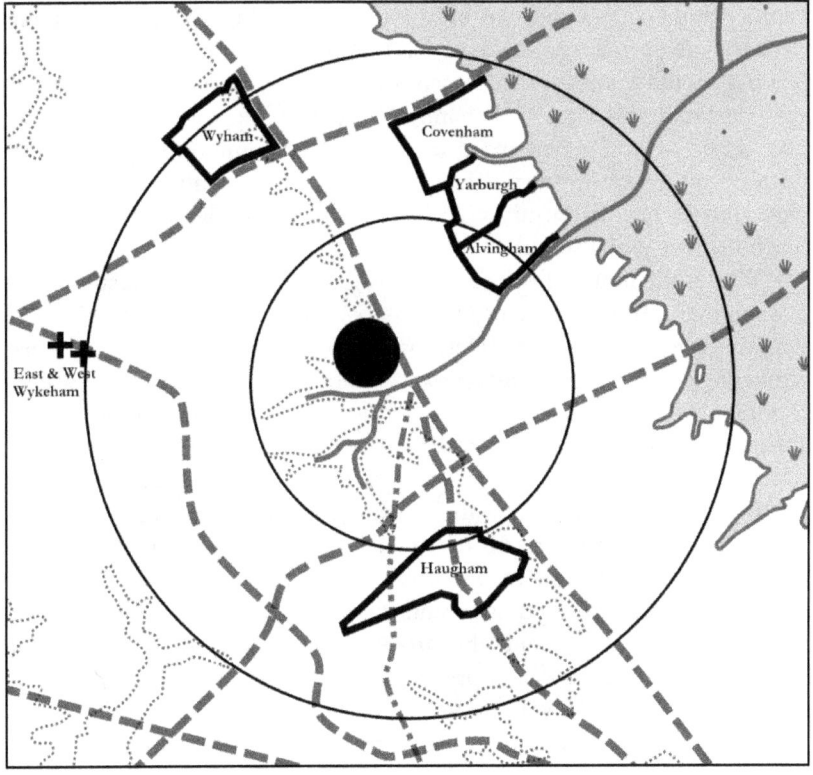

Figure 31: Early Anglo-Saxon place-names of the Louth region, showing the approximate coastline in this period and the parish boundaries currently associated with these names.

The only other potential source of information on the settlement sites of the Louth region in the Early Anglo-Saxon period comes from the corpus of surviving place-name evidence. Of particular significance here are those names that involve Old English *-ham* and *-ingas/-inga-*, as these elements are generally agreed to have been primarily used to form place-names in the period between the fifth and seventh centuries. Perhaps the most important of these names is found just beyond the western edge of our study zone, at a pair of Deserted Medieval Villages in Ludford parish named East and West Wykeham. 'Wykeham' derives from Latin *vicus* (a Romano-British term for a local administrative centre) + Old English *-ham* ('estate, settlement'), and place-names with this derivation are believed both to date from before the end of the sixth century and to be indicative of some sort of administrative continuity between the Late Roman and the Early Anglo-Saxon periods, in this case relating to the Roman 'small town' of Ludford that lies just the north-west of West and East Wykeham. Whilst this site is located outside of our survey zone, it is perhaps worth noting that some Early Anglo-Saxon pottery and a sixth-century sleeve-clasp have been found in the parish, as well as two eighth-century coins and four other pieces of eighth- to ninth-century metal-work.

Within the limits of our study zone, one particularly interesting name is Haugham, 'the high estate/settlement'. The description 'high' – Old English *heah* – can either refer to elevation or to some sort of pre-eminent status ('the chief *ham*'), though the former sense is topographically appropriate and so is perhaps best adopted here. Intriguingly, compounds of Old English *heah* + *ham* almost all seem to lie on high ground close to and overlooking Roman and prehistoric routeways, which has led to the suggestion that places with this name were established very early in the Anglo-Saxon period, perhaps by immigrants employed by the Britons to defend their territories. Certainly such a role for the early immigrants to eastern Lincolnshire has already been suggested above, and the present village of Haugham overlooks one of the likely north-south prehistoric routeways of the eastern Wolds, as well as being not too far from the east-west Roman road to Saltfleet and the possible north-south Roman route from Tetford/Horncastle to Louth (land in the parish also overlooks Barton Street and the Marshes, which may be significant given that nucleated villages only emerge after the Early Anglo-Saxon period). There is, it had to be said, currently no archaeological evidence available from the parish to support this scenario, but the very presence of the name-element -*ham* is, in any case, strongly indicative of there having been an Early Anglo-Saxon settlement somewhere here. Moreover, if the inhabitants made use of the cremation cemetery, then the lack of physical evidence is unsurprising given the paucity of archaeological settlement evidence from this region.

The two final early settlement-names to be considered are Covenham and Alvingham. Covenham is 'the estate/settlement of Cofa', and whilst further details on Cofa and his identity are completely lacking, in this case there are one or two sherds of Early Anglo-Saxon pottery – found to the north of Birkett Lane – that can help to locate at least one fifth- to seventh-century settlement/farmstead here. Alvingham is 'the estate/settlement (*ham*) of the *Ælfingas*', with *Ælfingas* being a population-group name meaning 'the people/dependents of a man named Ælf'. In general, place-names ending in -*ingaham* are now considered to date a little later than those that simply have the -*ham* suffix, perhaps being coined in the sixth or seventh centuries, with the *Ælfingas* probably being a local sub-group that developed around this time within the larger population-group that made use of the South Elkington-Louth cremation cemetery as its 'central place'. Two points need to be made with regard to these Early Anglo-Saxon place-names. The first is that Covenham and Alvingham are found either side of Yarburgh parish, a coincidence that is at the very least interesting given the possible Late/post-Roman fortification there. The second is that current reconstructions of the Anglo-Saxon period coastline indicate that all three parishes were then located at the edge of the coastal zone, on navigable creeks leading inland from what was effectively a sheltered lagoon protected by offshore islands.

Attention ought also to be directed to Wyham (Old English *Wihum*), the name of a Deserted Medieval Village found just to the west of Ludborough. This represents the Old English dative plural of *wig/wih* and hence means 'at the pagan shrines', a name that is obviously of relevance here. *Wig* is, alongside *hearg* ('Harrow'), one of two generic terms used for Early Anglo-Saxon pagan religious sites. Names in *hearg* appear to have described pagan sanctuaries occupying a prominent position on high land; these probably functioned as communal places of worship for a tribe and were perhaps focussed on a stone or cairn. In contrast, the term *wig* seems to have been used for open-air sanctuaries that could occupy a variety of topographic situations, including hill-tops

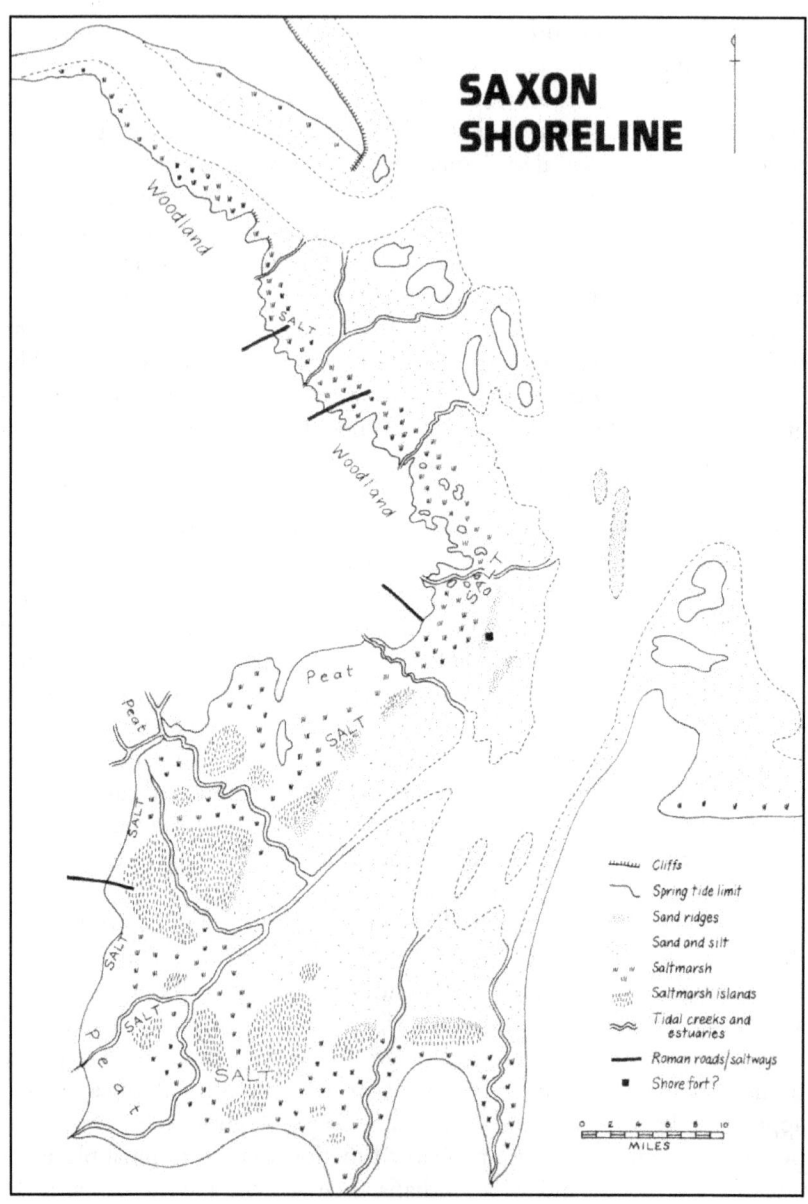

Figure 32: David Robinson's reconstruction of the Early Anglo-Saxon coastline of Lincolnshire, showing the offshore islands protecting the coast of the Louth region. Image used by kind permission of David Robinson.

and woodland groves, and which may have had as their focal point a wooden or stone pillar, perhaps carved in the image of a pagan god. They are usually located close to ancient routeways – Wyham lies just to the west of prehistoric Barton Street and to the north of the Roman road from Ludford to the coast – and this has led to the suggestion that they could have been wayside shrines, accessible to the traveller. Finally, names involving *wig/wih* and *hearg* have a curious and sparse distribution across the whole of England, which it has been argued is consistent with them having survived in use because they denoted shrines where pagan rites continued exceptionally late into the seventh century, after most other shrines had been repressed or Christianized.

In consequence, the place-name Wyham would appear to preserve the memory of a pagan Anglo-Saxon sanctuary site located in our region, just off the major north-south prehistoric trackway that ran through Louth and close to its junction with an important local Roman road. This sanctuary probably incorporated several shrines (given the plural form of the name) that are likely to have included wooden or stone pillars, perhaps with the images of gods carved upon them. Furthermore, this was probably one of the final centres of pagan Germanic religious activity in Lincolnshire to be suppressed by the Church after the conversion of the Anglo-Saxons of the kingdom of *Lindissi* in the 620s. Where, exactly, this sanctuary was located is uncertain, although it might be tentatively wondered whether the redundant church at Wyham doesn't overlay it. Certainly Pope Gregory instructed Bishop Mellitus in 601 not to destroy but to Christianize the 'temples' of the pagan Anglo-Saxons, and we have a letter written in the 680s by Aldhelm, Abbot of Malmesbury, which confirms that seventh-century Christians did indeed do this. He mentions in this letter a church being built to replace and Christianize a 'profane shrine' where 'crude pillars' carved with a likeness of a 'three-tongued serpent' and a stag 'were worshipped with coarse stupidity'. There is no evidence to suggest that the late pagan site at Wyham was similarly dealt with via the construction of a seventh-century church, but it is possible that the 'pagan shrines' here were Christianised in some other manner, perhaps via a free-standing cross, with this then being replaced by a church at some future point (the present church has some architectural details that have been claimed to belong to the eleventh century and so could provide a *terminus ante quem* for the first church on the site, although this dating has been disputed).

All told, the fifth, sixth and earlier seventh centuries do appear to have been a time of tremendous change for the people of the Louth region, even if the old notion that the Romano-Britons were driven out or exterminated in these centuries is no longer credible. Not only did they cease to be citizens of the Roman Empire and suffer a major economic collapse, but they also saw the arrival of Germanic immigrants – the Anglo-Saxons – from the Continent. These Anglo-Saxons eventually took control of the region, with the result that the Britons here ended up adopting the immigrant material culture, language and eventually ethnicity. Moreover, whereas the Louth region was largely peripheral to Roman Lincolnshire (although Louth itself was probably the site of a locally-significant settlement and a rural cult-site), in the post-Roman era the high ground above Louth became the site for one of the major 'central places' of Anglo-Saxon Lincolnshire. Needless to say, this is a point of considerable significance when considering the origins of Louth's medieval and modern importance. Finally, if there were tremendous upheavals for the inhabitants, there are also changes for the historian too. In particular, the availability of place-name evidence is significant – at the very least, it allows us for the first time to put a name to some of the people who lived in the Louth region (Cofa and Ælf), which is an important development.

5

The Middle Saxon Minster and Market at Louth, *c.* 650–870

The regional importance and centrality that Louth had developed in the Early Anglo-Saxon period appears to have been maintained into the Middle Saxon period and beyond. Louth is, for example, likely to have remained the meeting-place for a very sizeable secular district in the Middle Saxon period, given that the later-recorded wapentake of Louthesk probably had its origins in the pre-Viking era and may derive ultimately from the territory dependent upon the South Elkington-Louth cremation cemetery. Even more significant, however, is the fact that Louth also seems to have become a major monastic centre, or minster, during this period (it should be noted here that minster – Old English *mynster*, 'monastery' – is now usually used for such Anglo-Saxon sites, in order to avoid the narrower and anachronistic connotations of the Modern English word 'monastery'). This religious centre is first securely mentioned in relation to the events of AD 792, when Abbot Æthelheard of Louth minster (*Hludensis monasterii*) became the Archbishop of Canterbury, but it is likely to have been founded at some point considerably before this, perhaps in the later seventh century. Certainly, the other documented Middle Saxon minsters in Lincolnshire were all founded around this time, and two further points can be made in support of such a foundation date.

The first point relates to a Mercian royal charter granting lands to the Anglo-Saxon minster at *Medeshamstede* (Peterborough), which purports to date from 680, the year after Midland kingdom of Mercia had finally managed to gain permanent control of the Lincolnshire kingdom of *Lindissi*. Although the charter is clearly a later forgery, it probably reflects a genuine attempt to set out in a new and concise form the documented possessions and monastic colonies of pre-Viking *Medeshamstede*, which was founded in the mid-seventh century. In these circumstances, it is intriguing to note that a certain *Lodeshale/Lodeshac* is mentioned in this charter. *Lodeshale* appears to be a compound name and it has been proposed that the first element here is the place-name Louth (*Ludes* at Domesday). On the whole, this suggestion doesn't appear particularly unreasonable, especially as we already know there was a Middle Saxon minster at Louth. Whilst the spelling of the name with an -*o*- rather than the normal -*u*- has been seen as a source of concern, too much can perhaps be made of this, and Kenneth Cameron was reportedly willing to consider *Lodeshale* as a potential form of the name Louth. Of course, if the name *Lodeshale* does indeed refer to Louth then the implication of this would be that Louth was considered a pre-Viking monastic colony of *Medeshamstede*. Even ignoring the date assigned to the forged charter, this would support the view that Louth minster was a later seventh century foundation, given that this seems to be when most of *Medeshamstede*'s colonies were founded.

The second point derives from the Middle Saxon archaeology of the Louth region. It has been argued that the minsters of this era were amongst the most important centres of consumption and exchange away from the coast, acting as *foci* for pre-Viking markets and fairs. A high proportion of inland coin finds from this period certainly seem to occur at or near to minster sites, and the evidence from the Louth region accords well with this picture: there is now a significant quantity of Middle Saxon coinage known from Louth and its immediate vicinity, and this material is thought to result from a market or fair that was associated with the recorded minster here. This situation is of particular importance with regard to the present issue, as although many of the coins found in and around Louth belong to the later eighth and ninth centuries, the corpus also encompasses six late seventh- to mid-eighth-century silver coins or *sceattas*, including a Series E *sceat* of *c.* 700–10, a Series J *sceat* of *c.* 710–25, and two *sceattas* of *c.* 675–750. Needless to say, given the likely association between the coinage found here and the pre-Viking minster and its market, the presence of such early coins would appear to add considerable weight to the suggestion that Louth minster was in existence by the early eighth century at the latest.

Figure 33: Coins of two ninth-century kings of Mercia, Burgred (852–74) and Ludica (825–7). Coins of these rulers were found in Louth in the first half of the nineteenth century, but unfortunately no drawings were made of them; the two examples illustrated here were found in Oxfordshire and Staffordshire. Images used by kind permission of the Portable Antiquities Scheme; PAS find reference numbers SUR-453548 and WMID-7A2DC2.

If there was probably a Middle Saxon minster (monastery) at Louth by around AD 700, if not a decade or two before, where then was it located? David Stocker has tentatively suggested that the twelfth-century Louth Park Abbey may have been founded by the Cistercians on the same site as the pre-Viking minster, although he notes only that such a location 'may be worth consideration' and that there is 'no evidence' for it beyond the general semi-island-like topography of the area, which might bear comparison with some of the known sites of Middle Saxon minsters. In this context, it should be pointed out that the traditional view that Louth minster was located in the area of the present town still has considerable merit.

At the most basic level it needs to be remembered that the twelfth-century abbey was actually located a significant distance away from Louth, with the site being currently placed in a separate parish (Keddington). Moreover, the Cistercians are generally known for their preference for 'virgin' sites for their monasteries, rather than ones used previously by an earlier monastic community. Even more significantly, it has been recently argued that the Domesday and medieval market at Louth probably derived directly from the pre-Viking monastic one (five of the seven Lincolnshire markets at Domesday are, in fact, located at sites with significant early religious associations), something that would obviously strongly favour a location for the monastic market on the site of the medieval town itself. Indeed, a location for the pre-Viking minster and its associated market or fair in Louth would actually provide a reasonable explanation as to why a town had developed here by the later eleventh century. Certainly, it now seems clear that many Late Saxon and Anglo-Norman small towns in England grew up at or around the sites of pre-Viking minsters, developing from the role that these sites played as major market and economic centres for their surrounding regions. Finally, it is worth recalling that Louth was arguably already a British Christian cult-site by the seventh century (on the basis of the above interpretation of St Helen's spring in the town), and pre-existing British religious sites do appear to have provided a focus for Anglo-Saxon religious activity elsewhere in Lincolnshire and across Britain as a whole. For example, Bardney minster appears, at least partially, to have been located where it is in order to take control of the pre-existing British sacred and ritual activity in the Witham valley, and the continuing religious usage of the site of the fifth- to sixth-century British church of St Paul in the Bail in Lincoln is also of potential relevance here.

In addition to these arguments, we also have the evidence of Louth's own Anglo-Saxon saint, St Herefrith, whose name usually appears in medieval documents in the form Herefrid. This saint and his association with Louth is first recorded in an eleventh-century account, probably written between *c.* 1068 and 1085 at Thorney near Peterborough, of a raid undertaken by the monks of Thorney in the tenth century to steal St Herefrith's relics from Louth. After Æthelwold, bishop of Winchester, refounded the minster at Thorney in 970, he began to endow it with relics. Following the successful retrieval of the body of Benedict Biscop in around 973, Æthelwold is said to have

> heard of the merits of the blessed Herefrid bishop of Lincoln resting in Louth a chief town of the same church. When all those dwelling there had been put to sleep by a cunning ruse, a trusty servant took him out of the ground, wrapped him in fine linen cloth, and with all his fellows rejoicing brought him to the monastery of Thorney and re-interred him.

As Arthur Owen has observed, this passage is interesting for several reasons. One is that St Herefrith is described as a bishop, a claim repeated in various other credible sources, not least a *c.* 1040 calendar from Bury St Edmunds that mentions St Herefrith and his feast-day (27 February). In light of this, the obvious conclusion is that St Herefrith of Louth was considered one of the pre-Viking Anglo-Saxon bishops of Lindsey. This bishopric ceased to exist in the later ninth century, after the Viking takeover of the region, and it seems likely that the late eleventh-century account of the Thorney raid is simply a modernization of his title to the then-current one of 'bishop of Lincoln', which had been revived in 1072 (note also that 'Lindsey' and 'Lincolnshire' were used interchangeably in the contemporary Domesday Book). The only problem with this is that no Herefrith is mentioned in the surviving episcopal lists for Lindsey, but this is not a serious impediment here – the lists appear to have missed out the final bishops of Lindsey, who can only be tentatively reconstructed from late ninth-century Mercian charters. As such, it is more than credible that Herefrith was one of these final, poorly-recorded bishops, dealing with the consequences of the Viking conquests, a suggestion perhaps supported by a fifteenth-century description of St Herefrith as a martyr.

Another point of interest in the passage is that it suggests that there were people keeping watch over the relics of 'the blessed' St Herefrith at Louth and that they had to be 'put to sleep by a cunning ruse' – which surely means drugged – before the body could be stolen. In other words, St Herefrith appears to have been held in sufficiently high esteem in tenth-century Louth that his shrine was provided with resident custodians. Naturally, this Anglo-Saxon shrine, with its potential origins in the ninth century, is of considerable interest from the present perspective of trying to establish where the Anglo-Saxon-period ecclesiastical centre in the Louth area was. So, where was the Anglo-Saxon shrine of St Herefrith: Louth itself, or the site of the later Cistercian abbey in Keddington parish?

Fortunately, the people of Louth appear not to have forgotten St Herefrith quickly, despite their loss of his body. Not only was no manorial business allowed to take place on his feast day, 27 February, but there was also clearly a church of St Herefrith at Louth in the medieval period. Needless to say, this church has to be considered a very serious candidate indeed for the site of the documented shrine. The church of St Herefrith at Louth is actually mentioned multiple times in medieval documents. So, for example, an agreement concerning lands in Cockerington was made in the church of St 'Herefridus' of Louth in 1257; Richard of Farford wished to be buried 'in the church of the blessed Herefrid of Louth' in 1299; and the gild of St Mary of Louth was not only founded to provide seven candles to burn daily before the image of the Virgin in a chapel within the church of St Herefrith of Louth, but they also paid for a chaplain to celebrate services in St Herefrith's in 1318. On the whole, the evidence we have from these records strongly suggests that the church of St Herefrith was also the parish church for Louth, which is a little curious considering that the parish church is presently dedicated to St James and a church of St James is recorded in the town from 1235. This becomes even more intriguing when one realises that the later medieval references to the local cult of St Herefrith indicate that this cult was centred in the church of St James, and that the church of St James possessed Louth's only remaining relic of him – the 'come of ivery that was saynt Herefridis' – in 1486. The most plausible explanation for all of this is that we are here dealing with either a double dedication or a church where the dedication to the local Anglo-Saxon saint was gradually replaced over time with a more conservative dedication. Whatever the case may be, it would appear that the present church of St James was also the church of St Herefrith of Louth and so very likely the site of the Anglo-Saxon-era shrine, especially in light of the apparent presence of St Herefrith's ivory comb at the church and the description of Herefrith's shrine as lying 'in Louth' in the Thorney narrative.

Needless to say, this cannot prove that the Anglo-Saxon minster was located in Louth itself, but it does indicate that the core of the medieval and later town was the focus of significant Anglo-Saxon religious activity, which is highly suggestive. All told, when the above situation is placed alongside the points made previously, the case for the Anglo-Saxon minster at Louth having been located on the site of the present town appears to be more than credible. Of course, such a location doesn't really fit with the suggestion that many Middle Saxon minsters were founded on topographically-defined 'islands', unless we're willing to consider that the area bordered by the Lud, the Hubbard's Hills gorge, and the former route of Louth-Bardney railway, constituted a rather hilly monastic island (it does at least have clear physical boundaries and is smaller than some of the extensive pre-Viking 'monastic islands' that have been suggested), or that the 'island' of river terrace that Louth town is built upon was sufficiently island-like in the later seventh century. However, this is probably unnecessary. There is no sense that every Middle Saxon minster was founded on a topographically-defined island, only that a number were. Louth may simply be one of those minsters that were not, another being the late seventh-century minster at Stow Green, in the south of the county.

If the evidence we have available is probably best interpreted as indicating that the Middle Saxon minster at Louth was founded on the site of the present town core at some point around the later seventh century, perhaps partly due to the presence here of St Helen's spring, what else can be said about this ecclesiastical 'central place' and its effect upon the surrounding region? Three points in particular are worth making here. First and foremost, it would be a mistake to think of pre-Viking minsters as single, enclosed sites, rather than complex entities that pervaded their dependent territories. So, for example, it is likely that there was a range of local devotional *foci* and ecclesiastical sites associated with the minster at Louth and located throughout the region, including perhaps holy wells/springs, free-standing crosses, and hermitages. In this context, the Old English place-name Fulstow is particularly intriguing: of the several etymologies that have been proposed for this name, the most convincing is that it means 'Fugol's hermitage'. Who this Fugol was is unrecorded, but it is probable that he was associated with the minster at Louth, given that Anglo-Saxon hermitages tend to have strong monastic links. Similarly the status of the church at Withcall in Domesday Book is suggestive, as it is referred to there once as a church and once as a *monasterium*. Needless to say, it seems unlikely that there was ever a true Anglo-Saxon minster at this spot, especially in light of the proximity of

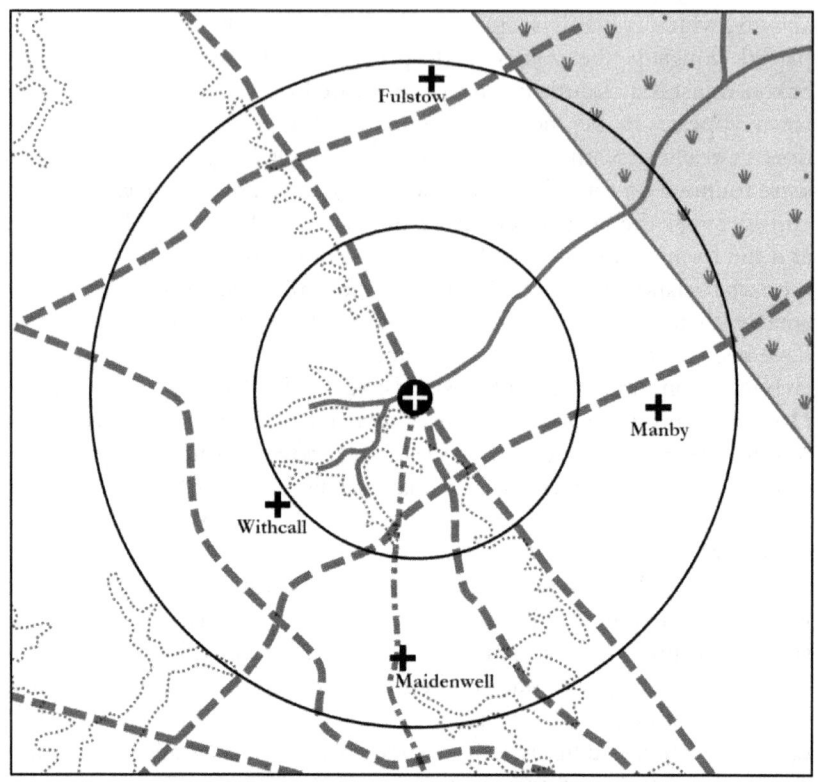

Figure 34: Possible local devotional foci and ecclesiastical sites associated with the Middle Saxon minster at Louth. The probable location of the minster is represented by the white cross within a circle; black crosses represent the sites referred to in the main text. Also shown is the suggested position of the Middle Saxon coastline.

Withcall to Louth. Instead, a more plausible solution may be that the church here and its confused status results from this being the site of dependent monastic possession (in later terminology, a 'grange') of Louth minster that was provided with its own church. Certainly such sites have been identified textually and otherwise elsewhere in Middle Saxon England, for example at *Osingadun* near Whitby, which had its church dedicated in the mid-680s when the Abbess of Whitby, Ælfflæd, stayed as this 'possession' of her minster with St Cuthbert. Alternatively, one might also consider the possibility that it represented what Bede in the eighth century termed a 'remoter house' (*mansio remotior*), that is to say a monastic site used by members of the main minster as a retreat, perhaps during Lent, although this may be less credible as an explanation. In addition, attention might also be drawn to a possible seventh-century Anglo-Saxon cross at Manby, although later dates have been suggested for this, and potentially to the reputedly petrifying holy spring at Maidenwell too. As to the latter, the name Maidenwell derives from Old English *mægden*, 'maiden, virgin' + *wella*, 'spring', and probably indicates a spring dedicated to the Virgin Mary, who was referred to by the term *mægden* in Old English (for example, Ælfric speaks of *þæt halige mæden Maria*, 'the holy Virgin Mary', in his tenth-century Old English 'Catholic Homilies'). Although the name given at Domesday to Maidenwell is simply *Welle*, it is by no means impossible that the fuller version of the name was in existence before the Norman Conquest and that it reflects a pre-Viking dedication of this spring.

Second, given that parish churches were a post-Viking phenomenon, it has been argued that most Middle Saxon minsters were actually expected to provide pastoral care to the inhabitants of their dependent territories. Their success in this is probably indicated by the fact that infant baptism was taken for granted in England by the middle of the eighth century, and that it was felt at that time that most ordinary people ought to expect at least some yearly contact with the church. Unfortunately, the exact methods by which such pastoral care was achieved are unclear, though one might suspect that the local *foci* mentioned above played a part, as did the market or fair that would have led to significant numbers of people gathering at the minster site. In any case, there seems little reason to think that the inhabitants of this region were not similarly served by the minster at Louth.

Third, early monastic estates appear to have been established through the redirection to the minster of the food-renders (and other services) that had been owed to the king by the inhabitants of at least part of a pre-existing Anglo-Saxon territory. As such, the initial establishment of the minster is unlikely to have had a major impact on the everyday economic life of the people of the Louth region. On the other hand, these traditional food-renders were primarily designed to support an itinerant royal court, which travelled around the whole kingdom, rather than a permanent community that lived in the area year-round. As a result, it is probable that 'inland' – a core of land around the estate-centre, which was directly exploited by the local lord instead of simply owing traditional renders and services – first emerged on monastic estates in the Middle Saxon period. Whilst the extent of this directly exploited core of land is still traceable around some pre-Viking minsters, this is not the case at Louth. Nonetheless, the change would have certainly been a major one for those who lived in that part of the region closest to Louth where it would have been instituted, with the local peasantry being subjected to a more exploitative and interventionist regime here than they had been previously used to.

Turning from the question of the minster and its likely effects to the more general one of what we can know about the region as a whole and its inhabitants in the Middle Saxon period, we are hampered by the paucity of the archaeological evidence. Although Middle Saxon graves are known from elsewhere in the county, they have proven far harder to locate than those of the Early Anglo-Saxon period, due to the fact that the use of grave-goods declines rapidly and unfurnished inhumation burial becomes the norm. As a result, no graves of this period have so far been discovered in the Louth region. On the other hand, we do at least have access to an increased corpus of numismatic evidence, almost all of which either comes from Louth itself or from sites near to the town. As was noted above, this material seems likely to derive ultimately from a market and/or fair associated with the minster at Louth, with the finds recovered from sites outside of the town perhaps representing, at least in some case, coin-losses at the settlements of people who made use of – and traded at – this market.

With regard to these sites, the closest to the town looks to have been somewhere in the vicinity of Thorpe Hall, on the basis of a Series E *sceat* from the Lower Rhineland or Frisia (dated to *c*. 720–30) apparently found in this area. Another site is represented by two *sceattas* of the period 675–750 and a coin of Offa of Mercia dating 792–6, found in the area to the north-west of Hallington village. Similarly, a ninth-century coin appears to have been found in the Acthorpe area (at the same site as the forged *tremissis* of 600–75, discussed in the previous chapter), and a coin of Offa and Archbishop Æthelheard (792–6) was found at a site to the east of Louth, probably in the Kenwick Road area. There may also have been pre-Viking activity of some sort at the former site of St Mary's church in Louth, north of the river, if some of the Middle Saxon coins that Robert Bayley recorded from the town in 1834 came from here. Unfortunately, however, his statement as to the findspots of these coins actually applies to all of the items that he records, which span the Roman to the medieval periods. As such, it is unclear whether the Middle Saxon coins he lists were found at all of the sites in Louth that he mentions, including St Mary's, or only at some or even one of them, most credibly his 'centre of the town' findspot in light of the above discussion of the probable location of the minster.

The only coinage of this period that doesn't seem to come from either Louth or its immediate environs is a small hoard of nine silver coins found at Walmsgate, on the edge of our survey area. This consisted of two Mercian coins of Burgred (852–74) along with seven West Saxon coins, and it was deposited at some point around 873; as such, it is

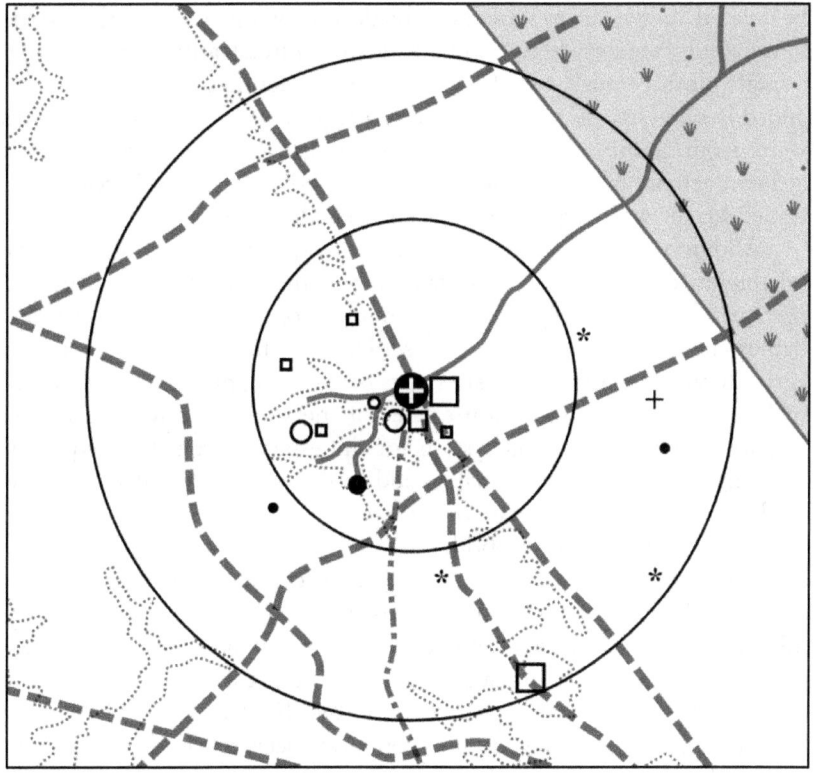

Figure 35: The Louth region in the Middle Saxon period. The minster is represented by the cross within a circle; filled circles are finds of metalwork; open circles indicate sceattas; squares represent late Middle Saxon coinage; stars indicate pottery finds; and the cross represents the possible cross from Manby. Where symbols differ in size, this reflects the varying quantity of finds.

probably to be associated with the Viking takeover of the region at this time. Aside from this, our available archaeological evidence is restricted to a handful of metal-detected items and a few sherds of pottery. Dealing with the former class first, the only site with more than one piece of metalwork is Maltby (in Raithby cum Maltby parish), near Louth. Here two ninth-century strap ends have been found, along with a copper-alloy pin head from a mid-eighth- to mid-ninth-century linked triple-pin-set and a substantial mount decorated with interlaced knotwork of the same period. Taken together, these finds suggest that there was a locally-significant Middle Saxon settlement site at this spot, which is probably to be related to whatever settlement made use of the Early Anglo-Saxon inhumation cemetery here. In contrast, from Little Carlton all we have is a single ninth-century strap end, although the fact that this is silvered and gilded is suggestive. As to the pottery, a large sherd of imported Ipswich ware from South Cockerington is potentially indicative of relatively affluent activity in the vicinity of this site, and there is a little regionally-traded Maxey ware from Authorpe and Haugham too.

Additional information on the region and its Middle Saxon inhabitants can potentially be obtained from the place-name evidence. In particular, it can be suggested that a number of local Old English place-names may refer to farms or settlements that had a specialized agricultural function. Such sites are often thought to have emerged within the major Anglo-Saxon estates of the seventh to tenth centuries as part of the provisioning system for the estate-centres. Consequently, these names have the potential to add to our knowledge of the people, landscape and estate structure of the Louth region at this time.

Two place-names – both involving Old English *tun*, 'farm/settlement/enclosure', an element rare before the eighth century – can, for example, be credibly interpreted as indicating settlements where the inhabitants were especially involved in the exploitation and management of woodland resources for a local Anglo-Saxon estate. One of these is Stewton, the 'stub- or stump-farm', from Old English *Styfic-tun*. As Eilert Ekwall long ago observed, the common occurrence of settlements named *Styfic-tun* in England suggests that the name had some special technical use beyond simply indicating a farmstead built near to (or from) one or more tree stumps, and in this context it seems very likely that the Anglo-Saxon inhabitants of Stewton and related places were actually engaged in coppicing. This is a woodland management process by which trees are cut back to the stump on a regular cycle and then allowed to regrow, in order to produce successive crops of rods and poles in different sizes that can be put to various uses, most especially in building and fencing work. Needless to say, such products would have been both valuable and necessary in the medieval period, and the provision of wagon-loads of rods and poles is mentioned a number of times in Anglo-Saxon charters. The other woodland-related Old English place-name in the Louth region is Reston, the 'brushwood-farm', from Old English *Hris-tun*. As was the case with *Styfic-tun*, this name – which occurs a number of times in England – has sometimes been seen as merely descriptive, being indicative of a farmstead surrounded by brushwood. However, it can equally be argued that Reston could have been so-named because its inhabitants were responsible for the provision of brushwood to a local estate-centre. Brushwood was another important woodland resource, particularly in terms of both fuel and the building of wetland causeways, and it is again mentioned in a number of Anglo-Saxon charters. So, for example, in the ninth century a certain Wulfred was required to provide twelve wagon-loads of brushwood (in addition to other items) to the minster at *Medeshamstede*, Peterborough, in return for the lease of an estate at Sempringham.

Other Old English place-names in the Louth region mention types of domesticated animal, and here the idea that these names referred to specialized farms seems even more credible: whereas both *Styfic-tun* and *Hris-tun* could conceivably merely describe the location of these settlements, this possibility doesn't really apply to names involving domesticated animals. Thus Gayton le Wold and Gayton le Marsh parishes both lie just within our survey zone and bear a name meaning 'goat-farm', from Old English *Gata-tun*: the clear implication is that the inhabitants here were specializing in the rearing of goats, potentially in order to provide for one or more local Anglo-Saxon estate-centres. Goats were not only a source of meat, thin leather, and perhaps milk in the Anglo-Saxon period, but their skins could also be used to make parchment for writing upon, which is suggestive from a monastic perspective. The settlement-name Oxcombe may be similarly significant, as it means 'ox-valley', from Old English *oxa* + *cumb*, a bowl-shaped valley. Although no farm is specified in the name itself, the easiest interpretation of this settlement-name is that it applied to a farm or settlement located in a valley that was especially associated with the breeding of cattle. Such animals were of considerable value in the Anglo-Saxon period, being used for ploughing, meat, milk, leather and – once again – vellum for scribes. Finally, mention ought to be made of the place-name Carlton (now preserved in Little, Great and Castle Carlton), which derives from Old English *Ceorlatun*, 'the settlement of the free peasant farmers'. This is another place-name that recurs all across England, including on many documented large Anglo-Saxon estates, and so is very likely to have had a specific technical sense. Exactly what this was remains open to debate, but it may be that Old English *Ceorlatun* indicated a settlement of 'free' peasant farmers, *Ceorlas*, who were required to provide labour services on the inland (the directly farmed land) of the local major estate. As such, it is also of potential interest here.

Of course, even if it is accepted that each of these place-names was of the type that referred to specialized farms or settlements, and that they were all linked to major local Anglo-Saxon estates of the seventh to tenth centuries, we still cannot be certain that in every case the estate-centre in question was the minster at Louth. Although this is likely to be the case for any specialized settlements close to the minster-site, such as Stewton, we don't actually know how extensive the territory granted to Louth minster was. Whilst the possible dependent sites discussed previously suggest it may have been reasonably large, there is no trace left of the minster-estate in Domesday Book, and the fact that there are two places with the name *Gata-tun* in the region could indicate that there was at least one more large Anglo-Saxon estate based in or close to our study zone. Furthermore, as such extensive estates broadly date from the seventh to the tenth centuries, it needs to be remembered that a number of these Old English names theoretically could have been coined after the end of the Middle Saxon period, in the later ninth or tenth centuries. On the other hand, even if some of the place-names fall just outside the Middle Saxon period or are associated with estates other than that of Louth minster, they do nonetheless still offer at least a potential insight into both the likely activities of the people who lived in this region around this time and the estate structures that may have developed here between the seventh and the tenth centuries, something which neither the archaeological nor the historical evidence can yet provide.

In conclusion, the Middle Saxon period clearly saw further development and reinforcement of Louth's role as a regional centre, with the driving force behind this being the foundation of an Anglo-Saxon minster here, probably on the site of the present town in the later seventh or early eighth century. The establishment of this monastic community looks to have transformed the river terrace on the south bank of the Lud into both a major religious centre and the site of a significant pre-Viking fair and/or market that served the surrounding area, with the Domesday and medieval market at Louth arguably deriving directly from this. As such, the minster deserves a central place in any explanation of how Louth came to be one of the most important towns in Lincolnshire in the medieval period, and the effects of its foundation provide a very credible solution as to why the focus of the region shifted from the hills above Louth to the site of the town itself. Moreover, the presence of the minster can be argued to have also bound the surrounding district ever more tightly to Louth in this period. It is, for example, highly likely that the minster provided pastoral care and religious instruction for the Middle Saxon population here, and a number of sites potentially associated with (or administered by) the minster can be identified throughout the region. Similarly, the demands of a permanent monastic community probably led not only to the development of an intensively exploited area of 'inland' in the immediate vicinity of the minster itself, but also to agricultural specialization within the wider region as part of the provisioning system for this estate-centre.

6

Vikings, Bishops and the Origins of Louth, *c.* 870–1086

It is difficult to say with confidence when the Viking raids on Lincolnshire began, due to the paucity of documentary sources concerned with events here. Certainly the Wessex-based 'Anglo-Saxon Chronicle' refers to many men in Lindsey having been killed by the Vikings in 841, but whether there were earlier attacks (or, indeed, further ones in the decade or so following this) must remain a matter of speculation. What is clear, however, is that 865 saw a major escalation of the Viking threat, as the 'Great Army' arrived and stayed in eastern Britain. This Viking army was probably active in northern Lincolnshire by 866, when it is recorded as having crossed the Humber into Northumbria (presumably from the Lincolnshire bank of the estuary), and it is believed to have been in control of at least Lindsey by the end of 869 – it certainly over-wintered at Torksey in 872–3. The effects of this domination and control of the region by the still-pagan Vikings are likely to have been both significant and potentially traumatic for the Anglo-Saxons who lived here. So, for example, even if St Herefrith of Louth wasn't martyred by the Vikings – he is only described as a martyr in one fifteenth-century reference, although such a death would certainly help to explain his tenth-century cult in Louth – it is likely that he was the last, or one of the last, bishops of Lindsey, as the Viking conquest of Lindsey appears to have led to the disappearance of this bishopric. Similarly, the hoard of Anglo-Saxon silver coins from Walmsgate, deposited sometime around 873, can probably be taken as a reflection of the instability and uncertainty that the Viking conquest engendered amongst the local Anglo-Saxons. However, the major impact on the region stemmed not from its initial conquest by the Vikings, but rather from the subsequent permanent settlement of Scandinavian immigrants in the Lincolnshire countryside (it should be noted that Scandinavian is used here in its true sense, to refer to immigrants from Norway, Sweden and/or Denmark).

According to the 'Anglo-Saxon Chronicle', at harvest time in 877 the Viking army took back a portion of the Midland kingdom of Mercia from their Anglo-Saxon puppet ruler, Ceolwulf, and shared it out amongst themselves. This annal is thought to record the permanent settlement of these Vikings in the lands that they had won, and the area they took control of and 'shared out' is usually assumed to have included Lindsey. Not only had Lindsey been a part of the kingdom of Mercia since the late seventh century, but there are also a considerable number of place-names of Scandinavian origin found here. Unfortunately, using these place-names to investigate the nature of the settlement of either these warriors or any subsequent Scandinavian immigrants to our region is problematical. In particular, the old theory that many of these names – most especially those involving the Old Danish element *-by*, 'village/farm' – represent brand-new settlements, founded in the later ninth or tenth centuries on previously unused 'virgin' land, now seems difficult to sustain. The idea that there were significant tracts of uninhabited and unexploited terrain in the pre-Viking landscape is no longer seen as credible, and it needs to be recognized that there is, in fact, archaeological evidence for earlier Anglo-Saxon activity in many of the parishes that currently bear Scandinavian names. For example, whilst Maltby near Louth (in Raithby cum Maltby parish) possesses a Scandinavian name – Old Danish *Malti* + *by*, 'Malti's farmstead/village' – and has even seen finds of Viking-style metalwork, there is also evidence for significant Early Anglo-Saxon and Middle Saxon activity here too.

If the Scandinavian place-names of the region consequently cannot be considered to simply result from Viking warriors and later Scandinavian immigrants colonizing unused land here, what then might they represent? Certainly, there seems little reason to doubt that names like Manby, Fotherby, Maltby, Utterby and Little Grimsby must be related in some way to the presence of Scandinavian immigrants. This is particularly the case given recent finds of Viking metalwork (such as a cast lead Viking disc brooch from North Ormsby, dated 850–975); the

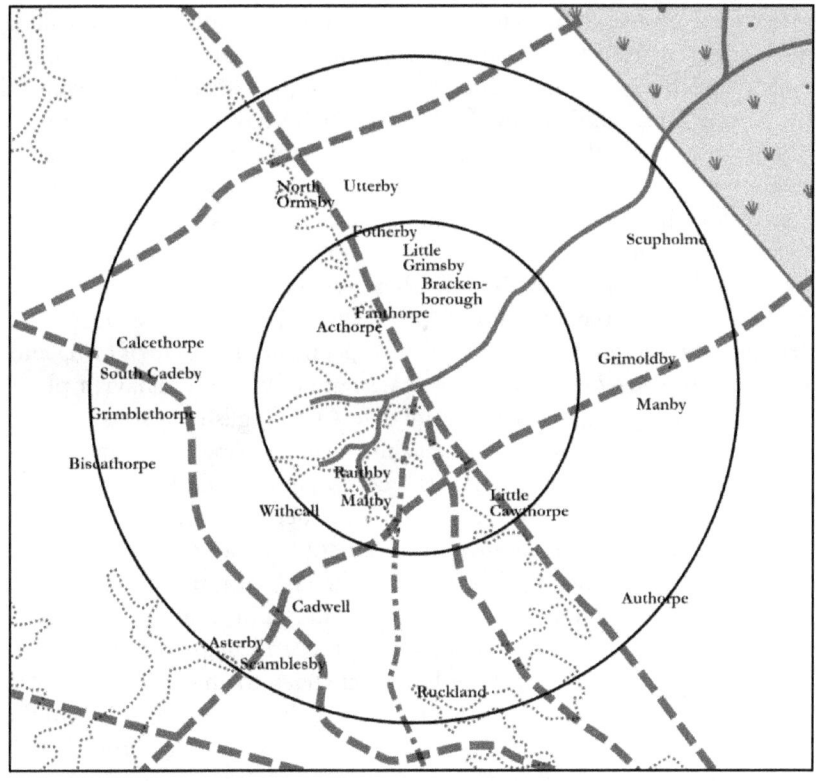

Figure 36: Scandinavian place-names in the Louth region.

evidence for a significant Scandinavian impact on the language and field-names of Lincolnshire; and the frequency of Scandinavian personal names in the Lincolnshire sections of Domesday Book (written 1086). All told, the evidence for a significant influx of Scandinavians into Lincolnshire during the later ninth century and after appears convincing. As such, it is not at all implausible that some of the above place-names do indeed represent settlements newly-founded by members of the Viking army or later immigrants from Scandinavia, albeit within what was probably an already farmed and exploited landscape, rather than virgin territory ripe for colonization. Others, however, could well have had a different origin, with immigrants perhaps moving into or taking over pre-existing settlements, which were then renamed. This certainly seems likely to have been the case at sites like Maltby near Louth, mentioned above. Not only has a significant quantity of pre-Viking material been found there alongside Viking-style artefacts (including a buckle attachment or belt-slide of *c.* 850–950, decorated in a fusion of the Viking Borre and Jellinge styles), but there have also been finds of ninth- to eleventh-century Anglo-Saxon-style artefacts, which is suggestive. Furthermore, some of the names involving Danish -*by* could conceivably have resulted from immigrants simply establishing lordship over pre-existing Anglo-Saxon settlements, rather than moving into them, with the new place-name then reflecting this new seigneurial relationship: the renaming of places when they gain new lords can certainly be demonstrated in better-documented parts of England. Finally, it is also worth observing that some of the Scandinavian place-names from this region actually involve Old English personal names, which again would tend to argue against a simple, single explanation for names such as these. So, Utterby is a compound of Old Danish -*by* with the Old English name Uhthere or Uhtred, rather than any Danish name.

The Scandinavian place-names of our study zone are therefore likely to have a rather more complex relationship with the settlement of Scandinavian immigrants in the ninth and tenth centuries than has sometimes been assumed. Nonetheless, they still help to confirm that this period saw major and long-lasting changes to this region, both in terms of its population and its language and culture. Indeed, although the Viking control probably only lasted until the 920s, when the Anglo-Saxon kings of Wessex won the overlordship of Lindsey from the Viking rulers of York, the evidence of Domesday Book indicates that local power and authority remained in the hands of people with Scandinavian names long after this. In this context, we need to ask just what the effects of all of this are likely to have been on the main focus of pre-Viking Anglo-Saxon activity in our region, Louth.

On the one hand, there seems little reason to doubt that Louth remained a major regional centre throughout the Anglo-Scandinavian (or Late Saxon) period. Louth was, for example, the focus and meeting-place for a large surrounding secular district – known as the wapentake of Louthesk – during this period, just as it probably had been in the pre-Viking era too. It also clearly functioned as a major religious focus well into the tenth century, being home to a significant shrine with resident custodians that was dedicated to St Herefrith, who appears to have been one of the last ninth-century bishops of Lindsey. Finally, Louth is likely to have remained the site of a major local market and/or fair throughout the Anglo-Scandinavian period. Not only is the Domesday market at Louth thought to derive directly from the pre-Viking monastic one, but the vast majority of the coin finds in the region also continue to come from sites 'near Louth', just as they had in the Middle Saxon period. Moreover, this Anglo-Scandinavian economic centrality for Louth is strongly supported by the apparent presence of a Late Saxon mint at Louth in the 970s. In common with the other new Lincolnshire mints of this time, very few of the coins minted here survive – only one or two examples are known from Louth, three from the new Horncastle mint, and four from the new Caistor mint in this period. However, the important point here is not the quantity of coinage that survives, but rather the simple fact that Louth was chosen as the site for one of these new royal mints of the 970s. It has been credibly suggested that this is, in itself, indicative of Louth having developed into a significant urban and trading centre within Lincolnshire by the later tenth century. In this context, it is perhaps interesting to note that the eleventh-century Thorney narrative of the theft of the bones of St Herefrith in *c.* 973 implies that Louth was, at that point, 'a chief town' of the Lincoln region – in light of the above, this does not seem a particularly implausible claim.

On the other hand, even though some major aspects of Louth's centrality to the region were maintained and even extended in the Anglo-Scandinavian period, there were also notable changes too. One might, for instance, point to the fact that Scandinavian speech became

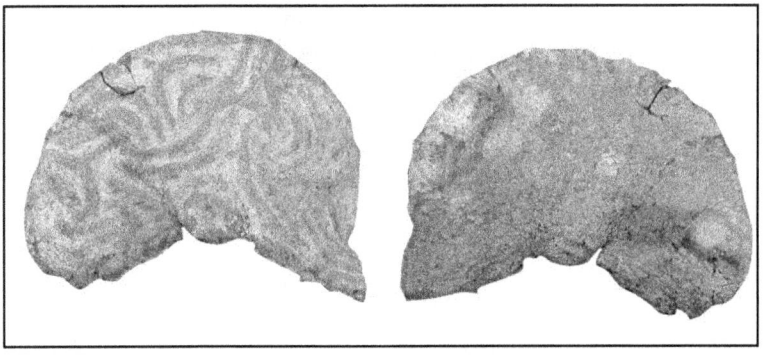

Figure 37: The front and rear of an incomplete cast lead Viking disc brooch from North Ormsby, dated 850–975. Image used by kind permission of the Portable Antiquities Scheme; PAS find reference number NLM-743AB7.

sufficiently widespread in this area to affect the local pronunciation of the name Louth itself, hence the presence of the Scandinavian *th* rather than the original Old English *d* in the modern form of the name. A more important change, however, was the loss of the Anglo-Saxon minster at Louth. Whilst Louth was still an important religious centre in the tenth century, there is no reason to think that the monastic community itself survived the Viking conquest and the disruptions to secular and ecclesiastical authority and control that this brought with it. Of course, there is nothing unusual in this – few if any of the Middle Saxon monastic communities of Lincolnshire survived the early part of this period in any meaningful way. Nonetheless, its loss must have had an impact on the region.

Equally significant is likely to have been the fragmentation of the minster-estate that was dependent upon Louth, which had disappeared by the time of Domesday. Place-names like Muckton ('Muca's village'), Hallington ('the settlement associated with Halla') and Manby ('Manni's village') probably all date broadly to the later Middle Saxon and Anglo-Scandinavian periods and reflect, in the main, both the dismemberment of the extensive Middle Saxon estates of the Louth region and their replacement by a large number of smaller estates under the control of local lords – both Anglo-Saxon and Scandinavian – who gave their names to these land-units. Moreover, it was not only sites with such diagnostic place-names that became the centres of small estates or manors during the break-up of the earlier units. Gayton le Wold, for example, bears a name which indicates that it was a *gata-tun*, 'goat farm', in the Middle Saxon period, but by the time of Domesday it too had become an estate-centre. This shift from large land-units to smaller, usually self-contained, estates is also believed to lie behind finds of tenth- and eleventh-century grave-covers and grave-markers in the Louth region, with potential examples identified from Gayton le Wold, Tathwell, Little Carlton and Manby. It has been argued that these items probably represent the memorials of the local resident lords of the tenth and eleventh centuries, founded at the sites of new parochial churches that were then being constructed under the influence of these lords to serve their new, small-scale estates.

If Louth therefore looks to have continued to dominate the region (despite the loss of the minster, a proliferation of small lordships or manors, and the beginnings of the medieval parochial system), can

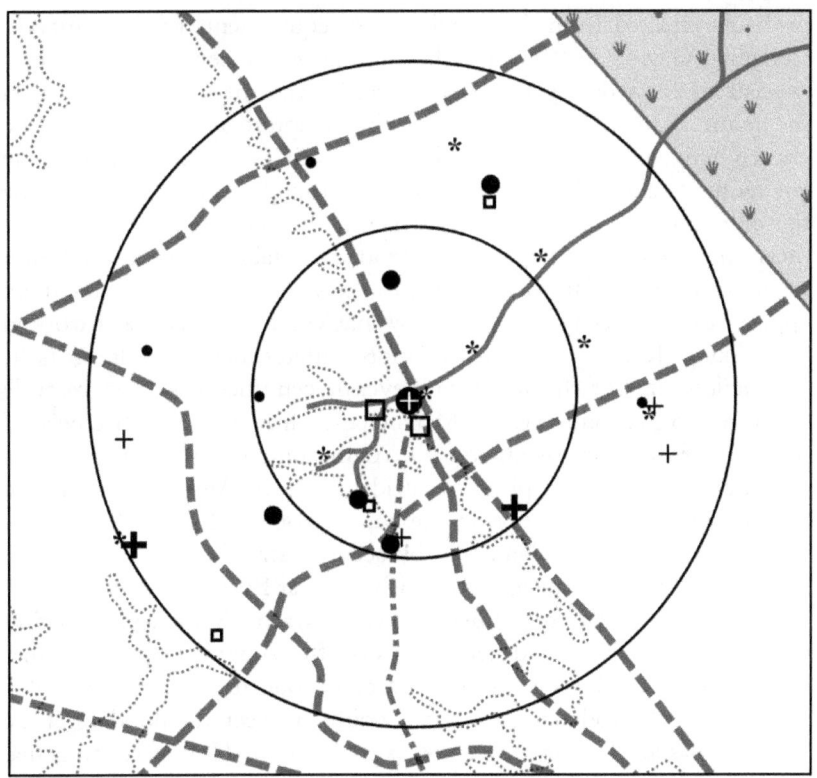

Figure 38: The Louth region in the Anglo-Scandinavian period. Bold crosses indicate settlement sites; normal crosses refer to grave-markers and grave-covers; filled circles are metalwork finds; squares indicate coin finds; and stars indicate other features, including pottery. Where symbols differ in size, this reflects the varying quantity of finds.

anything be said more generally about the everyday lives of the people here, be they of Scandinavian or Anglo-Saxon descent, between the later ninth and later eleventh centuries? On the whole, it seems likely that the people of this region continued to be primarily engaged in arable and pastoral farming, although finds of hammerscale – small fragments of iron oxide or slag that occur as a consequence of iron-working – and slag from Donington on Bain confirm a degree of local smithing. As to the kind of agricultural specialization discussed in the previous chapter, it seems unlikely that this survived the disintegration and demise of the large Middle Saxon estates here, given that this type of specialization probably resulted from the provisioning requirements of these estates. Certainly, Gayton le Wold had become an estate-centre rather than a specialized farm during the Anglo-Scandinavian period (most likely in the tenth century, on the basis of the sculpture recovered from the church here), and the same is probably true of Carlton too, in light of the late tenth- or eleventh-century grave-cover found at Little Carlton during the demolition of St Edith's church. On the other hand, this doesn't mean that there was no specialized production taking place in the Louth region or its immediate vicinity. Just to the south of the 10 km line there appears to have been a site at Ketsby that was producing metal-work in the Viking Jellinge style. Even more interestingly, a saltern (salt-production site) of the tenth to eleventh centuries has been recently excavated to the south-west of Marshchapel, around a kilometre beyond the northern borders of our region. At the time of the excavation this constituted the first physical evidence for Anglo-Saxon/Anglo-Scandinavian salt-production in the coastal zone of Lincolnshire, but it has recently been complemented by securely-stratified finds of eighth- and ninth-century briquetage from Fishtoft near Boston.

Whilst neither of the above excavations actually took place within the Louth area, as defined here, they do offer support to the view that people living in the easternmost parts of our region were probably involved in salt production at various points between the flooding of the Roman coastal zone and the Norman Conquest. However, the actual physical presence of salterns in the Louth region – as opposed to communities who utilized salterns – seems unlikely for much of the Anglo-Scandinavian era at least. The reason for this is that coastal zone appears to have moved entirely out of our study area during this period. For example, by the tenth century the edge of the coastal zone must have been found somewhere in the vicinity of Marshchapel, given that the saltern here was located a little to the south-west of the church and was processing sea-water brought to the site by an artificial channel. Moreover, further south we find evidence that the coastal zone was being permanently settled as the period progressed. Thus a late tenth- or early eleventh-century cross-head from Conisholme churchyard implies that there was probably a significant church here, and so a permanent settlement, by this time. Similarly, Grainthorpe is mentioned in the Domesday Book as not only the site of six eleventh-century salterns, but also a permanent settlement with sokemen, villains, ploughs and meadowland. Needless to say, this suggests that Grainthorpe was well-established and had been in existence for a reasonable amount of time before Domesday. Such a colonization and eastwards shift of the coastal zone is usually associated with an increasing level of salt-production all along the Outmarsh in the Anglo-Scandinavian period and after. This led to mounds of waste accumulating that provided solid ground for settlement and agriculture (as at Marshchapel, where the church was clearly constructed on top of a former saltern mound), with the land in-between the salterns then being reclaimed. These settlements were subsequently protected from the sea by newer saltern sites to their east and the construction of sea-banks, although the earliest identified major sea-bank (the A1301, known as Sea Dyke Way) must have post-dated the tenth- to eleventh-century Marshchapel saltern, as this lies to the west of the bank and thus would have been cut off from its supply of sea-water after the bank was built.

Although we are consequently able to say a reasonable amount about the development of the landscape and coastal zone to the east of the Louth region and the probable link between the changes here and the economic activities of the inhabitants of the eastern part of our region and the Outmarsh, saying much else about the landscape is difficult. Domesday Book does make mention of the woodland resources that were available, implying that the most heavily wooded parts of our region in the eleventh century were the neighbouring parishes of Louth and Stewton. This is, of course, interesting given the suggestion made in the previous chapter that Stewton was a settlement of people specialising in woodland management (coppicing) for a Middle Saxon estate based at Louth, and in this context it is perhaps worth noting that Domesday Book actually records coppiced woodland in Louth parish. Otherwise, most of our information on the Anglo-Scandinavian flora and fauna of the region comes from a handful of relevant place-names. So, the name Brackenborough (*Brachenberg* at Domesday, Old Norse *brakni* + *berg*) refers to hill covered by bracken. Similarly, the name Withcall (*Widcale*, *Withkale*) may indicate an area of woodland during the Anglo-Scandinavian period, if it derives from Old Norse *vithr*, 'a wood', + *kjolr*, 'a keel/ridge of land', although an arguably more plausible solution may be to treat the name as derivative of Scandinavian *with-kall*, 'echo', + *a*, 'stream'. Aside from these two names, there are three Scandinavian place-names that potentially refer to the animal-life of this region after the Viking conquests. The first is Ruckland, *Rocheland* in 1086, which is an Old Norse name meaning the small wood or grove (*lundr*) where rooks (*hrokr*) are found. The second is Cadwell (*Cathadala, Cattedale*), which appears to mean 'the valley where wild-cats are found' and is probably a purely Scandinavian name rather than an English-Scandinavian hybrid as has sometimes been thought. The most notable, however, is the third and final name, Wragholme (*Wargholm*), which is first recorded in the early thirteenth century but is likely to have had earlier origins. Although Wragholme lies just outside of our region between Grainthorpe and Marshchapel, its meaning – 'raised land amidst marshes frequented by wolves', from Old Norse *vargr* + *holmr* – is sufficiently interesting to be relevant here, offering as it does an intriguing perspective on the character and wildness of the reclaimed Outmarsh.

The overall picture of the Anglo-Scandinavian Louth region that emerges from all of the above is itself intriguing. Whilst there may have been wolves on the Marshes and wild-cats on the Wolds, it is nonetheless clear that by the end of this period the Louth region had begun to take on a recognizable form. For example, the coastal zone had been an almost constant part of this region from the Later Mesolithic onwards. However, as a consequence of the exploitation and reclamation of the saltmarsh, this zone had finally retreated out of our region and towards the present coastline by the eleventh century, with permanent settlements being established on the reclaimed land at sites such as Conisholme and Grainthorpe. Similarly, the extensive estates and

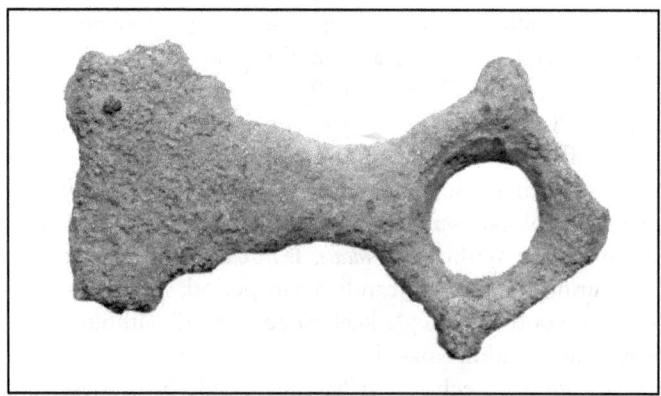

Figure 39: An incomplete eleventh-century horse harness link from Yarburgh. Image used by kind permission of the Portable Antiquities Scheme; PAS find reference number LIN-B4B3F6.

centralised pastoral care system of the pre-Viking era had largely disappeared, to be replaced by smaller-scale 'manors' and the beginnings of the medieval parochial system, with local churches and associated burial grounds evidently established in a number of places by the later eleventh century. Finally, comparative evidence from elsewhere in the country suggests that the nucleated villages and 'open fields' of the medieval and later Louth region probably also had their origins in the Middle Saxon and Anglo-Scandinavian periods. Even more important from the present perspective, however, is the fact that Louth too had started to become recognizable by the end of the Anglo-Scandinavian period, at least in terms of its role and status within local and regional society. Not only was it apparently the focal point for the surrounding district (Louthesk wapentake) and the site of a market, but one eleventh-century author also clearly considered it 'a chief town' of the Lincoln region, and its status as an urban and trading centre appears to be confirmed by the fact that it was briefly a royal mint in the tenth century. In one sense, therefore, the ultimate origins of Louth as a central place and market town can be said to clearly lie in the pre-Norman era. The question is, when did Louth also start to become recognizable in terms of its location, layout and structure?

As to the first element of this, the indications that we have suggest that settlement activity in Louth before the Norman Conquest was indeed concentrated at the heart of the later town, on the south bank and terrace of the Lud. This is where the Anglo-Saxon minster and the shrine of St Herefrith are likely to have been located, and it is similarly the probable location of the monastic and later market. Equally, despite the fact that the central area of Louth provides only limited scope for archaeological excavations and has potentially seen considerable destruction of the underlying archaeology by cellars and later development, this is the only part of Louth parish from which sherds of Anglo-Scandinavian pottery have been so far recovered, these having been discovered in possible association with a number of pits during the construction of Meridian House on Eastgate. Moreover, it ought to be remembered that the area to the south of the Lud is also the location of the neighbouring Aswell and St Helen's springs too. The latter, given its dedication, was probably a local cult-site throughout this period, and the former – 'the spring by the ash tree' – is a possible location for 'the ash tree at Louth' where the wapentake of Louthesk met to discuss and arrange the business and legal affairs of the surrounding district.

In contrast, there is little to indicate that there was any significant activity in the area to the north of the Lud in the pre-Norman period, despite frequent speculation to the contrary. Although it is sometimes suggested that the former church of St Mary had Anglo-Saxon origins and was the original parish church, there is no reason to think that this was actually the case. Indeed, one of the main modern proponents of this theory, Arthur Owen, has himself withdrawn the suggestion in recent years, noting that the evidence actually indicates that St Mary's was never more than a medieval chapel of ease and that most of the supposed references to this church actually relate to a chapel dedicated to St Mary in the parish church of St Herefrith-St James. Similarly, claims that Middle Saxon coins have been found at St Mary's are questionable, as was noted in the previous chapter – coins were clearly found there in the earlier nineteenth century, but whether they were Anglo-Saxon or instead medieval and/or Roman is unclear. Finally, whilst Cisterngate or Saxongate lies to the north of the Lud and bears a name involving Scandinavian *gata*, 'road', this cannot be taken to imply that there was significant Anglo-Scandinavian activity here. Given the extensive Scandinavianization of the local dialect, there is no necessity to see such a road-name involving *gata* as a pre-Norman coinage, and Cisterngate-Saxongate is, in fact, first recorded in 1396. Furthermore, it is worth pointing out that this road-name doesn't refer to Anglo-Saxon activity in this region, as has occasionally been suggested; instead, it appears to involve the personal name Saextan, hence the earliest form 'Saxtanegate'.

If the Anglo-Scandinavian town of Louth was thus likely to have been located in the same area as the medieval and modern town, what of the origins of Louth's street-plan and basic geography? With regard to this, a partial explanation may well lie in the deeds of the lord of Louth – the Bishop of Lincoln – in the latter half of the eleventh century. Exactly how long Louth had been under episcopal control before 1086, when it is assigned to Bishop Remigius in Domesday Book, is uncertain. However, a declaration by the jurors of Louthesk wapentake appended to the Lincolnshire Domesday does allow the potential start-date to be narrowed somewhat. This informs us that Bishop Remigius had stated his claim to lands apparently located in Louth Hundred – a sub-unit within Louthesk – because his predecessor, Bishop Wulfwig (1053–67), had purchased them from Alsi and Olgrim for £160 during the reign of Edward the Confessor. Needless to say, given both the probable location and high price of these lands, the above is usually and most easily interpreted as a record of the episcopal purchase of Louth and its immediate vicinity from these two laymen at some point between 1053 and 1066.

As to the effects of this new episcopal rule on Louth, Domesday Book remains the key source. In addition to confirming Louth as the site of an eleventh-century market and thirteen water-mills (which may indicate that Louth had, at some point, become a local milling centre), the Louth entry suggests that there was probably also a significant population increase for the town under the rule of the bishop. Whilst Anglo-Scandinavian Louth was potentially home to several hundred people, by the time of Domesday it looks likely to have at least doubled in size, largely through the establishment of 80 households of burgesses – probably representing around 400 or so people – in the town, an event that seems to have occurred between 1066 and 1086, given that no burgesses are listed as having lived in the town in 1066 (other towns with burgesses, such as Grantham, have totals for both 1086 and 1066 provided). This apparent episcopal encouragement of burgess households in Louth is important not simply in terms of the size of the town. First, burgesses held land in towns by burgage tenure, which is to say freely in return for money rents rather than labour services, without many of the normal customary obligations or restrictions over how the property could be disposed of. As such, the burgesses were free to pursue careers in commerce and industry, and the fact that the bishop had attracted 80 burgesses to set up in Louth by 1086 consequently testifies to his desire to develop and promote his town of Louth as a significant urban and trading centre within Lincolnshire as a whole. Indeed, in this context it should be noted that Louth was, in fact, one of only five towns (or 'boroughs') in Lincolnshire provided with burgesses by 1086, the others being Lincoln, Torksey, Grantham, and Stamford.

Second, the establishment of burgesses in a town did not simply involve the local lord waiving some of his rights in return for money rents and an increased level of commercial and industrial activity in his town – it actually required him to remodel the whole town in order to create burgage tenements for the burgesses to inhabit and work from. Across England, early (pre-1100) forms of tenement plots in towns were generally very long and narrow, with the thin ends fronting onto the street – this being where the place of business or workshop was based, the back part probably being used for growing produce, pasturing animals, and waste disposal – whilst plots initially marked out in the twelfth and thirteenth centuries tended to be less elongated. Once established, the boundaries of such plots were usually extremely long-lived features in towns and continued largely unchanged into the industrial era, being traceable even where the original plot had been multiply divided, and so it is in Louth too. Here the late nineteenth-century Ordnance Survey maps of the town and its property boundaries clearly show long and narrow early-style medieval plots fronting onto Mercer Row, and it is accordingly a reasonable conclusion that this road preserves on its south-side the original tenement boundaries created by the late eleventh-century remodelling of the town to allow burgesses to settle here. As to what lay to the north of these tenements, the answer is almost certainly the market site, but saying much more than this about the layout of the town at the time of Domesday is difficult. Similarly, the degree to which the layout of the Anglo-Scandinavian town was erased by this remodelling is unclear. Certainly, it was argued previously that the Late Saxon/Anglo-Scandinavian shrine of St Herefrith is likely to have been located on the same site as the medieval parish church of St Herefrith-St James. On the other hand, significant changes must have been made to the overall plan of the town in order to create the regular blocks of burgage tenements that are preserved here. At the very least, it is likely that the pre-Norman course of the main north-south routeway through Louth, Barton Street, was shifted to the present-day Upgate route as a result of the remodelling, with its original course through the town probably running under the new tenements.

Louth therefore saw significant changes in the latter half of the eleventh century, when it came under episcopal control. In particular, it appears that Bishop Remigius was concerned to fully exploit and develop the Anglo-Scandinavian town that his predecessor had bought for £160, with the result that by 1086 Louth had apparently become only the fifth town in Lincolnshire to have a community of burgesses living within it. This investment in Louth not only further increased its status and regional importance, but also led to important physical changes too, not least a notable increase in its population and a remodelling of the town to provide properties for the new craftsmen and traders who the bishop had attracted here. In sum, whilst the origins of Louth as a market-centre and town appear to lie in the pre-Norman era, it is also clear that key aspects of the modern geography of the town have their foundations just after this, in the period between 1066 and 1086, with the modern layout of at least the area to the south of Mercer Row being ultimately due to this early Norman and episcopal interest in the town.

7

Louth – Past, Present and Future

With the compilation of Domesday Book in 1086, the main body of this study reaches its conclusion. For much of the Louth region, this event marks the start of the documentary record and, as such, it provides a natural end-point for the current investigation. Moreover, the analysis in the preceding chapters suggests that if we are interested in the fundamental origins of this region, then the period before Domesday is where we primarily need to be looking. By 1086 our study zone had begun to take on a recognizable form, and the key basic elements of the region – including a reclaimed Outmarsh and Louth as an important market town – appear to have been largely in place. Arguably, therefore, we have gone as far as we need to. Nonetheless, given the overall focus here on the 'Origins of Louth', it seems worthwhile asking in this concluding chapter how the town of Louth continued its evolution and expansion after Domesday until it reached something approaching its modern form, and whether we can say anything about the likely future development of the region.

Domesday Louth stands at end of perhaps 400,000 years of intermittent human activity in this part of Britain, and for the vast majority of this almost inconceivably long period of time there is little reason to think that Louth was anything other than unremarkable within the surrounding region. Only in the Romano-British period do we start to get solid indications that Louth was a locally important centre, with probably at least one significant Romanized settlement and a rural cult-site located in the core area of the modern town. This local centrality for Louth and its immediate vicinity developed further in the subsequent

Anglo-Saxon era. A regionally-significant social, sacred and burial centre was established on the hills above Louth in the fifth century, and the Anglo-Scandinavian and Domesday town of Louth is likely to have had its origins in the foundation (sometime around AD 700) of an Anglo-Saxon minster and its associated monastic market on the site of the later town. Up until the Norman Conquest, however, there is little to suggest just how extensive Louth actually was during any of these earlier stages in its development or, indeed, what it looked like. It can be fairly assumed that the Anglo-Scandinavian town occupied approximately the modern central area of Louth between the church (the probable site of the shrine of St Herefrith) and the St Helen's and Aswell springs, but going beyond this is difficult. In contrast, in the period after the Conquest we start to be able to describe the town in more detail.

The first concrete indications as to the town's layout and extent come from the period immediately before 1086. As was discussed in the previous chapter, at least part of the central area of Louth was probably remodelled at this time by Bishop Remigius, in order to attract burgesses to the town that his predecessor had bought for £160. This remodelling laid out long burgage tenements (which can still be traced today to the south of Mercer Row) and the medieval market place, and it probably also shifted the main north-south route through Louth onto its present course along Upgate. At this point the town is unlikely to have extended much further south than the end of the tenements facing onto Mercer Row, and it may well be that there was only limited settlement activity to the west of these too. Certainly, excavations at the rear of the Greyhound Inn, which is situated immediately to the west of the above tenements, indicate that this site was only occupied from the twelfth century and lay on the edge of the town, with arable fields and wooded areas being located close by. With regard to the character of the medieval activity here, finds made include a substantial quantity of twelfth- and thirteenth-century pottery along with horse shoes and horse harness fittings, leading to the suggestion that the first buildings on this site were stables, perhaps associated with an inn.

Other evidence for twelfth-century activity in the town comes from the area around the parish church, where pottery dating to the twelfth century and later has been found in graves excavated in 1999. That there should have been activity in this area then is, of course, unsurprising, especially given that it now seems clear that Louth's parish church was always located here, with St Mary's never having been more than a chapel of ease. As to the medieval church of St Herefrith-St James itself, the earliest architectural evidence so far found within the present edifice belongs to a church constructed in the later twelfth century (c. 1170). However, in view of the fact that the parish church of Louth is actually first mentioned in 1146, this must represent a rebuilding of an earlier church, and it seems likely that this earlier church developed somehow from the recorded Late Saxon/Anglo-Scandinavian shrine of St Herefrith. In this context, it is worth noting that whilst there is no mention of a church in Louth at the time of Domesday, this does not mean that Louth lacked a church then. Domesday Book only notes a proportion of the churches that were in Lincolnshire in 1086 and even misses out some of the major pre-Norman churches, such as that at Edenham. In some cases this appears to have been due to lords failing to report that they owned a church to the survey, but in other cases it may simply be because the local lord received no revenue from the church and so Domesday just wasn't interested in it. The latter seems likely to be the case with regard to Louth, particularly in light of the fact that in 1146 the revenues from the parish church appear to have been assigned not to the local lord, the Bishop of Lincoln, but instead to a canon of Lincoln cathedral in order to support him in his duties.

The parish church was not the only part of Louth to be apparently improved upon during the course of the twelfth century. The market too was developed further, with Henry II in 1155–8 granting and confirming to the Bishop of Lincoln the right to hold two eight-day fairs in Louth, one beginning on the 6 July (the octave of St Peter and St Paul) and the other on the third Sunday after Easter Day. Both this and the rebuilding of the parish church around 1170 suggest that that the twelfth century was something of a boom period for Louth, perhaps partly encouraged by the foundation of Louth Park Abbey three kilometres to the east of the town in c. 1139 and the additional employment and prosperity that this must have brought to the region. This era of prosperity and expansion continued into the thirteenth century, with the church being rebuilt once again in the 1240s: the south doorway and pillars in the nave of the current fifteenth-century church date from this rebuild. The town also appears to have gained a school for local boys around this time – a certain Simon de Luda was the Master of this school in 1276 – and the wealth and status of some of the town's thirteenth-century inhabitants is confirmed by the grand tessellated pavement of this date discovered at Westgate House in 1801.

It is probable that much of the medieval layout of the modern town-centre beyond Mercer Row was in place by the end of this era too. Walkergate or Fullers' Street (modern Queen Street) was clearly in existence by the mid-thirteenth century, when it is first mentioned, although how far east it originally extended is unclear. Walkergate appears to have been the centre of the cloth-finishing industry in Louth from at least this time – the walkers, or fullers, after whom the street is named stamped on cloth in pure water to felt it and give it a smooth finish, and the presence of dye-works on this street is confirmed by the name of one its earliest inhabitants, Gilbert the dyer, who had a house and land that extended from the road to the Aswell spring at some point between 1235 and 1253. Both Westgate and Eastgate were likewise almost certainly in existence by the end of the thirteenth century. Whilst both are first mentioned in 1317, the former was clearly already the site of the some of the town's grander houses in the thirteenth century (by 1425 it had also become the home of the guildhall belonging to St Mary's Gild) and finds of pre-fourteenth-century material have been made on Eastgate. For example, Anglo-Scandinavian pottery was recovered from the site of Meridian House, along with probably medieval chalk rubble foundations. Equally, the block of preserved medieval property boundaries to the east of the Fish Shambles is complemented by a substantial quantity of twelfth-century and later pottery from 47–51 Eastgate (currently Peacocks, just to the north-east of the Fish Shambles), chalk wall foundations of probably medieval date, two pits and a possible gravel surface. Further evidence for activity in this part of Louth comes from 76a Eastgate, where medieval pottery sherds were found along with a red-brown baked clay layer that may reflect a medieval hearth or oven.

In addition to these main streets, Chequergate, Northgate and the western half of Kidgate are also likely to have emerged during this time, to function as back access-ways for the properties that fronted onto Eastgate and Mercer Row respectively. Northgate, for example, is recorded under its alternative name of Padehole ('toad-hollow') in 1317, and has seen finds of a late twelfth- or thirteenth-century buckle-plate and sherds of fourteenth- to fifteenth-century pottery; in neither case were the finds associated with medieval structural remains. Similarly, Gospelgate is twice mentioned in the thirteenth century and so must have existed by this point, although it probably chiefly functioned as simply a lane leading to the Goose Pool, one of the spring-fed pools of the town. The latter was located to the north of The Lodge, near to the western end of modern Gospelgate, although it may well have been only one of a number of medieval pools for keeping geese located along Gospelgate. Certainly, traces of another medieval pool have recently been found to the south of Gospelgate, during an archaeological watching brief at 9 Edward Street, and yet another was discovered through excavations behind the Greyhound Inn at the eastern end of this road. Aswell Lane almost certainly originated as an early access-way too, in this case running from Mercer Row and Walkergate to the important Aswell spring and its pool. This was not only potentially the meeting-place for the wapentake of Louthesk and probably venerated as a holy spring during the medieval period, in light of its later treatment and the dedication of its neighbour, but it was also a key source of fresh water for the town. Such medieval significance is reflected in the fact that fines were fairly frequently handed out for its defilement in this period, as in 1441 when John Baumburgh was fined 4d for washing sheepskins in its waters.

If the layout of the main core of the town was therefore probably established in its broad outlines before the mid-fourteenth century, and certainly seems to have been largely settled by the end of the medieval period, this is not to say that the town-centre area did not continue to develop in subsequent centuries. Nichol Hill, first mentioned in 1443, may have been a later addition to Louth's street-plan, linking Eastgate with its back access routes, and Vickers Lane and Cannon Street certainly were, being founded in the eighteenth and nineteenth centuries, respectively. Mercer Row and the medieval market place at the heart of the town also saw significant changes to their basic structure and character. Perhaps the most important of these was the conversion of the medieval butcher-stalls into two permanent blocks of buildings that cut Mercer Row off from the modern Cornmarket, although the erection of the Elizabethan Town Hall on the south side of the Market Place was also notable (it remained in this position until its demolition in the early nineteenth century).

The area around Aswell Lane and spring was similarly subject to alteration and development in the later medieval and early modern eras. In particular, at some point the road to the spring began to have properties established along it, with these cutting into land belonging to the earlier medieval plots that ran either side of the road and fronted onto Mercer Row and Walkergate. At the same time, the spring site itself

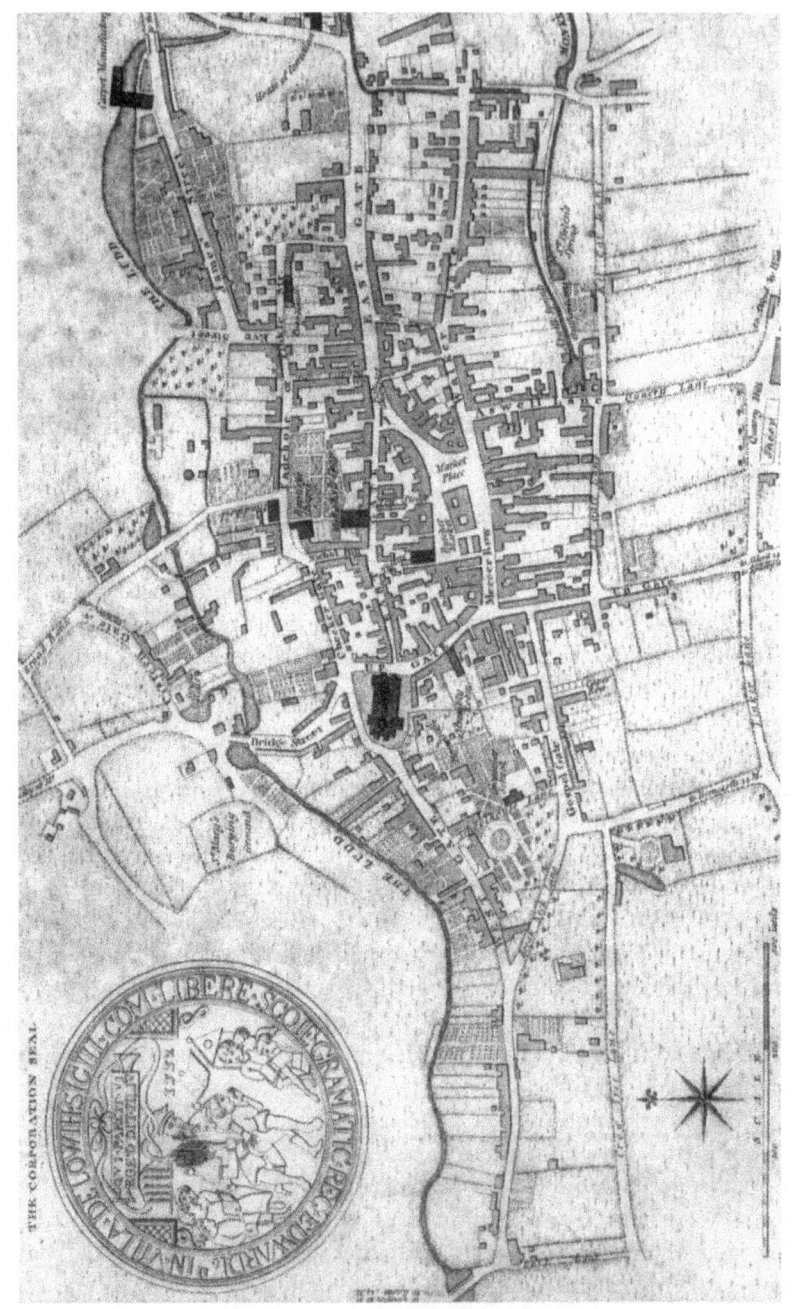

appears to have been the focus of considerable activity. The numerous references in the sixteenth and seventeenth centuries to relatively substantial payments being made for the dressing and cleaning of Aswell spring in preparation for its blessing and religious usage presumably continue a medieval veneration of this site – this devotion was apparently primarily focussed on Holy Thursday (Ascension Day), although there are indications that the spring was prepared for other festivals too, as in 1559 when one Mertyn Chapman was paid to dress the Aswell spring for Christmas. Moreover, there are also frequent accounts of large quantities of stone and timber being conveyed to Aswell in the aftermath of the Reformation, something which has been thought to indicate an unusual lavishing of attention on this area then. Some of this material was apparently being used 'for paveinge at Aswell... [and] the Raisinge of yt', as in 1621, but the quantities involved would imply that rather more substantial building works were also taking place. Although no trace of any such buildings now survive either on Aswell Lane or at the spring, in 1834 Robert Bayley observed that one of the much-decayed Tudor houses that persisted at Aswell to his day had 'some appearance of having been used for religious purposes', which may be significant here.

With regard to the expansion of the town beyond its central core, it is apparent that that the area to the north of Chequergate-Northgate saw at least some activity during the medieval period. There was, for instance, undoubtedly something going on in the fourteenth and/or fifteenth centuries near to the river at Spout Yard. A pit lined with wickerwork was recently excavated here, with straw and hay found deposited above this lining and a fill lying over this containing late medieval pottery, animal bone, and hammerscale from iron-working. In addition, two wooden stakes from a presumed associated superstructure were found adjacent to the pit. Quite what the function of this set-up was is unclear, however, and the environmental evidence preserved at this site indicates that this area of Louth was not a significant settlement or industrial zone in the medieval period, but was rather primarily a woodland habitat.

Moving north of the river, the evidence becomes more solid, with a chapel of ease dedicated to St Mary founded here at some point, although documentary confusion between the chapel of St Mary in the parish church of St Herefrith-St James and this site makes dating its

Figure 40 (opposite): Thomas Espin's map of Louth, 1808.

construction problematical in the absence of any architectural remains. Thus, for example, the supposed first reference in 1267 to St Mary's north of the river can no longer be relied upon as it has been, as it could just as easily – and perhaps more credibly – refer to an event taking place in the chapel of St Mary within the parish church instead. The excavated fourteenth- or fifteenth-century secular building on Mount St Mary is also important, but whether it stood alone (perhaps being associated with the above chapel of ease) or as part of a developing northern suburb of medieval Louth is unclear. Similarly, whilst Cisterngate was plainly in existence by the late fourteenth century, we currently have no indications as to the nature or density of the activity here. Certainly, in the 1540s and 1550s the street was apparently considered sufficiently remote from the main town community that a cottage there could be used as a 'plague house' to isolate victims in. Indeed, to judge from Thomas Espin's map of 1808, there was actually very little development of the town north of the Lud between the medieval era and the early nineteenth century, aside from the laying out of Broadbank in the eighteenth century. Only really in the middle years of the nineteenth century did this begin to change, with more buildings being mapped in this area by Robert Bayley in 1834 and a new workhouse (now part of Louth Hospital) being built at the top of Broadbank in 1837.

In contrast, the previously undeveloped area south of the river between the Lud and Chequergate-Northgate had clearly seen a notable increase in activity over the same period of time. By 1808 buildings had been established all along the north side of Padehole/Northgate, including the 'Free School' on the corner of Northgate and Broadbank. However, the nineteenth-century nickname of Northgate – Finkle Street, 'stinking street' or 'fart street' – suggests that this area wasn't considered an especially desirable part of Louth at that time, something perhaps also implied by the presence of the town's eighteenth-century workhouse here. Even more important was the construction of Eve Street and James Street in this area during the late eighteenth century. Together they linked the town to the new carpet factory on the Lud and to the Riverhead, the industrial village that had grown up around the point where the Louth canal terminated, and by 1808 a significant quantity of housing had been established along both of these streets. Finally, by the mid-nineteenth century the areas running down to the river behind Northgate and Chequergate had become the site of poor and over-crowded housing, in particular at Healey's Court and Ludgate (behind

Chequergate), with the majority of households in the former area being those of paupers supported by the parish.

To the south of the core of the town there is relatively little evidence for any expansion of medieval settlement activity beyond Kidgate, but this is not to say that this area was not in use both during and after this period. So, in the later medieval period the town gallows (first mentioned in 1274) and a leper hospital (first mentioned in 1314) were located on Spital Hill, to the south-west of the modern Newmarket-Upgate crossroads. This hospital was a religious and probably quasi-monastic institution and is last heard of in 1488; however, in 1572 its buildings appear to have still been in existence and were being used as a poor house for the town, and the site continued to be used in this fashion well into the seventeenth century. Likewise, at some point Aswell Lane was extended south of the Aswell spring to become an access road to the quarry, with this extension being known as Quarry Lane (now the southern half of Aswell Street). Although it is not clear when this happened, the quarry itself – located in the area of the present cattle market – provided the stone for Louth Park Abbey and so was in existence by the twelfth or thirteenth century. Moreover, this site also afforded the people of the town a venue for numerous different activities from the medieval period onwards.

In the 1430s, for example, William Guage and William Day were fined 2d each for playing tennis and other 'unlawful games' in the quarry, and in the sixteenth and seventeenth centuries it was the site of The Butts, where a yearly archery pageant took place. Subsequently it was home to both a Bowling Greene (from at least 1691) and tea-gardens, which were briefly established here in the eighteenth century. Perhaps most significantly, the quarry also functioned as a 'beast market' for the town from at least as early as 1551, when its role as such is mentioned in a charter of Edward VI. Nonetheless, even though it was evidently well-utilized, this southern district remained largely peripheral to the main town for much of the post-medieval era. The quarry was still separated from the centre of town by open fields in 1808, Quarry Lane was almost entirely devoid of housing well into the nineteenth century, and there was relatively little development on Upgate south of its junction with Kidgate either. On the other hand, by 1834 things were beginning to change here too, most notably with regard to Lee Street. This led from Kidgate to the quarry and had not only been laid out within the last twenty-five years, but was also already lined with cottages on both sides of the road. Similarly, there was clearly building taking place on Spital Hill and Newmarket by this time, with cheap housing being constructed at the former location in order to provide homes for itinerant Irish rural labourers. St Mary's Roman Catholic Church was also constructed around this time (1833) at the southern end of Upgate, presumably partly to cater for the Irish community in this area.

Looking west of the central core of the town, it is generally thought that the Louth had come to encompass the vast majority of Westgate within its bounds by the end of the medieval period, although the stages by which this was achieved are uncertain. In any case, in the post-medieval period this street appears to have retained its medieval status as the home of some of the wealthier inhabitants of the town. For example, in the sixteenth century John Bradley, a wealthy local wool merchant who played a major role in the refoundation of the grammar school in 1551, lived at 44 Westgate and owned numerous other properties here, including one where The Limes is currently sited. Similarly, modern Westgate derives in the main from the eighteenth century, when many of the houses here were either built or rebuilt, with the quality and size of these properties offering a stark contrast to the cheap terraced cottages being then constructed elsewhere in the town. Gospelgate's developing place and role within the town is less clear. Although this street was in existence by the thirteenth century and is shown as having buildings all along it on Armstrong's plan of Louth of 1778 and Espin's of 1808, its character in the intervening period is unclear. Certainly, excavations at the Greyhound Inn on the corner of Upgate and Gospelgate show that at least this part of Gospelgate was largely abandoned after the mid-fourteenth century and was only reoccupied in the eighteenth. Breakneck Lane is even more obscure, being first mentioned in 1456 but shown as largely undeveloped on all of the early maps of the town. There is equally no evidence for any development of the land fronting onto the modern Edward Street before the early nineteenth century, whilst Crowtree Lane served only a handful of properties up to that point, most notably The Lodge. This was built overlooking the Goose Pool at the end of the eighteenth century as a new boarding-block for the grammar school and house for its headmaster, with one of the first boarders to live there being the future Sir John Franklin, the Arctic explorer. Lastly, both George Street and Irish Hill were products of the nineteenth century expansion of the town, neither being shown on Espin's map of 1808, although the latter is present on Bayley's of 1834.

The only other significant street in this part of town is the modern Schoolhouse Lane, formerly Gulpyn Lane, which links Westgate with Gospelgate. Gulpyn Lane clearly had its origins during the medieval period, as in 1474–5 the accounts of St Mary's Gild mention that their Bedehouse was situated in Gulpyn Lane, with the almsfolk occupying the lower floor and the chamber above being let for 3s 4d annually. There was also at least one barn located on Gulpyn Lane before the Reformation, where the Gild of the Holy Trinity repaired and stored the pageants (either wheeled or on poles) that were carried in procession on Corpus Christi Day in 1528–9. As to what else was happening here during the medieval period, one potential clue comes from the name Gulpyn Lane itself, as 'gulp' or 'gulpin' appears to have been a dialect word used in Lincolnshire and elsewhere for a child. In light of this, it may be tentatively suggested that when the town's grammar school was moved from St Mary's church – which had been converted into a school following the refoundation of the grammar in 1551 – to Gulpyn Lane after only five years of being in that location, this was not so much a shift to a totally new site as a move to the street where the 'gulpins' of the town had been traditionally educated in the medieval period. Whatever the case may be on this, the grammar school remained primarily on this road from the mid-sixteenth century right the way through until the twentieth, as did the Bedehouses, the current incarnation of which were constructed in 1869, at the same time as the school buildings still found here.

Turning at last to the eastwards expansion of Louth beyond its central core, it is usually assumed that the town had probably come to encompass the whole of Eastgate and Walkergate/Queen Street down to Maiden Row (the northern part of modern Church Street) by the end of the medieval period. Just how built-up the most easterly parts of these roads were in the fourteenth and fifteenth centuries is, however, unclear. Maiden Row, which is first mentioned in the fifteenth century and links the eastern ends of Eastgate and Walkergate, certainly appears to have been largely undeveloped then, with the early references being to pasture here rather than anything else. Nonetheless, by the early nineteenth century this area had seen significant development and was clearly an important part of the town. It was home to Louth's House of Correction from the seventeenth century onwards, on the site now occupied by the Orme Almshouses, and by 1808 there were buildings along much of the south side of the eastern end of Eastgate (including 140–2 Eastgate, built

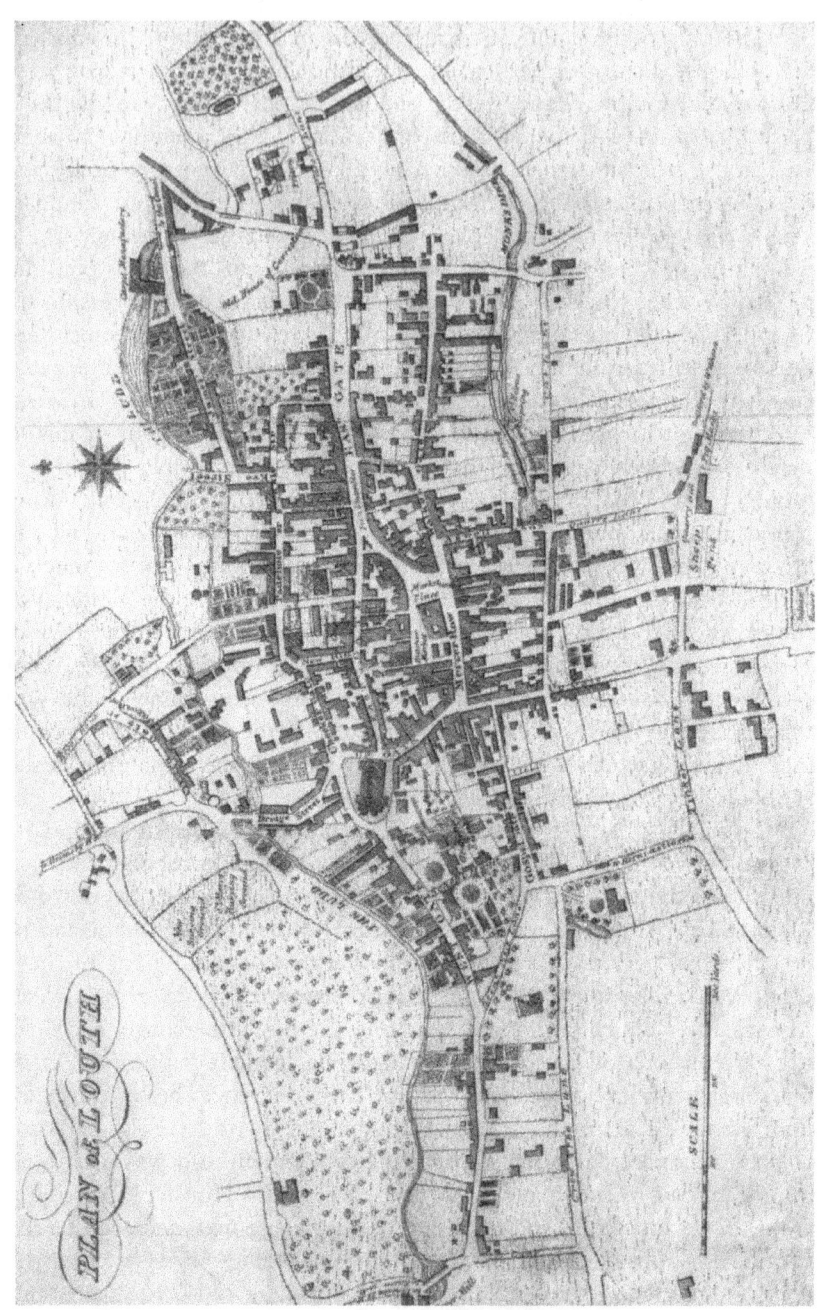

in 1794), with the Manor House standing on the north side. Indeed, although the latter building dates to the eighteenth century, it is worth noting that it stands above cellars belonging to an earlier structure. Similarly, there were buildings all along both sides of Walkergate and on Maiden Row by 1808, something that is to be explained largely by the industrial activity that was taking place in this area of Louth. Not only was it the centre of the medieval cloth-finishing industry in the town, but in later years the 460 gallons-per-minute put out by the Aswell spring were also used to power a fulling mill and a corn mill here (with the tailrace of the mill pond then running down the western side of Maiden Row) and for brewing too. The latter industry was, incidentally, first mentioned in 1449, and by the later nineteenth and early twentieth centuries it was a major activity in this part of the town.

In contrast, the area to the south of the Aswell spring and the mill pond appears to have remained largely peripheral to the town until a relatively late date. For example, the eastern part of Kidgate – also known as Kit Cat Lane – looks to have been only really used for housing from the latter part of the eighteenth century, with just eight buildings located on this road in 1808 and the property boundaries all being eighteenth- and nineteenth-century in character. Similarly, the Gatherums, lying in-between Walkergate and Kidgate, appears to have originated as a rough track or droveway (Scandinavian *gatu-rum*) running eastwards by the Aswell and St Helen's springs, the latter of which had been diverted in the Middle Ages to run down the Monks' Dyke to Louth Park Abbey. Although a few properties are recorded here in the eighteenth- and nineteenth centuries, they are generally rated at a low level compared to the town as a whole and include non-residential buildings, such as the 'Barne in the Gatherums' of Thomas Sutton in 1717 and the barn and stable here belonging to James Bond in 1823. Only from the mid-nineteenth century did this area really become a significant focus for residential activity, with the construction of tightly-packed terrace houses (these lasted for a relatively brief period before they were cleared as a slum in the twentieth century).

Finally, if there was little expansion of Louth to its south-east before the mid-nineteenth century, this was not true of area to the north-east of the town, which saw significant activity from the later eighteenth century onwards. The primary catalyst here was the creation of the Louth's

Figure 41 (opposite): Robert Bayley's map of Louth, 1834.

navigation canal, opened in 1770. For reasons of cost, the canal terminated somewhat short of the contemporary town (around 700 metres to the north-east of Maiden Row) and a new industrial village and docklands consequently grew up in this area. Not only were shipyards and warehouses built here, but there were also granaries, coalyards, breweries, a woodyard, a soapery, and a leather factory, and by 1790 a greater weight of fish was being landed daily at the Riverhead than at Grimsby. Moreover, non-industrial properties were established in this area as a result of this activity. So, the Woolpack Inn and houses such as 35 Eastfield Road were built here in the late eighteenth century, and the Lincolnshire Poacher Hotel and some of the grand houses near to Trinity Church were constructed to the south of Riverhead in the early nineteenth century, as was Trinity Church itself, this being consecrated in 1834. At the same time, Louth itself expanded eastwards in the direction of this new economic focus, with significant building and development occurring along Ramsgate and Watery Lane – now part of Eastgate, so-named due to the fact that the Aswell spring used to flow down this street after it exited Maiden Row – during the first half of the nineteenth century.

This, then, is the general course of Louth's evolution and expansion from the Norman Conquest through until the start of the Victorian era. It seems clear that the central core of the town had been established in its broad outlines during the medieval period. Subsequently Louth largely developed within the bounds of the medieval town until the eighteenth and nineteenth centuries, when it began to expand once again. By the time we reach the mid-nineteenth century, not only would most of the central area of modern Louth have been largely recognizable in terms of both its layout and its buildings, but those areas of the modern town beyond the central zone were also beginning to emerge too. Of course, the following decades saw continued expansion and development of the town and its periphery. For example, by the end of the nineteenth century residential housing had been established along Broadbank, High Holme Road, Edward Street, Church Street, and Quarry Lane (Aswell Street) as well as all along Eastgate towards the Riverhead, with Victoria Road being laid out in this period too (in 1869). Similarly, the era after the Second World War saw another wave of significant expansion, most especially with the laying out of the St Bernard's Avenue estates in the 1950s, those between North Holme and High Holme Roads in the

1970s, and the creation of the Fairfield Industrial Estate in the town's old North Field from the 1960s onwards.

As to the other concluding question raised at the start of this chapter, namely the likely future development of the Louth region, this is rather more difficult to answer. Futurology is in general a dangerous game to play, especially when it comes to predicting the course of human affairs. Consequently, no attempt can be seriously made to forecast how Louth and the surrounding villages will develop as settlements or fare economically in the coming decades and centuries. They could continue to prosper and thrive as they do now, but equally some of them – including Louth – could decline and even potentially disappear, just as did many of the Roman towns of Britain and the deserted medieval villages of the Wolds. On the other hand, if we concern ourselves chiefly with the physical aspects of our study region, then recent scientific research and analogues from the past do enable us to at least say something about the environmental and geological changes that are likely to affect this area in the future. Over the last 400,000 years the Louth region has sometimes been buried under glaciers and frozen into an arctic desert for thousands of years, with the coastline retreating to the north of Shetland, whilst at other times it has been so warm that elephants wandered across the Wolds and the sea inexorably rose to drown the eastern parts of our region. The question is, are the next hundred thousand years or so likely to bring further such dramatic changes with them?

Even in the short term there are likely to be important physical changes and challenges for the Louth region. In particular, recent research indicates that sea-level may well rise faster in this century than has been previously predicted, with between one and two metres of increase likely by 2100 and further rises already built in for the century to follow, even if greenhouse gas emissions are successfully stabilised. This is likely to put strain on Lincolnshire's coastal defences. If they are not properly maintained, or even abandoned as financially unviable, then land up to around five metres above the present mean sea-level (Ordnance Datum) could be affected by regular marine flooding, given that the annual mean high water during spring tides is around three metres above OD in this region. Moreover, if there is much more than $2°C$ of warming during the twenty-first century – as now seems likely – then current models indicate that this will probably ultimately lead to a very significant melting of at least the Greenland ice sheet and potentially the West Antarctic ice sheet too. A complete or near-complete melting of the Greenland ice sheet would eventually add six or seven metres to the sea-level, and the melting of the most at-risk part of the West Antarctic ice sheet would add several metres more.

It is usually thought that such a significant melting of the Greenland ice sheet would take several thousand years or more to complete, although recent modelling suggests that it is by no means impossible that half of Greenland's ice-volume could be lost within the first millennium of warming. Moreover, it has been argued that positive feedback effects may well lead to non-linear ice sheet disintegration, which might then occur over centuries rather than millennia. Whatever the case may be,

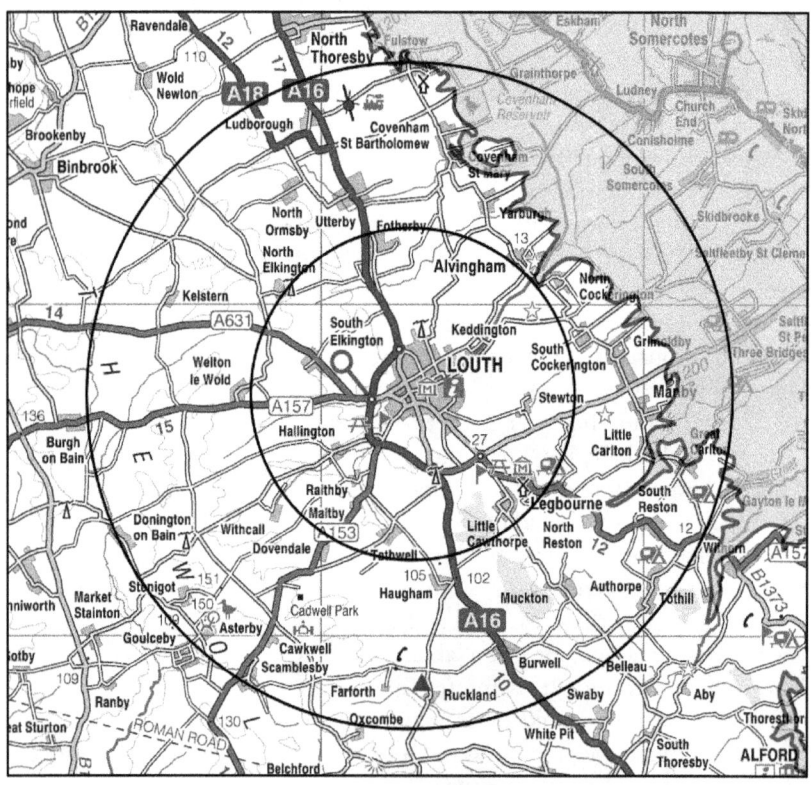

Figure 42: Map showing those parts of the Louth region that could be affected by spring tides in the future, if sea-level rises by two metres and sea-defences are not maintained. Image based on public domain NASA SRTM data.

these massive sea-level rises probably lie far in the future on the scale of a single human lifespan. However, from the present historical perspective they appear rather less distant. After all, both the Norman Conquest and the laying out of Mercer Row occurred nearly a thousand years ago; traffic still runs under the Newport Arch in Lincoln, despite the fact it has stood on that spot for nearing two thousand years; and monumental prehistoric barrows constructed five thousand years or more ago still stand on the Wolds today. Needless to say, it seems extremely unlikely that the coastal defences of Lincolnshire would be able to cope with five to ten or more metres of additional sea-level rise on top of that already predicted by 2100, even if it were spread over

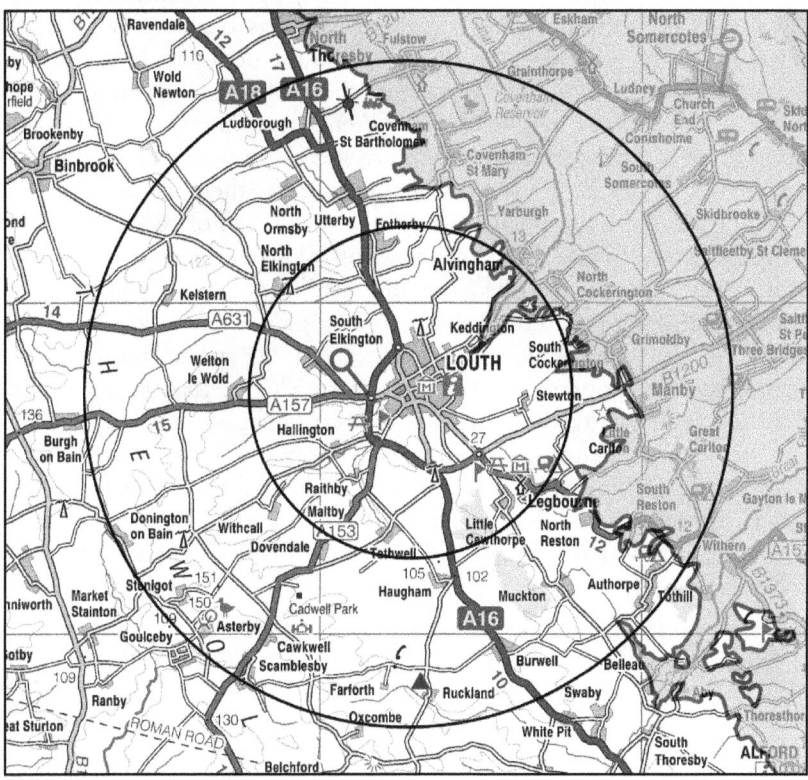

Figure 43: Map showing those parts of the Louth region that could be affected by marine flooding if the Greenland and West Antarctic ice sheets melt significantly. Image based on public domain NASA SRTM data.

several millennia, and it is consequently likely that the coastal zone will move decisively inland during this period. Louth will probably come to stand close to the edge of this coastal zone, which may perhaps be to its advantage if it still exists as a significant regional centre. On the other hand, not only will the sites of present-day villages like Grainthorpe and Somercotes (both constructed on land reclaimed from the sea around a thousand years ago) disappear beneath the rising tide, if they have not already done so, but the sea will also reach new heights and so probably inundate at least part of the Middle Marsh too, with Covenham, Yarburgh and Manby all being at risk.

In addition to their effects on the sea-level, the melt-waters from the Arctic and Greenland could themselves also impact significantly on the climate of the Louth region. In particular, it has been argued that the release of large quantities of melt-water into the ocean could lead to the weakening or even failure of the ocean thermohaline circulation, that is to say the 'conveyer belt' of ocean currents that warms Britain via the 'Gulf Stream'. If the circulation only weakens – as presently seems most credible, at least for the twenty-first century – then the cooling that should result from this would probably be more than offset by the rise in temperatures resulting from the build up of greenhouse gasses in the atmosphere. However, if the 'conveyor belt' does actually shut down at some point, then a significant local cooling of Britain could occur. The last time this happened was around 6200 BC, when mean annual temperatures temporarily dropped by up to 5°C for a period of several hundred years. As to when such a shutdown might occur, if it ever does, this remains a matter of controversy. Some suggest that it could theoretically occur within a few decades, whilst others maintain that any major impacts on the ocean thermohaline circulation are unlikely until after the twenty-first century, and then only if the Greenland ice sheet melts rapidly.

Moving from short- and medium-term changes to a longer view, it needs to be remembered that the Holocene – the current geological epoch, which began with the end of the Younger Dryas around 11,600 years ago – is actually an interglacial. Although the quantity of greenhouse gases likely to be emitted over the next few decades and centuries will almost certainly cause significant warming, environmental changes, and sea-level rises in the short- to medium-term, if emissions are brought under control and the warming trend doesn't become irreversible (a real and dangerous possibility according to some researchers, which could ultimately lead to sea-level reaching 75 metres OD and a massive die-off of species), then the Holocene Interglacial should eventually come to an end. In particular, glacial-interglacial climatic alternations appear to be largely controlled by variations in the Earth's orbit around the Sun, known as the Milankovitch orbital cycles. On the basis of these, current work indicates that the present interglacial ought to draw to a close around 50,000 years from now, with the climate of the Louth region subsequently starting to cool noticeably if future humans aren't able or willing to intervene somehow to prevent this happening. Initially the climatic conditions are likely to approximate those in the 'Little Ice Age' of *c.* AD 1550–1850, with winters in particular becoming much more severe, but continued cooling will inevitably lead to the disappearance of forests and woodland and the emergence of a shrub-dominated, steppe grassland across our region and more widely. This in turn will eventually give way to arctic tundra-like vegetation and permafrost in the Louth region, as mean annual temperatures drop by over 12°C. At this point most of the familiar interglacial fauna will probably retreat southwards towards warmer refuges on the Continent, along with any remaining significant human communities, whilst species such as reindeer and arctic fox are likely migrate into the region across the North Sea basin, which will once more be exposed by falling sea-levels as the glaciers expand.

The available models indicate that there will be a temporary reversal of this glacial cooling between about 63,000 and 71,000 years after present (AP), but after this the climatic decline will resume and the Next Glacial Maximum should peak sometime around 100,000 AP. It seems likely that this period will see the British and Scandinavian ice sheets expand southwards to bury much or all of the Louth region under glaciers, just as they did in earlier epochs, with this action potentially erasing most physical traces of the Holocene-era human civilization and settlements that once existed in this region, including Louth itself. What happens after this is can only be speculated about; however, the glacial-interglacial cycle will almost certainly continue, with the next interglacial predicted to begin sometime around 113,000 AP. If there are still recognizable humans living in Europe by this point, then what was once Britain and the Louth region may be re-colonized by them from the southern refuges where they have survived this future Ice Age, perhaps relatively quickly if they are both numerous and live in a technologically advanced society at a level equal to or above that of our own. Of course, given both the changes that any glaciation of the region will cause and the millennia that will have passed since the former Louth region was last inhabited, it is unlikely that any significant memory or trace of what once existed here will survive, and any re-colonization effort will probably represent an entirely fresh start for humanity here.

An Archaeological Gazetteer of the Louth Region

The following gazetteer includes all of the archaeological discoveries made within 10 km of Louth through until mid–late 2010, as recorded in the various datasets used in this study. The finds and sites are arranged by parish and each is given a code reflecting the dataset it derives from plus its reference code in that dataset: CASSS V, Corpus of Anglo-Saxon Stone Sculpture, Volume 5; CCI, Oxford Celtic Coin Index; EMASPP, East Midlands Anglo-Saxon Pottery Project; EMC, Corpus of Early Medieval Coin Finds, 410–1180; HER, Lincolnshire Historic Environment Record; PAS, Portable Antiquities Scheme; UKDFD, UK Detector Finds Database. Note, in some cases individual sites listed below can have tens (or even hundreds) of finds recorded from them in the PAS database. In such circumstances, only a representative sample of the associated PAS record numbers are cited below; full details of all of the relevant finds can usually be obtained from the PAS database (at finds.org.uk) by using its 'Find objects with a 2km radius of this artefact' option.

In addition to these datasets, reference is made in some of the entries to publications that either discuss finds/sites in more detail or offer the only record of them: *Treasure Annual Reports* are published by HMSO for the Department for Culture, Media and Sport; AAA 2009/016 refers to Allen Archaeological Associates, *Archaeological Evaluation Report: Trial Trenching at St Margaret's Church, Keddington, Lincolnshire* (April 2009, Report No. 2009/016); Alabaster and Straw, 1978 refers to C. Alabaster and A. Straw, 'The Pleistocene context of the faunal remains and artefacts discovered at Welton-le-Wold, Lincolnshire', *Proceedings of the Yorkshire Geological Society*, 41 (1976), 75–94; Aram *et al*, 2005 refers to J. Aram *et al*, *Towards an Understanding of the Ice*

Age at Welton le Wold (Heckington, 2005); Bayley, 1834 refers to R. S. Bayley, *Notitiæ Ludæ, or Notices of Louth* (Louth, 1834); Blackburn, 1993 refers to M. Blackburn, 'Coin finds and coin circulation in Lindsey, *c.* 600–900', in A. Vince (ed.), *Pre-Viking Lindsey* (Lincoln, 1993), pp. 80–90; Jones, 1999 refers to D. Jones, 'Romano-British Settlement in the Lincolnshire Wolds', in R. H. Bewley (ed.), *Lincolnshire's Archaeology from the Air* (Lincoln, 1999), pp. 29–65; Leahy, 1993 refers to K. Leahy, 'The Anglo-Saxon settlement of Lindsey', in A. Vince (ed.), *Pre-Viking Lindsey* (Lincoln, 1993), pp. 29–44; Owen, 1997 refers to A. E. B. Owen, 'Louth before Domesday', *Lincolnshire History and Archaeology*, 32 (1997), 60–4; Thompson, 1956 refers to F. H. Thompson, 'Anglo-Saxon sites in Lincolnshire: unpublished material and recent discoveries', *Antiquaries Journal*, 36 (1956), 181–99; Ulmschneider, 2000 refers to K. Ulmschneider, *Markets, Minsters and Metal-detectors: the Archaeology of Middle Saxon Lincolnshire and Hampshire Compared* (Oxford, 2000); Webster, 1952 refers to G. Webster, 'An Anglo-Saxon urnfield at South Elkington, Louth, Lincolnshire', *Archaeological Journal*, 108 (1952), 25–64; Youngs, 2005 refers to S. Youngs, 'After Oldcroft: a British silver pin from Welton le Wold, Lincolnshire', in N. Crummy *et al* (eds.), *Image, Craft and the Classical World* (Montagnac, 2005), pp. 249–54.

ASTERBY
Neolithic: A probable Neolithic-Bronze Age lithic working site represented by 335 flint objects (HER 43357).
Anglo-Scandinavian: A penny of Cnut, dated 1029–36 (UKDFD 25607).

ALVINGHAM
Bronze Age: A stone axe hammer (HER 41252); possible round barrow (HER 44078); stone axe hammer (PAS LIN-959B08).
Roman: Scatter of fourth-century Romano-British sherds (HER 41253); sherds of Romano-British pottery, mostly fourth-century (HER 41251); sherds of Romano-British pottery (EMASPP).
Anglo-Scandinavian: Saxo-Norman pottery of the late tenth to early thirteenth century associated with a possible hearth (HER 43680).

AUTHORPE
Neolithic: Two polished Neolithic stone axes (HER 42516, 42515).
Anglo-Saxon: Middle Saxon Maxey ware pottery (EMASPP).

BINBROOK
Bronze Age: Possible round barrow (HER 44077).
Roman: Cropmarks of a Romano-British settlement, associated with a sherd of greyware (HER 44585).

BRACKENBOROUGH WITH LITTLE GRIMSBY
Roman: A late first- to early second-century silver ring, a second-century bronze ring, and eleven first- and second-century silver coins from Little Grimsby (*Treasure Annual Report 2000*, p. 20).

BURWELL
Neolithic: Neolithic stone axe (HER 42369); three worked flints, Neolithic-Bronze Age (HER 42362); three Neolithic axes (HER 42372).
Bronze Age: Two earthwork round barrows (HER 43603); possible round barrow (HER 45070).
Roman: A possible Romano-British kiln producing light greyware pottery of the third-fourth centuries (HER 42370); scatter of Romano-British pottery (HER 42367); scatter of Romano-British pottery (HER 42365); copper-alloy coin of Trebonianus Gallus, 251–3 (HER 42363); scatter of Romano-British pottery (HER 42364); a cockerel-headed silver pin, thought to date from the Roman period (UKDFD 171).

CALCETHORPE WITH KELSTERN
Palaeolithic: A Lower Palaeolithic handaxe, with a suggested dating of around 280,000 BC (PAS NLM-54EC10).
Neolithic: A possible Neolithic long barrow (HER 43179); a scatter of Neolithic or Bronze Age worked flints (HER 40694); a probable Neolithic small long barrow (HER 43655); a significant number of Neolithic flints – suggested settlement site (HER 40698).
Bronze Age: Three round barrows (HER 43179); possible round barrow (HER 44090); possible round barrow (HER 44088); possible round barrow (HER 44089); a ploughed-out round barrow (HER 40705); a bronze axe, known as a palstave (HER 40706); a ploughed-out round barrow (HER 40703); a ploughed-out round barrow (HER 40707); possible round barrow (HER 44061); possible round barrow (HER 44076).
Iron Age: Two Iron Age silver coin fragments, *c.* 55–45 BC (PAS NLM7133); a cast copper-alloy Colchester brooch, dated *c.* 25–60 AD (PAS NLM-F90C12).

Roman: A second-century silver finger-ring and another, dated 185–300, inscribed ToT (PAS PAS-C1FCA5, LIN-94B8B4; *Treasure Annual Report 2001*, p. 20); two fragments of a fourth-century Roman lead font, found in a pit where they had been deliberately concealed (PAS LIN-E8F806; *Portable Antiquities Scheme Annual Report 2004/05*, p. 47); two undated Roman coins (NLM6563); a mid-late first-century dolphin brooch (PAS NLM6564).
Anglo-Scandinavian: A complete copper-alloy large Viking sword pommel of the tenth-century, decorated in the Borre style (PAS NLM-C3B377).

CAWKWELL
Neolithic: Neolithic-Bronze Age button scrapers and worked flints (HER 40803); A possible Neolithic saddle quern (HER 40804).
Bronze Age: Two possible round barrows (HER 40807); possible round barrow (HER 44141).
Roman: Ditches and hearths, four of which seem to be grain dryers, associated with late first- to late third-century pottery – settlement probably nearby (HER 46491); linear boundary ditch associated with sherds of first-century storage jar (HER 42873); sherds of Romano-British pottery (EMASPP).

CONISHOLME
Roman: Scatter of Romano-British pottery (HER 41371).

COVENHAM ST BARTHOLOMEW
Neolithic: A scatter of worked flints (HER 43727).
Iron Age: Possible Iron Age pottery sherd (HER 43726).
Anglo-Saxon: One or two sherds of fifth- to seventh-century pottery (HER 43725).
Anglo-Scandinavian: A ditch dated between the tenth and twelfth centuries and other associated finds and features (HER 44015).

COVENHAM ST MARY
Bronze Age: Possible round barrow (HER 46094).
Iron Age: Copper-alloy coin of the Durotriges (CCI 02.0556).

Donington on Bain

Mesolithic: A microburin, a waste product from the manufacture of stone tools, characteristic of the Mesolithic period (HER 43954); a number of flint artefacts associated with the Mesolithic microburin, of Late Mesolithic-Neolithic date (HER 43954).

Neolithic: A possible Neolithic rectilinear field system (HER 43689); a scatter of fifteen worked flints of Neolithic-Bronze Age date, including a barbed and tanged arrowhead (HER 44519); a Neolithic mortuary enclosure or long barrow (HER 43690).

Bronze Age: A nearly ploughed-out round barrow, related to a ditch containing Bronze Age pottery (HER 43624, 43687); possible round barrow (HER 43691); a ring ditch of a round barrow, associated with decorated Beaker-type pottery (HER 43686); possible round barrow (HER 44735); possible round barrow (HER 44106); re-worked bronze spearhead (HER 40731); barbed and tanged arrowhead (HER 40727); possible round barrow (HER 44739); possible round barrow (HER 44734); possible round barrow (HER 44103); possible round barrow (HER 44104); possible round barrow (HER 44105); possible round barrow (HER 44107); possible round barrow (HER 44108); possible round barrow (HER 44101); barbed and tanged arrowhead (HER 44519).

Iron Age: An excavated Late Iron Age occupation site (HER 43692); an Iron Age inhumation found beneath the above occupation site (HER 43694).

Roman: A first-century brooch and some sherds of Romano-British pottery suggest that the Late Iron Age domestic site continued in use into the Roman period (HER 43693); finds of brick, tile, a fragment of a glass vessel and mid-/late second- to fourth-century pottery indicate the presence of a Roman building (HER 43955); Romano-British finds, including penannular brooches, twenty coins (one a coin of Nero), hair-pins and samian ware pottery (HER 40726) – a pair of Romano-British copper-alloy tweezers and a miniature votive sword have also been found at or very near to this site (PAS LIN-E41E47, LIN-E42867); possible Romano-British enclosures and ring-ditch (HER 46977); a fourth-century crossbow brooch and two Roman coins, found at Welsdale, Donington on Bain (Louth Museum, A.47, A48.1, A48.2); sherds of Romano-British pottery from a number of locations (EMASPP).

Anglo-Saxon: A cremation cemetery was recorded here in 1834 and is sometimes thought to be of Anglo-Saxon date, though it could just as easily be earlier – perhaps best seen as Bronze Age, given the local context? (HER 40725).

Anglo-Scandinavian: Early medieval – tenth- to twelfth-century – pottery (HER 40728); a timber-built structure dating from the tenth- to eleventh-centuries seen in gullies, postholes and a stone-lined hearth – probably a domestic dwelling, measuring 12x5 metres, with some local smithing implied by finds of slag and hammerscale (HER 43956).

FOTHERBY

Neolithic: Late Neolithic scraper found along with five pieces of struck flint and a possible fragment of a Neolithic stone axe (HER 43190); a flint core of Neolithic-Early Bronze Age date (PAS LIN-8F2285).

Roman: A probable Romano-British settlement site, represented by a variety of finds: several sherds of samian pottery (PAS LIN-AE16C6, LIN-8EFC81); two headstud brooches, dated *c.* AD 70–150, a late third- or fourth-century gilded disc brooch, and a Romano-British copper-alloy mount perhaps from a box or piece of furniture (PAS LIN-720EC2, LIN-8E58E1, LIN-8EF102, LIN-8E6236); and a first- to third-century copper-alloy coin, a 'House of Constantine' coin of 330–5, a coin of Claudius II – dated 268–9 – and a coin of Crispus, struck 323–4 (PAS LIN-74ACB3, LIN-8EBEB5, LIN-8EAFB8, LIN-8E8877). From other sites in the parish have been found a second- or third-century 'lockpin' and two *c.* AD 70–150 brooches (PAS LIN-C2D525, LIN-C33803, LIN-C347A6); a first- or second-century terret (harness) ring (PAS LIN-71A9B5); a copper-alloy coin of Constans, 343–8 (PAS LIN-730707).

Anglo-Saxon: A sixth-century cruciform or small-long brooch and a sixth-century bun shaped bead from the same area as the probable Romano-British settlement – a possible Anglo-Saxon inhumation burial or small cemetery (PAS LIN-71FB55, LIN-8F11C3); a sixth-century small-long brooch, found at a separate site (PAS LIN-7206E6).

Anglo-Scandinavian: Three finds all from the same field – a terminal mount of an eleventh-century stirrup (PAS LIN-ADE591), an eleventh-century bridle fitting, perhaps a cheek piece (PAS LIN-AE7743), and an eleventh-century bridle fitting, perhaps a cheek piece in the Viking Ringerrike style (PAS LIN-C27541).

Fulstow
Bronze Age: Copper-alloy casting waste (PAS LIN-0735F7).
Iron Age: A sherd of Iron Age pottery (PAS LIN-E82466); sherd of coarseware pottery (PAS LIN-C47184); body sherd of a large storage vessel (PAS LIN-80E2C3).
Roman: Scatter of third-/early fourth-century pottery (HER 41180); finds indicative of a sizeable Roman site, including 26 coins chiefly of the third to late fourth centuries (e.g. PAS LIN-FB98C6, LIN-0C4BB1), Romano-British pottery sherds (e.g. LIN-DE21F7, LIN-C0B2B6), and lead tablets probably used in the forging of silver coins of Valens, 364–78 (LIN-57B091, LIN-57F021, LIN-5806B6; *Treasure Annual Report 2007*, p. 186).

Gayton le Marsh
Anglo-Saxon: A sixth-century cruciform brooch, found somewhere in this parish (PAS NLM4742).

Gayton le Wold
Neolithic: Partially polished Neolithic stone axe (HER 40685); a possible Neolithic-Bronze Age pit cluster (HER 44678).
Bronze Age: substantial earthwork remains of a round barrow, known as Grim's Mound (HER 43551); possible round barrow cemetery visible as cropmarks (HER 44085); possible round barrow (HER 44693); possible round barrow (HER 44691); possible round barrow (HER 44087); possible round barrow (HER 44086).
Iron Age: Fragment of a harness terret, dated *c.* 300–100 AD (PAS NLM5341).
Roman: Part of a Roman sword scabbard of the first to third century (PAS NLM5360); sherds of Romano-British pottery from a number of locations (EMASPP).
Anglo-Saxon: A small Early Anglo-Saxon inhumation cemetery, indicated by metalwork finds including a seventh-century triangular buckle (PAS NLM-0399A2, NLM-029B23).
Anglo-Scandinavian: Part of a mid-tenth- to mid-eleventh-century grave-marker, probably earlier rather than later, and part of a mid-tenth to early eleventh-century grave-cover – other references mention 'a number of Anglo-Saxon grave markers' to the north of the church (CASSS V, Gayton le Wold 1 and 3; HER 42949).

GREAT CARLTON
Neolithic: A struck flint flake of Neolithic or Bronze Age date (HER 44704); a fragment of a Neolithic polished stone axe (HER 42801).
Roman: A second- to fourth-century occupation site, including a hearth, Romano-British ditches and local domestic pottery, associated with a field system – small amounts of hammerscale may indicate local iron smithing in the area (HER 45873).

GRIMOLDBY
Roman: Scatter of Romano-British pottery (HER 41302).

HALLINGTON
Mesolithic: Abraded flint blade, of probable Mesolithic date (HER 43611).
Bronze Age: Possible round barrow (HER 44099); possible round barrow (HER 44095).
Roman: Scatter of Romano-British greyware pottery (HER 40830); a minor settlement or farmstead visible on aerial photography (Jones, 1999, p. 77).
Anglo-Saxon: Sherds of early Anglo-Saxon pottery (HER 43607).
Anglo-Scandinavian: Sherds of Late Saxon pottery (HER 43607).

HAUGHAM
Neolithic: A Late Neolithic or Early Bronze Age axe hammer (HER 43783).
Bronze Age: A ploughed-out round barrow (HER 41833); a round barrow (HER 40358); two broken flint blades (HER 43808); possible round barrow (HER 44129); possible round barrow (HER 44130).
Iron Age: Two gold Corieltavi coins (CCI 98.1907, 98.1929).
Roman: Scatter of Romano-British greyware and gritted ware pottery (HER 41831).
Anglo-Saxon: Middle Saxon Maxey ware pottery (EMASPP).

KEDDINGTON
Neolithic: A Neolithic-Early Bronze Age polished chalk axe (HER 41399).
Bronze Age: Possible round barrow cemetery (HER 46421); possible round barrow (HER 44098).

Roman: Coins of Maxentius, 306–12, and Alexander Severus, 222–35 from Louth Park Abbey (HER 41382); Roman headstud brooch (PAS LIN-E14F34); second- or third-century finger ring (PAS LIN-E16125); a single sherd of Romano-British pottery, recovered during work at St Margaret's Church (AAA 2009/016); a quantity of Roman coins may have been found at Louth Park Abbey before 1834 (Bayley 1834, p. 247).
Anglo-Saxon: A single Early Anglo-Saxon cruciform brooch (PAS NLM-2767B2).
Anglo-Scandinavian: A single sherd of ninth- or tenth-century pottery, recovered during work at St Margaret's Church (AAA 2009/016); possible pre-Norman features observed in the fabric of St Margaret's Church (HER 41385; Chris Bowen, pers. comm.).

LEGBOURNE
Palaeolithic: A Lower Palaeolithic handaxe (HER 41847).
Neolithic: A polished Neolithic flint axehead (HER 43904); a Neolithic light grey stone axe (HER 41841); a polished Neolithic flint axe (HER 41842); a Neolithic polished flint axe (HER 41945); a Neolithic grit stone axe (PAS LIN-73E8B0); a Neolithic leaf arrowhead (HER 41847).
Bronze Age: Perforated stone axe (HER 41947); barbed and tanged arrowhead (HER 41847).
Roman: Scatter of Romano-British pottery (HER 41836); Romano-British pottery from a grid reference in this parish (EMASPP).

LITTLE CARLTON
Iron Age: Late Iron Age bow brooch, 'Birdlip' type (PAS LIN-E412C2).
Roman: Silvered copper-alloy spoon of *c.* 150–200 (PAS LIN-E34076).
Anglo-Saxon: A copper-alloy silvered and gilt Anglo-Saxon strap end of the ninth century (PAS LIN-E33095).
Anglo-Scandinavian: part of a late tenth- or eleventh-century grave-cover found in the wall of St Edith's church (HER 43417; CASSS V, Little Carlton 1).

LITTLE CAWTHORPE
Neolithic: A Neolithic-Bronze Age flint scraper (PAS LIN-395F11).
Roman: A pit containing sherds of Romano-British pottery (HER 43350).

Anglo-Scandinavian: A gully dated to the tenth to twelfth century, thought to be indicative of the presence of a settlement of this period (HER 41923).

LOUTH

Mesolithic: Possible Late Mesolithic flints (including a possible microlith blade or core) occur as part of a scatter that dates between the Mesolithic and Bronze Age, found to the north of Lyndon Way off Keddington Road (HER 47054).

Neolithic: A small scatter of Neolithic or Bronze Age flints, including a transverse arrowhead, was observed on the Legbourne-Louth parish boundary east of Kenwick Road during the laying of a water pipe (HER 43604); 'many worked flints', of Neolithic or Bronze Age date, were found north of Halfpenny Lane, to the east of the southern entrance to Hubbard's Hills (HER 41393); a Neolithic-Bronze Age scraper, found within a scatter of Late Mesolithic-Bronze Age flints, found to the north of Lyndon Way off Keddington Road (HER 47054); a Neolithic flint knife was found during the excavation of Mount St Mary (HER 45610); also found in Louth have been a flint axe or chisel and a Neolithic polished axe (HER 41397; 41398).

Bronze Age: A residual Early (*c.* 2200–1500 BC) Bronze Age thumbnail scraper found in a post-medieval pit at Spout Yard – the lack of wear indicates that it was not deposited by river action (HER 43923); a barbed and tanged arrowhead was found on the school field at Monks' Dyke (HER 45522); a Bronze Age socketed axe found 'near Louth' (HER 41400).

Iron Age: Six coins of the Corieltavi have their findspot recorded as Louth, four silver and two gold (CCI 95.1181, 03.0516, 02.0055, 01.1010, 00.0571, 00.0372); a single large sherd of Iron Age pottery found on the Fairfield Industrial Estate (HER 46721); an odd ancient Greek coin, *c.* 500–250 BC, found north of Louth, likely a modern copy (PAS LIN-EDD313).

Roman: Roman ditch containing charcoal, burnt sandstone and pottery found west of the Kenwick Road – probably an enclosed farmstead or related to one nearby (HER 43612); unstratified fragments of Roman brick and tile found on Gospelgate suggest that a Roman building may have been located somewhere in the vicinity (HER 45626); a Roman coin of Domitian, AD 86, found on the corner of Charles Street and Newbridge Hill (HER 41389); two coins – one of Tetricus, 271–4, and one of Faustina the Younger, d. 175 – found somewhere in Louth (HER 41395); a considerable number of Roman coins, dating from the first to the fourth centuries, were found in Louth before 1834 (Bayley 1834, p. 247).

Anglo-Saxon: A single Early Anglo-Saxon cruciform brooch found in Louth cemetery (HER 41394); a late eighth-century silver coin of Offa of Mercia from Louth, no findspot recorded (PAS NLM6590); a small Early Anglo-Saxon inhumation cemetery found at an uncertain spot just within the parish boundary, indicated by metalwork finds including three small-long brooches (Leahy, 1993, p. 40); a number of ninth-century coins, mostly Mercian, were found in Louth before 1834, although the find-spot is uncertain (Bayley 1834, p. 247; Owen, 1997, p. 61). In addition to these finds, there is also a significant number of Middle Saxon coins known from sites described as 'near Louth'. Some of these find-spots are potentially identifiable from the date-specific maps in Blackburn, 1993, pp. 85–6: a Series E *sceat* from the Lower Rhineland or Frisia, dating around 720–30 (Blackburn, 1993, p. 88; from the Thorpe Hall area?); a plated forgery of a seventh-century Continental Merovingian gold *tremissis* and a late ninth-century coin of Alfred of Wessex (Blackburn, 1993, p. 88; from the Acthorpe area?); two *sceattas* of *c.* 675–750 and a coin of Offa of Mercia dating *c.* 792–6 (Blackburn, 1993, p. 88; from a site to the north-west of Hallington village?); a coin of Wulfred, Archbishop of Canterbury, dated *c.* 810 (Blackburn, 1993, p. 88; from a site to the south-west of South Elkington village?); a coin of Æthelheard, Archbishop of Canterbury, with Offa of Mercia, dating 792–6 (Blackburn, 1993, p. 88; from a site to the east of Louth, plotted in the Kenwick Road area). Other finds have no detailed location data other than 'near Louth', though they may well come from some of the above sites: a Series E English *sceat* of *c.* 700–10; a Series E Continental *sceat* of *c.* 700–50; a Series J English *sceat* of *c.* 710–25; a coin of Offa of Mercia, minted in East Anglia and dating between 770–92; a coin of Alfred of Wessex, dated 871–5; a cut quarter of a gold Frankish coin of Louis the Pious, dated 814–40 (EMC 2001.0699, 2001.0698, 2001.0045, 1999.0132, 1996.0199, 1997.0101).

Anglo-Scandinavian: Two sherds of Late Anglo-Saxon pottery from the site of Meridian House, Eastgate, possibly associated with pits (HER 43245); a York coin of 921–7, a coin of Harold Harefoot (dated 1036–8), and two coins of Edward the Confessor (dated 1042–4), all from a site 'near Louth' that has also produced a *sceat* (EMC 1986.0113, 1985.0037,

1985.0038, 1986.0114; from the Thorpe Hall area?); a coin of Edward the Confessor, dated 1053–6, from somewhere 'near Louth' (EMC 1985.0041); a coin of Cnut, dated 1029–36, from somewhere 'near Louth' (EMC 2001.0700); a coin of Edgar, dated 959–72, from somewhere 'near Louth' (EMC 1986.5025).

LUDBOROUGH
Neolithic: A Neolithic stone axe (HER 41195).
Iron Age: A gold coin of the Corieltavi (CCI 04.2619).
Anglo-Saxon: An imitation in silver of a 600–675 Continental Merovingian *tremissis* coin (EMC 2001.0978).

LUDFORD
Bronze Age: Possible round barrow (HER 44072).
Roman: Romano-British pottery (EMASPP).

MAIDENWELL
Palaeolithic: A Lower Palaeolithic handaxe (HER 45980).
Mesolithic: Late Mesolithic or Early Neolithic pyramidal flint core for the making of bladelets (HER 43169).
Neolithic: A Neolithic long barrow or chalk quarry (HER 43388); a Neolithic long barrow or chalk quarry (HER 42975); a probable long barrow associated with a probably Neolithic flint blade and the pyramidal flint core mentioned above (HER 43169); a scatter of Neolithic-Bronze Age worked flints (HER 41926); a flint point (HER 41938); an unpolished Neolithic flint axe (HER 41959).
Bronze Age: Possible round barrow (HER 44984); possible round barrow (HER 44128); possible round barrow (HER 44157); possible round barrow (HER 44158); possible round barrow (HER 44163); possible round barrow (HER 44153); possible round barrow (HER 44152).
Roman: Extensive cropmarks, including hut circles, associated with a scatter of Romano-British pottery – a Romano-British settlement site and possible villa (HER 44999; Jones, 1999, pp. 72–3, 77); an irregular enclosure, possibly representing a Romano-British farmstead involved in animal husbandry (HER 44979; Jones, 1999, pp.75–7); five features – ditches and pits – associated with late first- to early second-century pottery (HER 43352); Romano-British rubbish pit, possibly associated

with a skeleton (HER 41958); a ditch containing traces of burning, animal bones and probable Romano-British pottery (HER 41937).
Anglo-Saxon: A small Early Anglo-Saxon inhumation cemetery, indicated by metalwork finds including a bucket and cruciform brooch (HER 41391; Leahy, 1993, p. 40).

MANBY

Mesolithic: Flint end scraper with blue-white patina, of probable Mesolithic date (HER 43638).
Iron Age: Middle-Late Iron Age features – pits, gullies and ditches, including a possible drip gully formed by water dripping off a roof – associated with Iron Age pottery and sheep and cattle bones, suggest a probable settlement site here (HER 43633).
Roman: Features of Romano-British date from the Iron Age site above suggesting continuity of settlement, including ditches associated with Romano-British pottery (HER 43634); fourth-century coin of Constantius II, 337–61 (HER 41305).
Anglo-Saxon: An Anglo-Saxon cross with heavy interlaced band and cable decoration; possibly of the seventh century, although a later date has also been suggested (HER 41682; Ulmschneider, 2000, p. 143; see below).
Anglo-Scandinavian: A pit containing ninth- to tenth-century Torksey ware pottery (HER 43636); a ninth- to eleventh-century zoomorphic buckle (UKDFD 23347); the sculpture from Manby noted above has also been treated as part of a late tenth- or early eleventh-century grave-cover and a mid-tenth- to mid-eleventh-century grave-marker (CASSS V, Manby 1 and 2; Ulmschneider, 2000, p. 143).

MUCKTON

Roman: From the same area are a coin of Constantine, dated 330–1, and some Roman greyware and samian pottery (HER 42512); a Romano-British spindle whorl and two bronze rings (HER 42511); and sherds of Romano-British pottery (EMASPP).

NORTH ELKINGTON

Neolithic: Polished Neolithic stone axe (HER 40847).
Bronze Age: A round barrow (HER 40849).

North Ormsby

Bronze Age: A possible round barrow cemetery (HER 44065).
Roman: Fragment of an early second-century silver trumpet brooch (*Treasure Annual Report 2004*, p. 55).
Anglo-Saxon: A small Early Anglo-Saxon inhumation cemetery, indicated by metalwork finds including a sixth- or seventh-century copper-alloy, gold and garnet triangular buckle (PAS NLM-50B114); Early Anglo-Saxon pottery (EMASPP).
Anglo-Scandinavian: A cast lead disc brooch dated 850–975, decorated in the Viking Borre style (PAS NLM-743AB7).

Raithby cum Maltby

Neolithic: Many Neolithic-Bronze Age flints (HER 43432); scatter of worked Neolithic-Bronze Age flints recorded from two sites in 'Raithby' (HER 40832) – from their grid-references, one of the sites appears to be identical with HER 43432, above, and the other with the site where 'many worked flints' are recorded from Louth parish, HER 41393.
Bronze Age: A sherd of Bronze Age pottery (HER 40835).
Roman: Romano-British pottery (EMASPP).
Anglo-Saxon: A small Early Anglo-Saxon inhumation cemetery, indicated by metalwork finds including a fifth-century cruciform brooch – probably an heirloom piece – and a sixth- or seventh-century pyramid mount from a sword (HER 40833; UKDFD 226; K. Leahy, pers. comm.); Middle Saxon metal-detected finds from Maltby – two ninth-century Anglo-Saxon strap ends, a copper-alloy pin head from a mid-eighth- to mid-ninth-century linked triple-pin-set, and a substantial mount decorated with interlaced knotwork (UKDFD 222, 223, 173, 174); Early Anglo-Saxon pottery, along with some Roman or Middle Saxon pottery (EMASPP).
Anglo-Scandinavian: A silver penny of Cnut, 1016–35 (PAS LIN-38A751); several metal-detected finds from Maltby – a ninth- to tenth-century Anglo-Saxon strap end, a tenth- to eleventh-century Anglo-Saxon strap end probably in the Winchester style, a buckle attachment or belt-slide of *c.* 850–950 decorated in a fusion of the Viking Borre and Jellinge styles, a small buckle loop of *c.* 850 – 950 decorated with a Viking Borre style animal head, and a silver-plated buckle of the late tenth or eleventh century decorated with a Viking Urnes style beast (UKDFD 220, 230, 229, 224, 225).

SCAMBLESBY
Bronze Age: Possible round barrow (HER 44139); a bronze spearhead (HER 42284); possible round barrow (HER 44140).
Roman: Small Roman bust of a female figure with her hair in a bun (PAS NLM6757); a fragment of Roman mortarium (PAS NLM6636).

SOUTH COCKERINGTON
Neolithic: Eleven partly worked flints, of Neolithic-Bronze Age date (HER 43244).
Bronze Age: A possible fragment of a Bronze Age scraper (HER 43967).
Roman: Romano-British greyware in large patches of dark soil (HER 41380).
Anglo-Saxon: Middle Saxon pottery, including a sherd of Ipswich ware (HER 43242).
Anglo-Scandinavian: Late Saxon pottery, including two sherds of Late Saxon Stamford ware (HER 43242).

SOUTH ELKINGTON
Neolithic: A Neolithic flint axe with a polished cutting edge (HER 41166).
Bronze Age: An earthwork round barrow (HER 43580); a round barrow cemetery, visible as cropmarks (HER 44096); possible round barrow cemetery (HER 44063); possible round barrow cemetery (HER 44062); possible round barrow cemetery (HER 44064); possible round barrow (HER 44094).
Roman: Coin of Julia Maesa, d. 224, found just to the east of Thorpe Hall (HER 41163); sherds of Romano-British pottery from two sites in the parish (EMASPP).
Anglo-Saxon: A major Early Anglo-Saxon cremation cemetery, beginning in the fifth century and originally containing around 1200 burials – it is located just to the west of the parish boundary between Louth and South Elkington, to the east of Acthorpe Top (HER 41162; Webster, 1952).

SOUTH RESTON
Roman: Scatter of Romano-British pottery (HER 42501); sherds of Romano-British pottery (EMASPP).

Anglo-Saxon: Two pits, one containing 34 sherds of Early to Middle Saxon pottery (HER 43349)

SOUTH SOMERCOTES
Roman: Large quantity of Romano-British pottery found twelve feet down at Scupholme, mainly greyware but some samian and colour-coated ware, associated with bones and oyster shell (HER 41294).

STENIGOT
Neolithic: A possible Neolithic long barrow or mortuary enclosure (HER 43185).
Bronze Age: A round barrow (HER 43772); a round barrow (HER 43771); possible round barrow cemetery (HER 44100); two possible round barrows (HER 44844, 44845); possible round barrow (HER 44860).
Iron Age: Five gold coins of the Corieltavi (CCI 01.1676, 01.1670, 01.1667, 00.1539, 00.0702); six silver Corieltavi coins (CCI 00.1959, 01.0985, 01.1697, 03.1503, 03.1510, 03.1511); two copper-alloy coins, one Corieltavi and one Cantii (CCI 03.0743, 03.0943).
Roman: Two Roman silver rings, dated to 185–300, inscribed ToT (PAS LIN-944EE5, LIN-947B96); a minor settlement or farmstead visible on aerial photography (Jones, 1999, p. 77).
Anglo-Saxon: A seventh-century barrow burial, containing three individuals (HER 40785; Thompson, 1956, pp. 192–9).

SWABY
Bronze Age: Possible round barrow (HER 44174).

TATHWELL
Neolithic: An earthwork Neolithic long barrow (HER 43625); a probable long barrow (HER 43184); a Neolithic polished flint axe and a thin butted stone axe (HER 41922); a Neolithic or Bronze Age antler tool (HER 41921); a Neolithic or Bronze Age flint scraper (HER 43644).
Bronze Age: A group of seven round barrows at Bully Hills, arranged in a line running south-west to north-east – a Middle Bronze Age pottery sherd has been found at the site (HER 43562); barbed and tanged arrowhead (HER 41920); damaged barbed and tanged arrowhead (HER 41922); possible round barrow (HER 44124); possible round barrow (HER 44123); possible round barrow (HER 44115); possible round

barrow (HER 44118); possible round barrow (HER 44117); possible round barrow (HER 44125); possible round barrow (HER 44122); possible round barrow (HER 44127); possible round barrow (HER 44126).

Iron Age: Two ditches and a pit containing Iron Age pottery (HER 43351).

Roman: Five Early Romano-British brooches, including a first-century headstud brooch and a gilded second-century oval plate brooch with a glass boss (PAS NLM4731, NLM4757, NLM4760, NLM4732, NLM4759); Romano-British pottery from a grid reference in this parish (EMASPP); a minor settlement or farmstead visible on aerial photography (Jones, 1999, p. 77).

Anglo-Saxon: A small Early Anglo-Saxon inhumation cemetery, indicated by metalwork finds including a gilded sixth-century great square headed brooch (PAS NLM-857633), a later equal-armed brooch (NLM-86D990), and an enamelled sixth-century cruciform brooch (NLM4745).

Anglo-Scandinavian: A tenth- or eleventh-century Viking stirrup mount (PAS NLM4738); a tenth-century Anglo-Saxon strap fitting (PAS NLM4730); part of a late tenth- or early eleventh-century grave-cover (CASSS V, Tathwell 1).

UTTERBY

Mesolithic: A Mesolithic or Early Neolithic core (PAS LIN-B02974).

Neolithic: Eleven Neolithic/Bronze Age flint objects (for example, PAS LIN-2131F1).

Bronze Age: Four flint scrapers/knives (PAS LIN-F61F86, LIN-99DA92, LIN-E8B6A2, LIN-E8C5A7); possible fragment of a Bronze Age spear or sword (PAS LIN-F612B1).

Iron Age: An early gold coin of *c.* 60–50 BC (PAS LIN-B104B7); two silver Corieltavi coins (CCI 02.0762, 03.0011).

WALMSGATE

Bronze Age: Possible round barrow (HER 44165).

Roman: A third-century copper-alloy coin (HER 42415).

Anglo-Saxon: A hoard of nine silver Anglo-Saxon lunette pennies of the mid-ninth century, deposited around AD 873 (UKDFD 55).

WELTON LE WOLD

Palaeolithic: Palaeolithic handaxes and a retouched flake found in gravels at Welton Quarry, along with animal bones (HER 41200; Alabaster and Straw, 1978; Aram *et al*, 2005).

Neolithic: A Neolithic long barrow (HER 42979); a Neolithic long barrow (HER 43178); a Neolithic long barrow (HER 43654); a potential Neolithic long barrow (HER 43180); a Neolithic polished flint axe (HER 41159).

Bronze Age: A round barrow (HER 43525); possible round barrow cemetery (HER 44093); possible round barrow (HER 44092); possible round barrow (HER 44091); possible round barrow (HER 44097).

Iron Age: Three coins of the Corieltavi, one gold and two silver (CCI 02.0557, 02.0560, 03.0290); likely Iron Age stage to the Romano-British villa site here, from cropmarks (HER 43546; Jones, 1999, p. 75); Iron Age settlement cropmarks, including hut circle (HER 43545).

Roman: An extensive (650m by 300m) Romano-British settlement site visible on air photographs – a probable villa site, with finds of Romano-British pottery, oyster shell and possible tile from the central area (HER 43544, 41157; Jones, 1999, pp. 72–5); further extensive (500m by 400m) Iron Age to Romano-British settlement cropmarks, associated with a quern stone, samian ware and third- to fourth-century pottery – a possible dependent village of the Welton villa estate (HER 41153, 41154; Jones, 1999, pp. 74–5); metal-detected finds associated with the villa site – a mid-late first-century dolphin brooch, a first- or second-century trumpet brooch (PAS NLM-1758B3, NLM-178482), and 28 coins found in an area spanning around 250 metres, mainly of third- to late fourth-century date (e.g. PAS NLM-17BCB0, NLM-B77AE2, NLM-B6FCD2); a rare and important late fourth- or fifth-century high-status British silver proto-hand-pin, found on the villa site (Youngs, 2005; *Treasure Annual Report 2001*, pp. 43–4; PAS PAS-E91188); around 275 Roman coins, mainly belonging to the fourth century – the PAS database assigns them to Louth, but the detectorist who found them confirms they came from the same area as the 28 coins and proto-hand-pin listed above, which are also his finds (e.g. PAS NLM1539, NLM1619; M. Jones, pers. comm.); five Early Roman items, including a mid-first-century bow brooch and a Romano-Celtic button and loop fastener of *c.* AD 50–150 – again said to be from Louth but actually from the same area as the other finds (PAS NLM566, NLM567, NLM565, NLM563, NLM564; M. Jones, pers. comm.); a coin of Gratian, 367–83, found elsewhere in the parish (HER

41151); a ladder enclosure and pit at Gayton Top, potentially associated with the Roman villa (HER 44631; Jones, 1999, pp. 74, 77, 79).
Anglo-Scandinavian: A tenth-century Urnes-style Viking strap end, said to be from Louth on the PAS but actually from Welton (PAS NLM553; M. Jones, pers.comm.).

WITHCALL
Neolithic: An Early Neolithic flint flake (HER 43613).
Bronze Age: Possible round barrow (HER 44114); possible round barrow (HER 44111); possible round barrow (HER 44116); possible round barrow (HER 44113); possible round barrow (HER 44102); possible round barrow (HER 44112); possible round barrow (HER 44109); possible round barrow (HER 44110).
Roman: Romano-British occupation site with ditches and a trackway associated with a sizable quantity of Romano-British pottery, some datable to the late first or early second century (HER 43610); scatter of mainly mid-late fourth-century pottery, along with slag from the base of an iron smithing hearth – occupation site possibly located to the north (HER 43609); Romano-British pottery found somewhere in the parish (HER 40811).
Anglo-Saxon: A pair of decorated tweezers, dating broadly *c.* 600–900 (UKDFD 233).
Anglo-Scandinavian: Three items metal-detected from Withcall parish – a ninth- or tenth-century Anglo-Saxon strap end, an eleventh- or early twelfth-century Anglo-Scandinavian Romanesque strap end, and a ninth- or tenth-century Ansate brooch (UKDFD 232, 231, 172).

WYHAM CUM CADEBY
Neolithic: Two polished Neolithic stone axes (HER 41139, 43052); Neolithic-Bronze Age flint scraper (HER 42951).
Bronze Age: Two Bronze Age axe hammers (HER 41137, 43051).
Roman: Two scatters of Romano-British pottery (HER 41138, 43050); a small dolphin brooch dated to *c.* AD 55–80 from this parish (PAS NLM-B33F44).

YARBURGH
Anglo-Saxon: A sixth- or seventh-century copper-alloy pin (PAS LIN-B4C292).

Anglo-Scandinavian: Two items from the same location – an eleventh-century stirrup mount (PAS LIN-B4F5E6) and an eleventh-century copper-alloy horse harness link (PAS LIN-B4B3F6); a York coin of 905–10 found somewhere in the parish (EMC 2005.0040).

Further Reading and Notes

The following section offers a brief bibliographic discussion of some of the earlier scholarship and research upon which this study and its conclusions depend. The references given in the captions accompanying figures in the main text refer to works listed below. Where the reference is given in the form Shennan *et al*, 2000a, this is due to there being two works with the same author and year listed in that chapter's 'further reading'; in such circumstances, 'Shennan *et al*, 2000a' refers to the first such work, 'Shennan *et al*, 2000b' the second, and so forth.

CHAPTER ONE

On the earliest human activity in Britain, see especially C. Stringer, *Homo Britannicus* (London, 2006), who also provides a good general overview of the Palaeolithic period in Britain. For another general overview of the Palaeolithic period, see N. Barton, *Stone Age Britain* (London, 1997), pp. 116–35, reissued and revised in 2005 as *Ice Age Britain*. A detailed account of the new Happisburgh finds and their dating can be found in S. A. Parfitt *et al*, 'Early Pleistocene human occupation at the edge of the boreal zone in northwest Europe', *Nature*, 466 (2010), 229–33. For the Lincolnshire Lower Palaeolithic handaxes and the Tetford-Salmonby area field-walking project, see T. W. Bee, 'Palaeolithic handaxes from the Lymn valley, Lincolnshire', *Lithics*, 22 (2001), 47–52, and T. W. Bee, 'New finds of Palaeolithic handaxes from Lincolnshire', *Lithics*, 26 (2005), 90–100. The landscape of Lincolnshire and East Anglia before its erosion during the Anglian and subsequent eras is reconstructed in K. M. Clayton, 'Glacial erosion of the Wash and Fen basin and the deposition of the chalky till of eastern England', *Quaternary Science Reviews*, 19 (2000), 811–22. For the dating of the boundaries of the Marine Isotope Stages, see especially L. E. Lisiecki and M. E. Raymo, 'A Pliocene-Pleistocene stack of 57 globally distributed benthic $\delta^{18}O$ records', *Paleoceanography*, 20 (2005), PA1003, and L. E. Lisiecki, 'Ages of MIS boundaries', archived at http://www.lorraine-lisiecki.com/LR04_MISboundaries.txt (accessed 29 December 2010). See also P. L. Gibbard and K. M. Cohen, 'Global chronostratigraphical correlation table for the last 2.7 million years', 2010, http://www.quaternary.stratigraphy.org.uk/correlation/chart.html (accessed 29 December 2010).

On the Welton le Wold finds and their dating, see C. Alabaster and A. Straw, 'The Pleistocene context of the faunal remains and artefacts discovered at Welton-le-Wold, Lincolnshire', *Proceedings of the Yorkshire Geological Society*, 41 (1976), 75–94; J. Wymer and A. Straw, 'Hand-axes from beneath glacial till at Welton-le-Wold, Lincolnshire', *Proceedings of the Prehistoric Society*, 43 (1977), 355–60; A. Straw, *Glacial and Pre-Glacial Deposits at Welton-le-Wold, Lincolnshire* (Exeter, 2005); J. Aram *et al*, *Towards an Understanding of the Ice Age at Welton le Wold* (Heckington, 2005), in particular Joanna Hambly's 'Discussion', pp. 45–51; and J-L. Schwenninger *et al*, *Welton-le-Wold, Lincolnshire: Optically Stimulated Luminescence (OSL) Dating of Pleistocene Glacial Tills and Interglacial Gravels*, English Heritage Research Department Report Series no. 36/2007. The notion that the Calcethorpe Till belongs to the Anglian glaciation is present in, for example, R. M. S. Perrin *et al*, 'The distribution, variation and origins of pre-Devensian tills in eastern England', *Philosophical Transactions of the Royal Society B*, 287 (1979), 535–70; S. G. Lewis, 'Eastern England', in D. Q. Bowen (ed.), *A Revised Correlation of Quaternary Deposits in the British Isles* (Bath, 1999), pp. 10–27; and J. A. Catt *et al*, 'Quaternary: ice sheets and their legacy', in P. J. Brenchley and P. F. Rawson (eds.), *The Geology of England and Wales*, 2nd edition (Bath, 2006), pp. 429–68.

For the revised model of the glaciation of Britain, which allows more than two glaciations in the Pleistocene including one in MIS 6, see C. D. Clark *et al*, 'Pleistocene glacial limits in England, Scotland and Wales', in J. Ehlers and P. L. Gibbard (eds.), *Quaternary Glaciations – Extent and Chronology, Part I: Europe* (Kidlington, 2004), pp. 47–82, and J. Rose, 'Early and Middle Pleistocene landscapes of eastern England', *Proceedings of the Geologists' Association*, 120 (2009), 3–33. On the significance of the Bout coupé handaxes, see, for example, M. J. White and R. M. Jacobi, 'Two Sides to Every Story: *Bout Coupé* Handaxes Revisited', *Oxford Journal of Archaeology*, 21 (2002), 109–33. M. J. White, 'Things to do in Doggerland when you're dead: surviving OIS 3 at the northwestern-most fringe of

Middle Palaeolithic Europe', *World Archaeology*, 38 (2006), 547–75, has a good discussion of MIS 3 and Neanderthals in Britain. The evidence for *Homo sapiens-Homo neanderthalensis* interbreeding is presented in R. E. Green *et al*, 'A draft sequence of the Neandertal genome', *Science*, 328 (2010), 710–22. The Upper Palaeolithic blade core from Fulletby has been published as T. W. Bee, 'Classic blade core from Lincolnshire', *Lithics*, 20 (1999), 11.

CHAPTER TWO

With regard to the last glaciation of eastern Lincolnshire, it has been argued that there were two entirely separate Devensian advances by the ice sheets onto the Lincolnshire Wolds: see most recently A. Straw, *The Last Two Glaciations in East Lincolnshire* (Louth, 2008), which also includes a detailed discussion of the physical evidence for Devensian glacial activity in this region. However, this model is rejected here in favour of the more orthodox view that there was a single glaciation that reached Holderness and Lincolnshire *c.* 20,000 BC. The case for two Devensian glaciations does not seem to have been widely accepted, and some of the arguments and supposed evidence in favour of it has been questioned and/or refuted. See further J. A. Catt, 'The Pleistocene glaciations of eastern Yorkshire: a review', *Proceedings of the Yorkshire Geological Society*, 56.3 (2007), 177–207; J. A. Catt *et al*, 'Quaternary: ice sheets and their legacy', in P. J. Brenchley and P. F. Rawson (eds.), *The Geology of England and Wales*, 2nd edition (Bath, 2006), pp. 429–68; and C. D. Clark *et al*, 'Pleistocene glacial limits in England, Scotland and Wales', in J. Ehlers and P. L. Gibbard (eds.), *Quaternary Glaciations – Extent and Chronology, Part I: Europe* (Kidlington, 2004), pp. 47–82. For the extent of the single-stage Devensian ice sheet, see C. D. Clark *et al*, 'Map and GIS database of landforms and features related to the last British Ice Sheet', *Boreas*, 33.4 (2004), 359–75. For a brief account and illustrations of the formation of the Hubbard's Hills gorge, see D. N. Robinson, *The Book of Louth* (Buckingham, 1979), and D. N. Robinson, *The Story of Hubbard's Hills* (Louth, 2007).

General surveys of the Late and Final Upper Palaeolithic periods in Britain can be found in N. Barton, *Stone Age Britain* (London, 1997), pp. 116–35, reissued and revised in 2005 as *Ice Age Britain*; N. Barton, 'The Lateglacial or Latest Palaeolithic occupation of Britain', in J. Hunter and

I. B. M. Ralston (eds.), *The Archaeology of Britain* (London, 2009), pp. 18–52; and C. Stringer, *Homo Britannicus* (London, 2006), who also looks at the Mesolithic. There are numerous good surveys available of human activity in Britain from the Mesolithic period through until the Iron Age, including F. Pryor, *Britain BC: Life in Britain and Ireland Before the Romans* (London, 2004). For the Mesolithic, V. Gaffney *et al, Europe's Lost World, the Rediscovery of Doggerland* (London, 2009), is especially important from the perspective of the present chapter, and M. Parker Pearson, *Bronze Age Britain* (London, 1993, reissued and revised in 2005), remains – despite its title – a useful analysis of both Neolithic and Bronze Age activity in Britain.

For a detailed analysis and discussion of the post-glacial prehistoric archaeology and changing environment of the Lincolnshire Marshes, see especially S. Ellis *et al* (eds.), *Wetland Heritage of the Lincolnshire Marsh: an Archaeological Survey* (Hull, 2001); R. Van der Noort, *The Humber Wetlands: The Archaeology of a Dynamic Landscape* (Macclesfield, 2004); D. N. Robinson, 'Coastal evolution in north-east Lincolnshire', *East Midland Geographer*, 5 (1970), 62–70; D. N. Robinson, *The Book of the Lincolnshire Seaside* (Buckingham, 1981); and D. N. Robinson, 'The buried forests of Lincolnshire', in N. Field and A. White (eds.), *A Prospect of Lincolnshire* (Lincoln, 1984), pp. 6–10. An overview of the prehistoric archaeology of the Wolds has recently been provided in M. Bennet, 'The Wolds before AD 1000', in D. N. Robinson (ed.), *The Lincolnshire Wolds* (Oxford, 2009), pp. 17–30, with a fully-referenced version of this article available online at http://www.lincolnshire.gov.uk/Download/9344 (file accessed 27 December 2010). An old but still useful general discussion of the prehistoric archaeology of Lincolnshire can be found in J. May, *Prehistoric Lincolnshire* (Lincoln, 1976), with updates by the same author on Neolithic and Iron Age archaeology in S. Bennett and N. H. Bennett, *A Historical Atlas of Lincolnshire* (Chichester, 2001). Also useful are the various Lincolnshire and East Midlands working-papers from 'The East Midlands Archaeological Research Framework', for example, J. McNabb, *An Archaeological Resource Assessment and Research Agenda for the Palaeolithic in the East Midlands (Part of Western Doggerland)*, 2001. These are available online at http://www.le.ac.uk/ar/research/projects/eastmidsfw.

The knife from just to the south of our region has been published as T. W. Bee and J. Owen, 'Upper Palaeolithic Knife from Fulletby', *Lincolnshire History and Archaeology*, 28 (1993), 66. The theory that the Younger Dryas was caused by a cometary impact was first outlined in R.

B. Firestone *et al*, 'Evidence for an extraterrestrial impact 12,900 years ago that contributed to the megafaunal extinctions and the Younger Dryas cooling', *Proceedings of the National Academy of Sciences of the United States of America*, 104 (2007), 16016–21. A restatement and attempted rebuttal of various criticisms of the theory can be found in R. B. Firestone, 'The Case for the Younger Dryas Extraterrestrial Impact Event: Mammoth, Megafauna, and Clovis Extinction, 12,900 Years Ago', *Journal of Cosmology*, 2 (2009), 256–85; for continued criticism, see, for example, T. L. Daulton *et al*, 'No evidence of nanodiamonds in Younger–Dryas sediments to support an impact event', *Proceedings of the National Academy of Science*, 107 (2010), 16043–7. The recent work from Ireland that suggests that the initial Younger Dryas cooling could have occurred over the course of only a few months was reported in K. Ravilious, 'Mini ice age took hold of Europe in months', *New Scientist*, issue 2734, 11 November 2009, p. 10.

On Doggerland and its disappearance, see B. J. Coles, 'Doggerland: a speculative survey', *Proceedings of the Prehistoric Society*, 64 (1998), 45–81; Gaffney *et al*'s *Europe's Lost World*; and I. Shennan *et al*, 'Modelling western North Sea palaeogeographies and tidal changes during the Holocene', in I. Shennan and J. Andrews (eds.), *Holocene Land-Ocean Interaction and Environmental Change Around the North Sea* (London, 2000), pp. 299–319. S. Ellis *et al*'s *Wetland Heritage of the Lincolnshire Marsh* provides details of recent boreholes and the chronology of the flooding of what is now the Lincolnshire Marshes – see also I. Shennan *et al*, 'Holocene isotasy and relative sea-level changes on the east coast of England', in I. Shennan and J. Andrews (eds.), *Holocene Land-Ocean Interaction and Environmental Change Around the North Sea* (London, 2000), pp. 275–98. For the North Somercotes cross-section, see Environment Agency, *Donna Nook Managed Realignment Scheme* (November 2009), pp. 252–55. On the '8.2 kiloyear event' and its impact, see D. C. Barber *et al*, 'Forcing of the cold event of 8,200 years ago by catastrophic drainage of Laurentide lakes', *Nature*, 400 (1999), 344–8, and, most recently, M. P. Hijma and K. M. Cohen, 'Timing and magnitude of the sea-level jump preluding the 8200 yr event', *Geology*, 38.3 (2010), 275–8. The Storegga Slide tsunami and its effects on Doggerland are modelled in B. Weninger *et al*, 'The catastrophic final flooding of Doggerland by the Storegga Slide tsunami', *Documenta Praehistorica*, 35 (2008), 1–24.

For the Neolithic barrows around Swinhope and their associated environmental evidence, see P. Phillips (ed.), *Archaeology and Landscape*

Studies in North Lincolnshire, 2 volumes (Oxford, 1989). On the Neolithic change to a sedentary, agricultural lifestyle being a rapid one, see for example P. Rowley-Conwy, 'How the West was lost: a reconsideration of agricultural origins in Britain, Ireland and southern Scandinavia', *Current Anthropology*, 45 (2004), 83–113, and M. Collard *et al*, 'Radiocarbon evidence indicates that migrants introduced farming to Britain', *Journal of Archaeological Science*, 37 (2010), 866–70. For the Bronze and Iron Ages in Lincolnshire, see in general the works cited above; Jeffrey May's *Dragonby: Report on Excavation at an Iron Age and Romano-British Settlement in North Lincolnshire*, 2 volumes (Oxford, 1996) is also important for its consideration of the Late Iron Age in Lincolnshire and the centrality of Lindsey to the territory of the Corieltavi. A map of the Late Iron Age territories dependent upon Ludford and Ulceby Cross is available in the above volume and in Jeffrey May's 'The later Iron Age', in S. Bennett and N. Bennett (eds.), *An Historical Atlas of Lincolnshire* (Chichester, 2001), pp. 12–13. Finally, it should be noted that where uncalibrated radiocarbon ages were given in the above works, these have all been converted into calibrated calendar years (using version 6.0 of M. Stuiver and P. J. Reimer, 'Extended ^{14}C database and revised CALIB radiocarbon calibration program', *Radiocarbon*, 35 (1993), 215–30, and the INTCAL09 dataset, online at http://calib.qub.ac.uk/calib/calib.html) in order to both standardize on one system and ease analysis. Similarly, where radiocarbon dates were calibrated some time ago and the uncalibrated result is given, these have also been recalibrated in the same manner.

CHAPTER THREE

There are a large number of good, general discussions of Roman Britain, including M. Todd (ed.), *A Companion to Roman Britain* (Oxford, 2004); M. Millett, *Roman Britain* (London, 1995, reissued and revised in 2005); M. Millett, *The Romanization of Britain* (Oxford, 1990); and P. Salway, *The Oxford Illustrated History of Roman Britain* (Oxford, 1993). For Lincolnshire, B. Whitwell, *Roman Lincolnshire*, 2nd edition (Lincoln, 1992), remains a valuable synthesis, which has recently been supplemented by S. Malone and M. Williams (eds.), *Rumours of Roman Finds: Recent Work on Roman Lincolnshire* (Heckington, 2010). See also, for brief overviews, B. Whitwell, 'Roman Lincolnshire', in S. Bennett and N. Bennett (eds.), *An*

Historical Atlas of Lincolnshire (Chichester, 2001), pp. 14–15, and M. Bennet, 'An Archaeological Resource Assessment of the Roman Period in Lincolnshire', http://www.le.ac.uk/archaeology/research/projects/eastmidsfw/pdfs/23linrom.pdf (accessed 28 December 2010). For the Wolds, D. Jones, 'Romano-British Settlement in the Lincolnshire Wolds', in R. H. Bewley (ed.), *Lincolnshire's Archaeology from the Air* (Lincoln, 1999), pp. 29–65, is particularly significant. There is also a good brief discussion in M. Bennet, 'The Wolds before AD 1000', in D. N. Robinson (ed.), *The Lincolnshire Wolds* (Oxford, 2009), pp. 17–30; a fully-referenced version of this is available at http://www.lincolnshire.gov.uk/Download/9344 (accessed 27 December 2010). For the Lincolnshire Marshes, S. Ellis *et al* (eds.), *Wetland Heritage of the Lincolnshire Marsh: an Archaeological Survey* (Hull, 2001), and R. Van der Noort, *The Humber Wetlands: The Archaeology of a Dynamic Landscape* (Macclesfield, 2004), are both important, although none of the sites discussed in them actually fall within our region.

On Totatis in Lincolnshire, see A. Daubney, 'The cult of Totatis: evidence for tribal identity in mid Roman Britain', in S. Worrell *et al* (eds.), *A Decade of Discovery: Proceedings of the Portable Antiquities Scheme Conference 2007* (Oxford, 2010), pp. 109–20. The Marshchapel settlement site from within the coastal zone is published in S. Ellis *et al* (eds.), *Wetland Heritage of the Lincolnshire Marsh*. The Roman font from Calcethorpe with Kelstern has been examined along with related items by S. Malone, 'A group of Romano-British lead tanks from Lincolnshire and Nottinghamshire', in S. Malone and M. Williams (eds.), *Rumours of Roman Finds: Recent Work on Roman Lincolnshire* (Heckington, 2010), pp. 138–42; see also 'A fourth-century font from near Ludford, Lincolnshire', in the *Portable Antiquities Scheme Annual Report 2004/05*, p. 47. The church in the *forum* at Lincoln has been discussed on numerous occasions – see especially M. J. Jones, 'St Paul in the Bail, Lincoln: Britain in Europe?', in K. Painter (ed.), *Churches Built in Ancient Times: Recent Studies in Early Christian Archaeology* (London, 1994), pp. 325–47; M. J. Jones, 'The Colonia era: archaeological account', in D. Stocker (ed.), *The City by the Pool: Assessing the Archaeology of the City of Lincoln* (Oxford, 2003), pp. 56–138 at pp. 127–9, 137; T. Green, 'The British kingdom of Lindsey', *Cambrian Medieval Celtic Studies*, 56 (2008), 1–43 at 18–22; and T. Green, *Britons and Anglo-Saxons: a Study of the Lincoln Region, c. 400–650* (Lincoln, forthcoming), chapter two. The nineteenth-century finds of Roman coins in Louth are discussed in R. S. Bayley, *Notitiæ Ludæ, or Notices of Louth* (Louth, 1834), pp. 246–7. The significance of dedications to St Helen is discussed in G. Jones, 'Holy wells and the cult of St Helen', *Landscape History*, 8 (1986), 59–75; B. Yorke, 'Lindsey: the lost kingdom found?', in A. Vince (ed.), *Pre-Viking Lindsey* (Lincoln, 1993), pp. 141–50 at p. 142; and Green, *Britons and Anglo-Saxons*, chapter three.

For Arthur Owen's reconstruction of the Roman road network of this region, see A. E. B. Owen, 'Roads and Romans in south-east Lindsey', in A. R. Rumble and A. D. Mills (eds.), *Names, Places and People* (Stamford, 1997), pp. 254–68. His theory as to the Roman origins of Louth is contained in A. E. B. Owen, 'Louth before Domesday', *Lincolnshire History and Archaeology*, 32 (1997), 60–4. The case for a Late or post-Roman fort at Yarburgh is made in B. Cox, 'Yarboroughs in Lindsey', *Journal of the English Place-Name Society*, 28 (1994–5), 50–60, and the Late/post-Roman fortification at Yarborough is discussed in K. Leahy, *The Anglo-Saxon Kingdom of Lindsey* (Stroud, 2007), pp. 111–14.

CHAPTER FOUR

The Early Anglo-Saxon/post-Roman period in Lincolnshire has been discussed a number of times in recent years. See especially B. Eagles, 'Lindsey' in S. Bassett (ed.), *The Origins of Anglo-Saxon Kingdoms* (London, 1989), pp. 202–12; K. Leahy, 'The Anglo-Saxon settlement of Lindsey', in A. Vince (ed.), *Pre-Viking Lindsey* (Lincoln, 1993), pp. 29–44; K. Leahy, *The Anglo-Saxon Kingdom of Lindsey* (Stroud, 2007); T. Green, 'The British kingdom of Lindsey', *Cambrian Medieval Celtic Studies*, 56 (2008), 1–43; and T. Green, *Britons and Anglo-Saxons: a Study of the Lincoln Region, c. 400–650* (Lincoln, forthcoming). On the economic and cultural collapse of the early fifth century, a key analysis remains S. Esmonde-Cleary, *The Ending of Roman Britain* (London, 1989). For the de-intensification of land exploitation in East Anglia after the end of Roman taxation and imperial demand, see P. Murphy, 'The Anglo-Saxon landscape and rural economy: some results from sites in East Anglia and Essex', in J. Rackham (ed.), *Environment and Economy in Anglo-Saxon England* (York, 1994), pp. 23–39.

That the Anglo-Saxon immigrants of the fifth and sixth centuries were more than a small elite now seems widely accepted, see particularly C. Scull, 'Approaches to the material culture and social dynamics of the migration period in eastern England', in J. Bintliff and H. Hamerow (eds.), *Europe Between Late Antiquity and the Middle Ages* (Oxford, 1995), pp. 71–83. On the environmental evidence and its lack of support for the kind of massive reduction in population in the post-Roman period that would be expected if the Britons were driven out or massacred, see, for example, S. P. Dark, 'Palaeoecological evidence for landscape continuity and change in Britain *ca* A.D. 400–800', in K. R. Dark (ed.), *External Contacts and the Economy of Late Roman and Post-Roman Britain* (Woodbridge, 1996), pp. 23–51; O. J. Rackham, *The History of the Countryside* (London, 1986), pp. 75–85; and Murphy, 'Anglo-Saxon landscape and rural economy'. The Victorian belief that the lack of British words in Old English requires an assumption of genocide has been effectively challenged by a number of researchers, including B. Ward-Perkins, 'Why did the Anglo-Saxons not become more British?', *English Historical Review*, 115 (2000), 513–33, and H. L. C. Tristram, 'Why don't the English speak Welsh?', in N. J. Higham (ed.), *Britons in Anglo-Saxon England* (Woodbridge, 2007), pp. 192–214. The estimate of the total number of 'archaeologically visible' Anglo-Saxons in Lindsey is that of Leahy, *Kingdom of Lindsey*, pp. 82–3.

The British territory of *Lindes* and its impact on the Anglo-Saxon immigrants is discussed at length in Green, 'The British kingdom of Lindsey', and Green, *Britons and Anglo-Saxons*; the latter also includes a brief discussion of the names Lud, Cockerington and Crake in chapter five. For the South Elkington-Louth and Cleatham cremation cemeteries, see G. Webster, 'An Anglo-Saxon urnfield at South Elkington, Louth, Lincolnshire', *Archaeological Journal*, 108 (1952), 25–64, K. Leahy, *'Interrupting the Pots': The Excavation of Cleatham Anglo-Saxon Cemetery* (York, 2007), and also Leahy, *Anglo-Saxon Kingdom of Lindsey*. For cremation cemeteries as the 'central places' of Early Anglo-Saxon Lincolnshire, see particularly H. Williams, 'Cemeteries as central places – place and identity in Migration Period eastern England', in B. Hårdh and L. Larsson (eds.), *Central Places in the Migration and Merovingian Periods* (Stockholme, 2002), pp. 341–62, and H. Williams, 'Assembling the dead', in A. Pantos and S. Semple (eds.), *Assembly Places and Practices in Medieval Europe* (Dublin, 2004), pp. 109–34. The suggestion that 'Charnwood ware' was distributed and exchanged at the large cremation cemeteries of our region was first made in A. G. Vince and D. F. Williams, 'The characterization and interpretation of early to Middle Saxon granitic tempered pottery in England', *Medieval Archaeology*, 41 (1997), 214–20. On the significance of the place-names Ludborough and Ludford, see, for example, A. E. B. Owen, 'Roads and Romans in south-east Lindsey' in

A. R. Rumble and A. D. Mills (eds.), *Names, Places and People* (Stamford, 1997), pp. 254–68 at p. 263; A. E. B. Owen, 'Louth before Domesday', *Lincolnshire History and Archaeology*, 32 (1997), 60–4; and Green, *Britons and Anglo-Saxons*, chapter five, and 'British kingdom of Lindsey', p. 16.

For the Anglo-Saxons continuing to draw a distinction between those of British and immigrant descent into the seventh century, see M. G. Thomas *et al*, 'Evidence for an apartheid-like social structure in early Anglo-Saxon England', *Proceedings of the Royal Society*, 273 (2006), 2651–7; A. Woolf, 'Apartheid and economics in Anglo-Saxon England', in N. J. Higham (ed.), *Britons in Anglo-Saxon England* (Woodbridge, 2007), pp. 115–29; and H. Härke, 'Changing symbols in a changing society: the Anglo-Saxon weapon burial rite in the seventh century', in M. O. H. Carver (ed.), *The Age of Sutton Hoo* (Woodbridge, 1992), pp. 149–65. A key guide to the chronology of English place-names is B. Cox, 'The place-names of the earliest English records', *Journal of the English Place-Name Society*, 8 (1976), 12–66. See also B. Cox, 'The significance of the distribution of English place-names in *-hām* in the Midlands and East Anglia', *Journal of the English Place-Name Society*, 5 (1972–3), 15–73; J. Kuurman, 'An examination of the *-ingas, -inga-* place-names in the East Midlands', *Journal of the English Place-Name Society*, 7 (1974–5), 11–44; and M. Gelling, *Signposts to the Past. Place-names and the History of England*, 2nd edition (London, 1988). On place-names such as Wykeham, see M. Gelling, 'English place-names derived from the compound *wīchām*', reprinted in K. Cameron (ed.), *Place-name Evidence for the Anglo-Saxon Invasion and Scandinavian Settlements* (Nottingham, 1977), pp. 8–26; Gelling, *Signposts to the Past*; and C. J. Balkwill, 'Old English *wīc* and the origin of the hundred', *Landscape History*, 15 (1993), 5–12. Cox, 'English place-names in *-hām*', especially p. 71, discusses place-names derived from Old English *heah + ham*. On place-names such as Wyham, see D. Wilson, 'A note on OE *hearg* and *weoh* as place-name elements representing different types of pagan Saxon worship sites', *Anglo-Saxon Studies in Archaeology and History*, 4 (1985), 179–84; D. Wilson, *Anglo-Saxon Paganism* (London, 1992); J. Blair, 'Anglo-Saxon pagan shrines and their prototypes', *Anglo-Saxon Studies in Archaeology and History*, 8 (1995), 1–28; and A. Meaney, 'Pagan English sanctuaries, place-names and Hundred meeting places', *Anglo-Saxon Studies in Archaeology and History*, 8 (1995), 29–42.

CHAPTER FIVE

On the probable pre-Viking origins for many of Lincolnshire's wapentakes, including Louthesk, see P. Sawyer, *Anglo-Saxon Lincolnshire* (Lincoln, 1998), pp. 84, 125–6, 134–6, 138; D. M. Hadley, *The Vikings in England: Settlement, Society and Culture* (Manchester, 2006), pp. 90–2; S. Turner, 'Aspects of the development of public assembly in the Danelaw', *Assemblage*, 5 (2000), archived online at http://www.assemblage.group. shef.ac.uk/5/turner.html (accessed 29 December 2010); and T. Green, *Britons and Anglo-Saxons: a Study of the Lincoln Region, c. 400–650* (Lincoln, forthcoming), chapter five. For the use of 'minster' instead of 'monastery', see, for example, J. Blair, *The Church in Anglo-Saxon Society* (Oxford, 2005), especially pp. 2–3. Archbishop Æthelheard's previous role as the abbot of Louth minster is mentioned in a manuscript of the 'Anglo-Saxon Chronicle', see P. S. Barker (ed.), *The Anglo-Saxon Chronicle. A Collaborative Edition. Volume 8 – MS. F* (Cambridge, 2000). Important discussions of other Anglo-Saxon minsters in Lincolnshire include D. Stocker, 'The early Church in Lincolnshire: a study of the sites and their significance', in A. Vince (ed.), *Pre-Viking Lindsey* (Lincoln, 1993), pp. 101–22, and D. Roffe, 'The seventh century monastery of Stow Green, Lincolnshire', *Lincolnshire History and Archaeology*, 21 (1986), 31–3. The *Medeshamstede* charter and its origins have been discussed in F. M. Stenton, 'Medeshamstede and its Colonies', in D. M. Stenton (ed.), *Preparatory to Anglo-Saxon England* (Oxford, 1970), pp. 179–92; see, for example, C. Hart, *The Early Charters of Eastern England* (Leicester, 1966), p. 97, for the identification of *Lodeshale* as Louth. Sawyer, *Anglo-Saxon Lincolnshire*, p. 241, finds the -o- in *Lodeshale* concerning. The late Kenneth Cameron's contrasting view that this name does reflect Louth is reported in R. N. Benton, *Louth in Early Days* (Cheddar, 1985); unfortunately Cameron's own volume on the place-names of Louthesk has not been published.

On Middle Saxon minsters as centres of consumption and exchange, the coins from around Louth being associated with Louth minster and its market, and the Domesday market at Louth deriving from the monastic one, see, for example, Blair, *The Church in Anglo-Saxon Society*; K. Ulmschneider, *Markets, Minsters and Metal-detectors: the Archaeology of Middle Saxon Lincolnshire and Hampshire Compared* (Oxford, 2000); K. Ulmschneider, 'Settlement, economy, and the 'productive' site: Middle Anglo-Saxon Lincolnshire A.D. 650–780', *Medieval Archaeology*, 44 (2000),

53–79; and Sawyer, *Anglo-Saxon Lincolnshire*. For the coins themselves, see the Gazetteer. See also R. S. Bayley, *Notitiæ Ludæ, or Notices of Louth* (Louth, 1834), pp. 246–7; M. Blackburn, 'Coin finds and coin circulation in Lindsey, c. 600–900', in A. Vince (ed.), *Pre-Viking Lindsey* (Lincoln, 1993), pp. 80–90; and A. E. B. Owen's two articles on Louth, listed below. The suggestion that Louth minster was at Louth Park is made in Stocker, 'The early Church in Lincolnshire'; it is repeated by R. Gurnham, *A History of Louth* (Stroud, 2007). For the link between Late Saxon and Anglo-Norman small towns and pre-Viking minsters, see especially Blair, *Church in Anglo-Saxon Society*. For the foundation of minsters to take advantage of the British sacred and ritual landscape of the Witham, see D. Stocker and P. Everson, 'The straight and narrow way: Fenland causeways and the conversion of the landscape in the Witham valley, Lincolnshire', in M. O. H. Carver (ed.), *The Cross Goes North: Processes of Conversion in Northern Europe, A.D. 300–1300* (Woodbridge, 2002), pp. 271–88, and P. Everson and D. Stocker, '"Coming from Bardney..." – the landscape context of the causeways and finds groups of the Witham valley', in S. Catney and D. Start (eds.), *Time and Tide, The Archaeology of the Witham Valley* (Sleaford, 2003), pp. 6–15.

St Herefrith of Louth is discussed at length in A. E. B. Owen, 'Herefrith of Louth, saint and bishop: a problem of identities', *Lincolnshire History and Archaeology*, 15 (1980), 15–19; see also A. E. B. Owen, 'Louth before Domesday', *Lincolnshire History and Archaeology*, 32 (1997), 60–4. The suggestion that the area between the Lud, the Hubbard's Hills gorge and the former route of Louth-Bardney railway was an extensive monastic island belongs to the latter. A good discussion of the characteristics of minster estates and their dependent sites can be found in Blair, *Church in Anglo-Saxon Society*. The etymology of Fulstow preferred here was first proposed in E. Ekwall, *The Concise Oxford Dictionary of English Place-Names*, 4th edition (Oxford, 1960). Good discussions of Middle Saxon pastoral care and the economics of minster estates can be found in Blair's volume and R. Faith, *The English Peasantry and the Growth of Lordship* (London, 1997). See Ekwall, *Oxford Dictionary of English Place-Names*, on Old English *Styfic-tun* having a specific technical usage. On Anglo-Saxon coppicing, see, for example, O. J. Rackham, *The History of the Countryside* (London, 1986), and O. J. Rackham, 'Trees and woodland in Anglo-Saxon England: the documentary evidence', in J. Rackham (ed.), *Environment and Economy in Anglo-Saxon England* (York, 1994), pp. 7–11. See Ekwall's *Dictionary* and K. Cameron's *Dictionary of*

Lincolnshire Place-Names (Nottingham, 1998) on the other place-names mentioned at the end of this chapter; the notion that place-names like Gayton may reflect specialized settlements that were components of large Anglo-Saxon estates has been frequently discussed, for example in Faith's *English Peasantry* and M. Costan's *The Origins of Somerset* (Manchester, 1992). On places named *Ceorlatun*, see especially H. P. R. Finberg, 'Charltons and Carltons', in H. P. R. Finberg, *Lucerna: Studies of Some Problems in the Early History of England* (London, 1964), pp. 144–60, and Faith, *English Peasantry*.

CHAPTER SIX

The course of the Viking conquests and their impact on Lincolnshire is discussed in P. Sawyer, *Anglo-Saxon Lincolnshire* (Lincoln, 1998), and K. Leahy, *The Anglo-Saxon Kingdom of Lindsey* (Stroud, 2007). A good general overview is available in D. M. Hadley's *The Vikings in England: Settlement, Society and Culture* (Manchester, 2006), and her *The Northern Danelaw: Its Social Structure, c.800–1100* (London, 2000) is useful. Kenneth Cameron's studies of place-names of Scandinavian origin, including his theory that most names in *-by* reflect new immigrant settlements on virgin sites, are collected together in K. Cameron (ed.), *Place-name Evidence for the Anglo-Saxon Invasion and Scandinavian Settlements* (Nottingham, 1977). Sawyer, *Anglo-Saxon Lincolnshire*, notes some arguments against this theory, including the fact that it can be no longer be credibly maintained that there were vast tracts of unexploited non-marginal land in pre-Viking England. On Scandinavian place-names, see also L. Abrams and D. N. Parsons, 'Place-names and the history of Scandinavian settlement in England', in J. Hines *et al* (eds.), *Land, Sea and Home* (Leeds, 2004), pp. 379–431; this supports the argument that the Scandinavian influence on place-names, field-names and personal names is together sufficient to indicate that there was a substantial influx of Scandinavian immigrants into Lincolnshire. Recent finds of Viking-style metalwork point in the same direction, as Leahy, *Anglo-Saxon Kingdom of Lindsey*, observes. With regard to the renaming of places when they gain new lords, see, for example, M. Gelling, *Signposts to the Past. Place-names and the History of England*, 2nd edition (London, 1988), chapter seven.

    The mint at Louth is primarily represented by a coin in the distinctive style of Lincoln and its subordinate mints with a damaged mint-mark that begins LV, although there is one other possible coin from this mint: Sawyer, *Anglo-Saxon Lincolnshire*, pp. 193, 201. See P. Stafford, *The East Midlands in the Early Middle Ages* (London, 1985), p. 46, on the mint being indicative of Louth having developed into an urban centre within Lincolnshire by the late tenth century. On the Thorney narrative, see A. E. B. Owen, 'Herefrith of Louth, saint and bishop: a problem of identities', *Lincolnshire History and Archaeology*, 15 (1980), 15–19, and A. E. B. Owen, 'Louth before Domesday', *Lincolnshire History and Archaeology*, 32 (1997), 60–4. With regard to place-names involving personal names and their origins, see, for example, Sawyer, *Anglo-Saxon Lincolnshire*, pp. 111–13, and Gelling, *Signposts to the Past*, chapter seven. A very brief discussion of the likely origins of the Domesday estate based at Gayton le Wold can be found in Hadley, *Northern Danelaw*, p. 148. The grave-covers and markers of Anglo-Scandinavian Lincolnshire are discussed in detail in P. Everson and D. Stocker, *Corpus of Anglo-Saxon Stone Sculpture, Volume 5: Lincolnshire* (Oxford, 1999).

For the Anglo-Scandinavian saltern at Marshchapel, see S. Ellis *et al* (eds.), *Wetland Heritage of the Lincolnshire Marsh: an Archaeological Survey* (Hull, 2001). The recent Fishtoft finds are to be published in P. Cope-Faulkner, *Clampgate Road, Fishtoft. Archaeology of a Middle Saxon Island Settlement in the Lincolnshire Fens* (Heckington, forthcoming). The question of salt-making and the settlement of the Outmarsh has been discussed a number of times – see especially A. E. B. Owen, 'Salt, sea banks and medieval settlement on the Lindsey coast', in N. Field and A. White (eds.), *A Prospect of Lincolnshire* (Lincoln, 1984), pp. 46–9, and D. M. Grady, 'Medieval and post-medieval salt extraction in north-east Lincolnshire', in R. H. Bewley (ed.), *Lincolnshire's Archaeology from the Air* (Lincoln, 1999), pp. 81–95. For further discussion of place-names that may include Anglo-Scandinavian terms referring to flora and fauna, see K. Cameron's *Dictionary of Lincolnshire Place-Names* (Nottingham, 1998); R. Coates, 'Reflections on some major Lincolnshire place-names. Part one: Algarkirk to Melton Ross', *Journal of the English Place-Name Society*, 40 (2008), 35–95; and R. Coates, 'Reflections on some major Lincolnshire place-names. Part two: Ness wapentake to Yarborough', *Journal of the English Place-Name Society*, 41 (2009), 57–102.

R. Gurnham, *A History of Louth* (Stroud, 2007), p. 13, similarly suggests the Aswell spring as the possible meeting-place of Louthesk wapentake in the Anglo-Scandinavian period. Arthur Owen's withdrawal of his suggestion that St Mary's was the original parish church can be found in Owen, 'Louth before Domesday'. On Cisterngate-Saxongate as originally including the personal name Saextan rather than 'Saxon', see the early form Saxtanegate – E. G. Kimball (ed.), *Records of Some Sessions of the Peace in Lincolnshire, 1381–1396. Volume II: The Parts of Lindsey* (Lincoln, 1962), p. 208 – and N. Field, *Louth: the Hidden Town* (Lincoln, 1978); D. N. Robinson, *The Book of Louth* (Buckingham, 1979). That Bishop Wulfwig had purchased Louth itself from Alsi and Olgrim is accepted by Sawyer, *Anglo-Saxon Lincolnshire*, p. 152, amongst others. On the 'urban' settlements of Lincolnshire in Domesday Book – Lincoln, Stamford, Torksey, Grantham and Louth – see, for example, H. C. Darby, *The Domesday Geography of Eastern England*, 3rd edition (Cambridge, 1971), pp. 78–83. On medieval plot patterns in towns, a good brief discussion is available in D. M. Palliser *et al*, 'The topography of towns 600–1300', in D. M. Palliser (ed.), *The Cambridge Urban History of Britain I, 600–1540*, (Cambridge, 2000), pp. 153–86 at pp. 169–72; the medieval plots in Louth are discussed in Gurnham, *History of Louth*, pp. 16–18, and Field, *Louth: the Hidden Town*.

CHAPTER SEVEN

On the medieval and later history of Louth, see especially N. Field, *Louth: the Hidden Town* (Lincoln, 1978); D. N. Robinson, *The Book of Louth* (Buckingham, 1979); and R. Gurnham, *A History of Louth* (Stroud, 2007). Older but still useful are J. E. Swaby, *A History of Louth* (London, 1951); R. W. Goulding, *Annals of Louth, 1086–1600* (Louth, 1918); and R. S. Bayley, *Notitiæ Ludæ, or Notices of Louth* (Louth, 1834). D. N. Robinson and C. Sturman, *William Brown and the Louth Panorama* (Louth, 2001), is also very useful for Early Victorian Louth, whilst details of recent excavations in the town are available from the Lincolnshire Historic Environment Record, especially record number 44506. The medieval and later development of the Outmarsh and coastline, not discussed here, is dealt with in D. N. Robinson, *The Book of the Lincolnshire Seaside* (Buckingham, 1981), and D. M. Grady, 'Medieval and post-medieval salt extraction in north-east Lincolnshire', in R. H. Bewley (ed.), *Lincolnshire's Archaeology from the Air* (Lincoln, 1999), pp. 81–95. With regard to St Mary's, see Chapter Six and A. E. B. Owen, 'Louth before Domesday', *Lincolnshire History and Archaeology*, 32 (1997), 60–4; on Eve Street and James Street, see now D. N. Robinson, *Adam Eve and Louth Carpets*

(Louth, 2010). As to the etymologies of Finkle Street and Gulpyn Lane, see R. Coates, 'A breath of fresh air through Finkle Street', *Nomina*, 18 (1995), 7–36, and J. Wright, *The English Dialect Dictionary*, six volumes (Oxford, 1898–1905), s.v. Gulp. The etymology of the Gatherums is discussed in R. Coates, 'Azure Mouse, Bloater Hill, Goose Puddings, and One Land called the Cow: continuity and conundrums in Lincolnshire minor names', *Journal of the English Place-Name Society*, 39 (2007), 73–143. Louth's House of Correction, which was founded on the far eastern edge of the town, is discussed in B. Painter, *The Story of Louth House of Correction, 1671–1872* (Louth, 2004).

There is a useful general summary of the possible future geological and environmental development of England and Wales in P. L. Gibbard *et al*, 'The future: climate and sea-level change, glaciation and northward drift', in P. J. Brenchley and P. F. Rawson (eds.), *The Geology of England and Wales* (Bath, 2006), pp. 469–75. For a recent analysis of the likely sea-level rise across the twenty-first century, see M. Vermeer and S. Rahmstorf, 'Global sea level linked to global temperature', *Proceedings of the National Academy of Sciences of the United States of America*, 106 (2009), 21527–32, and S. Rahmstorf, 'A new view on sea level rise', *Nature Reports Climate Change*, 4 (2010), 44–5. On the response of the Greenland ice-sheet to the warming expected to occur this century and after, the following offer useful insights: J. M. Gregory *et al*, 'Threatened loss of the Greenland ice-sheet', *Nature*, 428 (2004), 616; J. A. Lowe *et al*, 'The role of sea-level rise and the Greenland ice sheet in dangerous climate change: implications for the stabilisation of climate', in H. J. Schnellnhuber *et al* (eds.), *Avoiding Dangerous Climate Change* (Cambridge, 2006), pp. 29–36; J. Hansen, 'A slippery slope: How much global warming constitutes "dangerous anthropogenic interference"?', *Climate Change*, 68 (2005), 269–79; J. Hansen *et al*, 'Climate change and trace gases', *Philosophical Transactions of the Royal Society A*, 365 (2007), 1925–54; J. Hansen *et al*, 'Earth's energy imbalance: confirmation and implications', *Science*, 308 (2005), 1431–5; J. Ridley, 'Thresholds for irreversible decline of the Greenland ice sheet', *Climate Dynamics*, 35 (2009), 1049-57. On the possible disruption of the thermohaline circulation, see for example Q. Schiermeier, 'Climate change: a sea change', *Nature*, 439 (2006), 256–60, and M. Vellinga and R. A. Wood, 'Impacts of thermohaline circulation shutdown in the twenty-first century', *Climatic Change*, 91 (2008), 43–63.

On the ending of the Holocene Interglacial and subsequent developments, see M. F. Loutre and A. Berger, 'Future climatic changes: are we entering an exceptionally long interglacial?', *Climatic Change*, 46 (2000), 61–90; A. Berger and M. F. Loutre, 'An exceptionally long interglacial ahead?', *Science*, 297 (2002), 1287–8; M. F. Loutre, 'Clues from MIS 11 to predict the future climate: a modelling point of view', *Earth and Planetary Science Letters*, 212 (2003), 213–24. For the alternative view that the glacial-interglacial cycle will fail under the pressure of human greenhouse gas emissions, with runaway warming instead laying ahead of the present, see, for example, J. Hansen, *Storms of My Grandchildren* (New York, 2009). It should be noted that the maps of the possible effects of future potential sea-level rises on the Louth region are derived from NASA's Shuttle Radar Topography Mission, via http://flood.firetree.net. This data has a number of sources of inaccuracy and the maps cannot be relied upon to be completely accurate as to the areas likely to be affected; nonetheless, the data is good enough to at least offer an impression of the general impact of future potential sea-level rises in this region.

Index

8.2 kiloyear event, 22, 128
Aby Grange, 14, 17
Acthorpe Top, 61, 66, 69, 71, 73, 88, 145
Ælfflæd, abbess of Whitby, 86
Ælfingas, the, 75
Ælfric, 87
Æthelheard, abbot of Louth minster, 79, 88, 141
Æthelwold, bishop of Winchester, 82, 83
Agriculture, 25, 26, 28, 29, 30, 34, 36, 38, 46, 50, 60, 90, 91, 92, 93, 100, 101, 103, 112, 142
Alauna (pagan water-goddess). *See* Louth: St Helen's Spring
Aldhelm, abbot of Malmesbury, 77
Alsi, owner of Louth, 106
Alvingham, 31, 75, 132
Animals
    arctic foxes, 15, 129
    aurochs, 20
    bison, 20
    brown bears, 15
    cattle, 20, 36, 47, 91, 119, 143
    elephants, 4, 9, 125
    goats, 91, 100
    hares, 15
    hippopotamuses, 9
    horses, 4, 11, 15, 16, 20, 36, 38, 112
    hyenas, 9
    lions, 9, 11
    pigs, 36
    red deer, 4, 15
    redwing/thrush, 36
    reindeer, 17, 18, 129
    rhinoceroses, 9, 11
    rooks, 104
    sheep, 36, 47, 143
    wild-cats, 104
    wolves, 15, 104
    woolly mammoths, 11, 15, 16, 38
Asterby, 28, 132
Authorpe, 90, 132
Bain, river, 7, 72
Barton Street, 54, 55, 56, 74, 77, 108
Bayley, Robert, 51, 88, 117, 118, 120, 123
Bede, 86
Binbrook, 54, 133
Bishop of Lincoln, 50, 83, 106, 107, 108, 113
Bishop of Lindsey, 83, 95
Boston, 102
Boswell Barrow, 31
Boxgrove (Sussex), 1
Brackenborough, 37, 103, 133
Bradley, John, 120
Brock a Dale plantation, 28
Brooches
    ansate, 149

bow, 139, 148
Colchester, 36, 133
crossbow, 48, 135
cruciform, 71, 136, 137, 139, 141, 143, 144, 147
disc, 96, 99, 136, 144
dolphin, 134, 148, 149
equal-armed, 147
great square headed, 147
headstud, 136, 139, 147
penannular, 46, 65, 135
plate, 147
small-long, 136, 141
trumpet, 144, 148
Buckles, 72, 98, 137, 143, 144
Bully Hills (Tathwell), 30, 31, 146
Burgesses, 107, 108, 112
    burgage tenements, 107, 108, 112
Burgred, king of Mercia, 81, 89
Burwell, 47, 133
Bury St Edmunds (Suffolk), 83
Cadeby, 149
Cadwell, 104
Caistor, 54, 99
Calcethorpe, 3, 4, 5, 8, 9, 33, 36, 50, 51, 133
Cameron, Kenneth, 80
Cannibalism, 1, 16
Castle Carlton, 92
Cawkwell, 46, 134
Celtic Coin Index, 36, 37
Ceolwulf, king of Mercia, 96
Chapel Point, 22, 34
Charnwood Forest (Leicestershire), 69
Christianity
    Anglo-Saxon, 66, 77, 79–87, 143
    Anglo-Scandinavian, 98, 100, 106
    Medieval, 112, 115, 117
    Romano-British, 50, 51, 52, 53, 60, 63, 64, 65, 66, 134
Churches
    Conisholme, 102
    Edenham, 113
    Gayton le Wold, 100, 102, 137
    Keddington, 139
    Little Carlton, 100, 102, 139
    Lincoln
        Cathedral, 113
        St Paul in the Bail, 50, 63, 82
    Louth
        St Herefrith's shrine, 83, 84, 98, 105, 108, 112, 113
        St Herefrith-St James, 84, 106, 108, 112, 113, 117
        St Mary, 88, 106, 112, 118, 121
        St Mary's Roman Catholic Church, 120
        Trinity, 124
    Manby, 100
    Marshchapel, 103
    Osingadun, 86
    Tathwell, 100
    Withcall, 86
    Wyham, 77
Claudius, Roman emperor, 41
Coastal defences, 125, 127
Coastal zone, 22, 24, 25, 27, 33, 34, 46, 47, 48, 49, 55, 75, 102, 103, 104, 128
Cocker, river-name, 66
Cockerington, 66, 84
    North, 66
    South, 49, 90, 145
Coins
    Ancient Greek, 140
    Anglo-Scandinavian, 99, 132, 141, 142, 144
    Carolingian, 141

Iron Age, 36, 37, 39, 133, 134, 138, 140, 142, 146, 147, 148
Merovingian, 72, 73, 141, 142
Middle Saxon, 74, 80, 81, 88, 89, 106, 141, 147
Roman, 44, 45, 46, 47, 50, 51, 52, 59, 60, 133, 134, 135, 136, 137, 139, 140, 141, 143, 145, 147, 148
Comet impact, 17
Conisholme, 102, 104, 134
Coppicing, 90, 103
Corieltavi tribe, 34, 36, 41, 43, 49, 138, 140, 142, 146, 147, 148
Covenham, 31, 75, 128, 134
    Covenham St Mary, 31, 134
    Covenham St Bartholomew, 75, 134
    Birkett Lane, 75
Crake, river, 66
Cremation cemeteries
    Anglo-Saxon, 60, 61, 62, 63, 64, 68, 69, 70, 71
    Bronze Age, 31, 136
    Cleatham, 68
    Elsham, 63
    Loveden Hill, 71
    South Elkington-Louth, 61, 64, 66, 68, 69, 71, 75, 79, 112, 145
    West Keal, 64, 68, 71
Cresswell Crags (Derbyshire), 16
Cropmarks, 36, 45, 133, 137, 142, 145, 148
Cult-sites, 52, 56, 65, 75, 77, 78, 82, 84, 87, 105, 111, 115
Doggerland, 13, 14, 17, 18, 20, 21, 22, 23, 24, 38, 129
Domesday Book, xi, xiii, 69, 80, 82, 83, 85, 87, 92, 93, 97, 98, 99, 100, 102, 103, 106, 107, 108, 111, 112, 113

Donington on Bain, 26, 31, 33, 35, 36, 43, 44, 48, 50, 51, 52, 101, 135
Dragonby, 34
East Anglia, 1, 3, 5, 8, 17, 60, 141
Edward the Confessor, king of England, 106, 141, 142
Espin, Thomas, 54, 117, 118, 120
Farforth, 54, 84
Fens, the, 3
Fishtoft, 102
Forging, coins, 46, 47, 137
Fotherby, 44, 55, 96, 136
Franklin, Sir John, 120
Freeman, E. A., 61
Fugol, hermit, 85
Fulletby, 10, 16
Fulstow, 33, 36, 44, 45, 46, 47, 51, 85, 137
Gayton le Marsh, 91, 137
Gayton le Wold, 42, 91, 100, 102, 137
Gildas, 65
Glacial lakes, 15, 22
    Hallington and Raithby, 14
    Lake Agassiz, 17
    Lake Humber, 13
Glacial tills
    Calcethorpe Till, 3, 5, 9
    Marsh Till, 5
    Welton Till, 5, 6, 7, 9
Glaciations
    Anglian, 1, 3, 4, 5, 7
    Devensian, 5, 10, 13, 15
    future glaciations, 129
    Tottenhill, 9
Gough's Cave (Chedder Gorge), 16
Grainthorpe, 54, 102, 104, 128
Grantham, 107
Grave-covers, 102, 137, 139, 143, 147
Grave-markers, 137, 143
Great Carlton, 47, 92, 138

Great Langdale 'axe factory' (Cumbria), 26, 29
Greenhouse gases, 125
Greenland ice sheet, 125, 126, 128
Gregory the Great, pope, 77
Grim's Mound (Gayton le Wold), 137
Grimoldby, 138
Gulf Stream, 17, 19, 128
Gulpin, 121
Hallington, 14, 66, 88, 100, 138, 141
Happisburgh (Norfolk), 1, 2
Harlaxton, 9
Haugham, 36, 74, 90, 138
Hermitages, 85
Holderness (Yorkshire), 13, 14
Homo antecessor, 1
Homo heidelbergensis, 1, 7
Homo neanderthalensis, 1, 7, 9, 10
Homo sapiens, 1, 10, 13
Horncastle, 26, 54, 74, 99
Horse tack, 104, 112, 136, 137, 147, 150
Hubbard's Hills, 14, 28, 33, 39, 85, 140
Human sacrifice, 49
Humber, river, 34, 95
Hunter-gatherers, 16, 17, 19, 22, 24, 26, 28, 29, 30, 38
Ice sheet disintegration, 126
Immingham, 22
Industrial activity, 21, 33, 36, 46, 47, 48, 49, 101, 102, 107, 108, 114, 117, 118, 123, 124, 136, 137, 138, 149
Ingoldmells, 16
Inhumation cemeteries
    Anglo-Saxon, 70, 71, 72, 90, 136, 137, 141, 143, 144, 146, 147
    Anglo-Scandinavian, 102, 137, 139, 143, 147

Iron Age, 135
Medieval, 112
Romano-British, 72, 143
Interglacials
    Aveley, 8
    future interglacials, 129
    Holocene, 10, 19, 128, 129
    Hoxnian, 6, 7, 8, 12
    Ipswichian, 2, 3, 9
    Purfleet, 8
Ipswichian cliff, 2, 9
Ipswichian wave-cut platform, 2, 9, 10, 14, 23
Keddington, 19, 28, 31, 38, 82, 84, 138, 140
Kelstern, 3, 4, 8, 28, 33, 36, 43, 49, 50, 51, 133
Kenwick Farm, 4
King Arthur's Cave (Herefordshire), 16
Kirmington, 34, 42, 50, 55
Langford (Nottinghamshire), 31
Late Glacial (Windermere) Interstadial, 14, 16, 19
Laurentide ice sheet (America), 17
Legbourne, 4, 25, 26, 139, 140
Leland, John, 54
Lincoln, 50, 63, 64, 66, 82, 83, 99, 105, 106, 107, 113, 127
Lincolnshire Marshes, 9, 23, 24, 25, 50, 65, 74, 104
    Middle Marsh, 14, 25, 28, 29, 31, 128
    Outmarsh, 14, 22, 23, 25, 42, 48, 49, 103, 104, 111
Lindes, post-Roman polity, xiii, 63, 64, 65, 66
Lindissi, kingdom of, 64, 66, 77, 80
Lindsey, 34, 63, 64, 73, 83, 95, 96, 98
Little Carlton, 90, 92, 100, 102, 139
Little Cawthorpe, 139
Little Grimsby, 44, 55, 96, 133

'Little Ice Age', 129
Lodeshale, 80
Long barrows, 26, 27, 28, 30, 31, 127, 133, 135, 142, 146, 148
Long Bennington, 31
Louth
   Aswell Lane. *See* Aswell Street
   Aswell spring, 105, 112, 114, 115, 117, 119, 123, 124
   Aswell Street, 52, 115, 117, 119, 124
   Bedehouses, 121
   Bowling Greene, 119
   Brackenborough Road, 37
   Breakneck Lane, 120
   Broadbank, 54, 118, 124
   butcher-stalls, 115
   Butts, the, 119
   Cannon Street, 54, 115
   carpet factory, 118
   cattle market and quarry, 119
   Charles Street, 44, 140
   Chequergate, 114, 117, 118, 119
   Church Street, 121, 124
   Cisterngate, 106, 118
   Cornmarket, 115
   Crowtree Lane, 120
   Eastfield Road, 124
   Eastgate, 105, 114, 115, 121, 124, 141
   Edward Street, 115, 120, 124
   Eve Street, 118
   Fairfield Industrial Estate, 37, 125, 140
   Fanthorpe Lane, 38
   Finkle Street, 118
   Fish Shambles, 114
   Free School (Northgate), 118
   Fullers' Street. *See* Walkergate
   Gatherums, the, 52, 123
   George Street, 120
   Gild of St Mary, 84, 114, 121
   Gild of the Holy Trinity, 121
   Goose Pool, the, 114, 120
   Gospelgate, 45, 52, 114, 115, 120, 121, 140
   grammar school, 113, 120, 121
   Greyhound Inn, 45, 52, 112, 115, 120
   Grimsby Road, 54
   Gulpyn Lane. *See* Schoolhouse Lane
   Healey's Court, 118
   High Holme Road, 124
   House of Correction, 121
   Irish Hill, 120
   James Street, 118
   Keddington Road, 19, 28, 38, 140
   Kenwick Road, 88, 140, 141
   Kidgate, 114, 119, 123
   Kit Cat Lane. *See* Kidgate
   Lee Street, 119
   leper hospital, 119
   Limes, the, 120
   Lincolnshire Poacher Hotel, 124
   Lodge, the, 115, 120
   Ludgate, 118
   Lyndon Way, 28, 140
   Maiden Row, 121, 123, 124
   Manor House, the, 123
   Market Place, 108, 112, 115
   Mercer Row, 108, 109, 112, 114, 115, 127
   Meridian House, 105, 114, 141
   mint, Late Saxon, 99, 105
   Monks' Dyke, 33, 123, 140
   Mount St Mary, 118
   Newbridge Hill, 44, 140
   Newmarket, 119, 120
   Nichol Hill, 54, 115
   North Holme Road, 124
   Northgate, 54, 114, 117, 118
   Orme Almshouses, 121
   Padehole. *See* Northgate

plague house, 118
Quarry Lane, 119, 124
Queen Street. *See* Walkergate
Ramsgate, 124
Riverhead, 118, 124
Saxongate, 106
Schoolhouse Lane, 121
Spital Hill, 119, 120
Spout Yard, 33, 117, 140
St Bernard's Avenue, 124
St Helen's spring, 52, 53, 65, 82, 85, 105, 112, 123
Thorpe Hall, 88, 141, 142, 145
Town Hall, Elizabethan, 115
Upgate, 45, 52, 108, 112, 119, 120
Vickers Lane, 115
Victoria Road, 124
Walkergate, 114, 115, 121, 123
Watery Lane, 124
Westgate, 113, 114, 120, 121
Westgate House, 113
workhouse, 118
Louth navigation canal, 118, 124
Louthesk wapentake, xiii, 69, 70, 79, 98, 105, 106, 115
Lud, river, xiii, 66, 85, 93, 105, 106, 118
Ludborough, 69, 73, 75, 142
Ludford, 34, 43, 48, 50, 54, 69, 74, 77, 142
Ludica, king of Mercia, 81
Maidenwell, 4, 43, 54, 72, 87, 142
Maltby by Louth, 33, 90, 96, 97, 144
Manby, 36, 43, 87, 89, 96, 100, 128, 143
Marine Isotope Stages, 5, 6
    MIS 3: 9, 10
    MIS 4: 9
    MIS 5e: 3, 9
    MIS 6: 6, 7, 9
    MIS 7: 8, 9
    MIS 8: 8
    MIS 9: 8
    MIS 10: 7, 8
    MIS 11: 6, 7
    MIS 13: 5
    MIS 15: 5
Markets and fairs, 80
    Anglo-Scandinavian, 98, 105
    Domesday, xi, 82, 93, 99
    eight-day fairs, 113
    Louth minster, 80, 82, 87, 93, 105, 112
    Medieval, 113
Marshchapel, 22, 34, 48, 102, 104
Meers Bank (Mablethorpe), 69
Mercia, kingdom of, 79, 81, 83, 88, 89, 96, 141
Milankovitch orbital cycles, 129
Minsters. *See* Monasteries and minsters
Monasteries and minsters
    Bardney, 82
    Louth minster, 79, 80, 81, 82, 84, 85, 86, 87, 88, 92, 100, 112
    Louth Park Abbey, 31, 81, 84, 113, 119, 123, 139
    Medeshamstede (Peterborough), 79, 80, 91
    seventh-century charter, 79, 80
    Stow Green, 85
    Thorney (near Peterborough), 82, 83, 84, 99
    Whitby (Yorkshire), 86
    Withcall, 85
Muckton, 44, 100, 143
Neanderthals. *See Homo neanderthalensis*
Nettleton, 42
Newport Arch (Lincoln), 127
Norman Conquest, xi, 87, 102, 105, 112, 124, 127

North Cockerington. *See* Cockerington
North Elkington, 143
North Ormsby, 72, 73, 96, 99, 144
North Somercotes, 23, 34, 128
Nucleated villages, 74, 105
Ocean thermohaline circulation, 17, 128
Olgrim, owner of Louth, 106
Optically Stimulated Luminescence (OSL) dating, 6
Owen, Arthur, 53, 54, 55, 83, 106, 141
Oxcombe, 91
Pakefield (Suffolk), 1
Place-name elements
  (ge)mære, 69
  a, 103
  berg, 103
  brakni, 103
  by, 96, 98, 100
  ceorlas, 92
  cumb, 91
  eorð-burh, 55
  gata (goat), 91, 92, 100
  gata (road), 106
  gatu-rum, 123
  ham, 74, 75
  heah, 74
  hearg, 75, 77
  hlude, xiii, 66
  holmr, 104
  hris, 91
  hrokr, 104
  ingas, 74, 75
  kjolr, 103
  lundr, 104
  oxa, 91
  stow, 85
  styfic, 90, 91
  tun, xiii, 66, 90, 91, 92, 100
  vargr, 104
  vicus, 74
  vithr, 103
  wig, 75, 77
  with-kall, 103
Plants
  alder, 19
  ash, 69, 105
  birch, 14, 17, 19
  bracken, 103
  cereals, 25
  elm, 19
  grasses and sedges, 14, 15, 16, 17, 38, 129
  hazel, 19, 25
  juniper, 14
  lime, 19
  oak, 19, 24, 25
  pine, 19
  sea-buckthorn, 14
  willow, 14
Pottery
  Anglo-Scandinavian, 105, 114, 132, 138, 139, 141, 143, 145
  Bronze Age, 32, 33, 135, 144, 146
  Charnwood ware, 69
  colour-coated ware, 146
  Early Anglo-Saxon, 72, 74, 75, 134, 138, 144
  Early to Middle Saxon, 146
  greyware, 45, 47, 133, 138, 143, 145, 146
  gritted ware, 138
  Ipswich ware, 90, 145
  Iron Age, 36, 37, 39, 134, 137, 140, 143, 147
  kiln, 133
  Maxey ware, 90, 132, 138
  Medieval, 112, 114, 117
  Middle Saxon, 90, 132, 138, 145
  mortaria, 46, 145
  Romano-British, 41, 43, 44, 45, 46, 47, 49, 59, 132, 133, 134, 135, 136, 137, 138,

175

139, 140, 142, 143, 144,
  145, 146, 147, 148, 149
samian ware, 44, 135, 136, 143,
  146, 148
Saxo-Norman, 132
Stamford ware, 145
Torksey ware, 143
Proto-hand-pin, 45, 65, 148
Querns, 46, 134, 148
Raithby, 14, 28, 33, 90, 96, 144
Remigius, bishop of Lincoln, 106,
  108, 112
Rings, 133, 134, 139, 143
Risby Warren, 9, 16
Roman army, 41, 42
Roman Bank, 54
Roman font, 50, 51, 134
Roman grain dryers, 134
Roman villas, 43, 45, 46, 51, 52,
  142, 148, 149
Round barrows, 30, 31, 32, 33, 132,
  133, 134, 135, 137, 138, 142,
  143, 144, 145, 146, 147, 148,
  149
Rowley-Conwy, Peter, 29
Ruckland, 103
Salmonby, 4, 7, 16, 19
Salterns, 48, 49, 102, 103
Saltfleet, 74
Saltfleetby St Clement, 16
Saltfleetby St Peter, 49
Saltmarsh, 21, 24, 27, 34, 38, 47,
  48, 49, 104
Scamblesby, 33, 145
Scunthorpe, 16
Scupholme, 44, 49, 146
Sea Dyke Way, 103
Sea-level, rise and fall, 2, 9, 10, 13,
  14, 23, 34, 47, 49, 55, 125, 126,
  127, 128, 129
Sempringham, 91
Severn estuary, 24
Sierra de Atapuerca (Spain), 1

Simon de Luda, 113
Skegness, 54
Skendleby, 25, 28
Sleeve-clasps, 74
South Cockerington. *See*
  Cockerington
South Elkington, 31, 61, 64, 68, 69,
  70, 72, 75, 79, 141, 145
South Reston, 145
South Somercotes, 44, 49, 146
St Cuthbert, 86
St Herefrid. *See* St Herefrith
St Herefrith, 82, 83, 84, 95, 98, 105,
  108, 112
Stamford, 107, 145
Stenigot, 35, 36, 43, 44, 49, 50, 70,
  72, 146
Stewton, 90, 92, 103
Storegga Slide tsunami, 23, 24
Strap ends, 90, 139, 144, 149
Swaby, 146
Swanscombe man, 7
Swinhope, 25, 26, 28
Tathwell, 14, 26, 30, 31, 33, 43, 54,
  71, 100, 146, 147
Tetford, 4, 7, 19, 54, 74
Teutates. *See* Totatis
Theddlethorpe, 22
Tools and weapons
  Ahrensburgian tanged points,
    17
  antler tool, 146
  arrowheads, 29, 33, 135, 139,
    140, 146
  axes, 25, 26, 27, 29, 33, 132,
    133, 136, 137, 138, 139,
    140, 142, 143, 145, 146,
    148, 149
  blade core, 10
  Bout coupé handaxes, 9
  chisel, 140
  handaxes, 3, 4, 5, 7, 8, 9, 133,
    139, 142, 148

knives, 16, 140, 147
leaf-shaped arrowheads, 29
palstave, 33, 133
scrapers, 33, 134, 136, 139, 140, 143, 145, 146, 147, 149
seax, 72
shouldered point, 16
spearheads, 33, 135, 145, 147
swords, 33, 42, 134, 135, 137, 144, 147
Torksey, 95, 107, 143
ToT rings, 43, 44, 49, 134, 146
Totatis (pagan god), 43, 49
Triple-pin-sets, 90, 144
Ulceby Cross, 35, 43
Utterby, 33, 36, 96, 98, 147
Vikings, 95–8
  Great Army, 95
Walmsgate, 89, 95, 147
Wash, the, 3, 15
Washingborough, 64
Water-mills, 107
Welton le Wold, xi, 4, 5, 6, 7, 12, 14, 36, 43, 44, 45, 46, 50, 51, 60, 65, 66, 132, 148
  Welton quarry, 4, 5, 6, 7, 148
Wessex, kingdom of, 89, 95, 98, 141
West Antarctic ice sheet, 126
West Keal, 64, 68, 71
Wispington, 42
Witham, river, 64, 82
Withcall, 47, 85, 86, 103, 149
Wolds, Lincolnshire, 3, 4, 5, 7, 9, 13, 14, 25, 28, 29, 30, 31, 38, 41, 43, 46, 48, 50, 55, 74, 104, 125, 127
Wragholme, 104
Wulfwig, bishop of Lincoln, 106
Wyham, 75, 77, 149
Wykeham, East and West, 74
Yarborough Camp, 55, 56, 64

Yarburgh, 31, 55, 56, 57, 65, 75, 104, 128, 149
Younger Dryas (Loch Lomond Stadial), 16, 17, 18, 19, 25, 128

www.ingramcontent.com/pod-product-compliance
Lightning Source LLC
Chambersburg PA
CBHW071709090426
42738CB00009B/1720